THIRD PARTIES
IN AMERICA

THIRD PARTIES IN AMERICA

Citizen Response to Major Party Failure

Second edition, revised and expanded

STEVEN J. ROSENSTONE
ROY L. BEHR
EDWARD H. LAZARUS

PRINCETON UNIVERSITY PRESS

PRINCETON, NEW JERSEY

Copyright © 1984 by Princeton University Press
Preface and Chapter 9 for the second edition © 1996
by Princeton University Press
Published by Princeton University Press, 41 William Street,
Princeton, New Jersey 08540
In the United Kingdom: Princeton University Press,
Chichester, West Sussex

Library of Congress Cataloging-in-Publication Data

Rosenstone, Steven J.
    Third parties in America : citizen response to major party
failure / Steven J. Rosenstone, Roy L. Behr, Edward H.
Lazarus. — 2nd ed., rev. and expanded.
        p.   cm.
    Includes bibliographical references and index.
    ISBN 0-691-02613-0 (pbk.: alk. paper)
    1. Third parties (United States politics)—History.   2. Elec-
tions—United States—History.   I. Behr, Roy L., 1958– .
II. Lazarus, Edward.   III. Title.
JK2261.R67   1996
324.273'09—dc20   96-510

This book has been composed in Linotron Palatino.

Princeton University Press books are printed on acid-free paper,
and meet the guidelines for permanence and durability of the
Committee on Production Guidelines for Book Longevity of the
Council on Library Resources

First printing of the expanded edition, 1996

Printed in the United States of America
by Princeton Academic Press

1   3   5   7   9   10   8   6   4   2

CONTENTS

TABLES AND FIGURES

PREFACE TO THE SECOND EDITION

OUR INTEREST in third parties began back in 1980 as an effort to explain John Anderson's performance in that year's presidential contest. There was little to guide our initial work. The national press had relatively little to say about Anderson, his campaign, or his level of electoral support. Few social scientists paid much attention to Anderson in the scholarship that surfaced in the wake of the election. What historical writings there were tended to be descriptive accounts of individual third party movements or their leaders. There were no general theories of third party voting that we could draw upon to explain when third parties were likely to flourish.

The several years that we spent together at Yale University were devoted to developing such a theory and testing it against data. We argued that three forces motivate third party voting: major party deterioration, attractive third party candidates who present a viable alternative to the major party nominees, and an influx of voters with weak allegiance to the two major parties. Working against these forces are a set of formidable constitutional, legal, and political constraints that make it difficult for people to cast a third party ballot. Our analysis of the interplay between these motivations and constraints culminated in the first edition of *Third Parties in America*, which Princeton University Press published in 1984.

Over the ensuing decade, we all left New Haven to pursue other interests. Rosenstone settled at the Institute for Social Research at the University of Michigan to resume research on political participation and to direct the National Election Studies. Behr and Lazarus established themselves as political consultants: Behr in California; Lazarus in Washington, D.C.

Then came Ross Perot. Perot's 19 percent of the 1992 presidential vote surprised most everyone—us included. Not since 1912, when former President Theodore Roosevelt ran as the Bull Moose candidate, did so many Americans vote for an independent challenger. In the weeks following the 1992 election, Malcolm DeBevoise, our editor at Princeton University

Press, suggested that we update our book to include Perot. Malcolm's encouragement provided the incentive for us to resurrect our collaboration. Two of us (Rosenstone and Behr) took up his challenge.

Our strategy in this new edition is not to recant our original theory, but to see how well it accounts for Perot's phenomenal success. Thus, the initial eight chapters appear exactly as they did in the original publication. The new material that focuses on Ross Perot appears as a new section—chapter 9. Our purpose is not only to explain Perot's vote, but to put him in historical perspective by pointing out the similarities and differences between Perot and his predecessors.

Part of the story behind Perot's success, we argue, is that like "successful" third party candidates before him, he was able to tap into the deep disaffection that citizens felt toward politics, the major parties, and their candidates. Disaffection, however, turns out to be only part of the story. The reason Perot did so well in 1992 is that he was able to break through many of the constraints that had impeded independent challengers before him. The $73 million that Perot pumped into his crusade, his extensive and relatively positive media coverage, and his participation in the presidential debates all boosted his vote total way beyond what it would have been had Perot been just an ordinary third party challenger.

The kernel of this argument first appeared in "Electoral Myths, Political Realities," which Rosenstone published in the January/February 1993 issue of the *Boston Review.* Rosenstone remains grateful to Josh Cohen for providing the opportunity to contribute to that issue of the *Review.* A roundtable discussion at the 1993 Annual Meeting of the American Political Science Association on "Third Parties in American Politics: Obstacles and Opportunities" that Joel Rogers organized provided an occasion for Rosenstone to elaborate the original claims with some data. Over the subsequent two years, Rosenstone and Behr worked out the argument and supporting evidence in much finer detail.

As in the first edition, we draw upon several kinds of data: journalists' insights into Perot and his organization; Perot's own words and deeds; and data on public opinion over the course of the campaign. Precise comparisons of the 1992 electorate with voters in earlier eras can only be done by relying on data that is gathered in a comparable fashion over time. Here, as in the first edition, we draw upon the National Election Studies conducted by the University of Michigan's Center for Political Studies under grants from the National Science Foundation. These data were provided by the Inter-University Consortium for Political and Social Research. Neither the original collectors of these data nor the ICPSR are responsible for our analysis and interpretations.

We benefited from the advice and generosity of several colleagues. John Zaller, Hanes Walton, Jr., and Adam Berinsky closely read an early draft of the manuscript and provided detailed comments and helpful suggestions. Berinsky prepared the figures that appear in chapter 9, tracked down some of the published data, and diligently checked our citations. We appreciate his many contributions. We are also indebted to Malcolm Litchfield (who later took over as our editor at the Press) and Joy Abellana for their editorial advice and the skill with which they supervised production of the book. Rosenstone also gratefully acknowledges the support he received from the Center for Political Studies of the Institute for Social Research at the University of Michigan.

ACKNOWLEDGEMENTS

DAVID R. MAYHEW gave generously of his advice. We also appreciate the close reading and detailed comments of Michael R. Kagay, Donald R. Kinder, Walter R. Mebane, Jr., and several anonymous reviewers. Christopher H. Achen, John Mark Hansen, Douglas W. Rae, Edward R. Tufte, and Raymond E. Wolfinger also provided helpful suggestions. We are indebted to Sandy Thatcher of Princeton University Press for his editorial advice and the skill with which he supervised the production of the book. Margo Carter and Jack Harriett prepared the figures with great care.

We are grateful for support provided by the Falk Fund, the Mag Foundation, and the Yale Institution for Social and Policy Studies.

The survey data from the National Election Studies of the University of Michigan's Center for Political Studies were provided by the Inter-University Consortium for Political and Social Research. Survey data gathered by the American Institute of Public Opinion were made available by the Roper Center. Neither the original collectors of these data, the ICPSR, nor the Roper Center are responsible for our analysis and interpretations. Donald DeLuca and Jane Draper of the Yale Roper Center and JoAnn Dionne of the Yale Social Science Data Archives aided in our acquisition of these data.

THIRD PARTIES
IN AMERICA

CHAPTER 1

INTRODUCTION

IN A DEMOCRACY there exists an unwritten contract between the people and their political leaders. Citizens support the political system because politicians provide certain benefits: peace, prosperity, government responsiveness, and competent, trustworthy leadership. As long as elected officials uphold their end of the bargain, citizens lend them their support and agree to work within the political order rather than circumvent it.

The two-party system in the United States embodies this unspoken pact, and the arrangement has rarely been challenged. A major party candidate wins nearly every election. The leaders of the two major parties organize both houses of the U.S. Congress and all but one state legislature. For well over a century the president has been either a Democrat or a Republican.

To the American voter, the two parties are as legitimate as any institution formally prescribed in the U.S. Constitution. Children grow up learning about the president, the Congress, and the Democrats and Republicans. Most have never even heard about Libertymen, Greenbacks, or Prohibitionists. Voters are socialized into a two-party norm that is constantly reinforced by the common portrayal of elections as contests between Democrats and Republicans.

It is an extraordinary act for Americans to vote for a third party candidate. Loyalty to the two-party system is a central feature of their political being. To vote for a third party, citizens must repudiate much of what they have learned and grown to accept as appropriate political behavior, they must often endure ridicule and harassment from neighbors and friends, they must pay steep costs to gather information on more obscure candidates, and they must accept that their candidate has no hope of winning.

But third party voting occurs nonetheless. In every presidential election, some portion of the American electorate abandons the major parties to support third party alternatives. Minor parties have managed to capture over 5 percent of the popular vote in a third of the presidential elections since 1840; they have won over 10 percent of the vote in one out of five contests. Because of third party strength, 14 of the last 36 presidents (40 percent) have entered the White House without a popular vote majority. Through the years, third parties have controlled enough votes in the right states to have theoretically changed one-third of the Electoral College results.

The level of third party support varies considerably from one election to the next. On several occasions—1856, 1860, and 1912—over a fifth of the electorate deserted the major parties. Yet in other presidential contests—1868, 1940, and 1960 among them—minor parties were unable to lure even one-half of one percent to their causes. (See figure 1.1.)

Periods of third party strength indicate that the major parties are not representing citizens' political demands. What specifically prompts citizens to seek a third party alternative?

FIGURE 1.1
Third Party Vote for President, 1840-1980

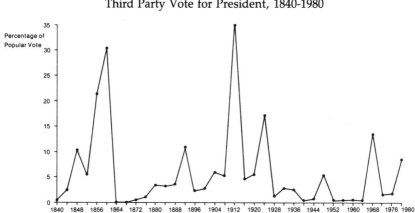

Year

When is this defection from the major parties likely to occur? What causes the two-party system to fail? What kinds of conditions, events, or conflicts is the American two-party system incapable of managing? What factors produce third party strength? What persuades voters that they should give up trying to change the policies of the major parties and opt instead for a new alternative? Are certain types of people consistently more likely to vote for third party candidates? What prompts politicians to mount third party campaigns? By focusing on periods of major party weakness, we can identify deficiencies in the two-party system. As Samuel Lubell noted, third parties shed "penetrating light on the inner torments of the major part[ies]" (1965, p. 205).

There has, of course, been no shortage of historical accounts of third party activity. The problem, though, is that scholars generally have examined only one minor party movement at a time. As a result, we are left with a different explanation (or sometimes more than one) for each third party. There is no general theory of third party voting that can be applied across instances or can be used to predict when the two-party system is likely to deteriorate and third parties flourish. This book develops such a theory.

At first it may seem unlikely that any single explanation can account for more than a few bursts of minor party activity. Third parties, after all, have represented nearly every political point of view, from the Communist Party on the left to the American Independent Party on the right. In some years, as in 1968, voters support a conservative party; at other times, like 1912, a progressive party captures their votes. Third parties have pushed for abolition (Liberty Party), Prohibition, Right-to-Life, States' Rights, even "Down with Lawyers." The candidates have included three ex-presidents, two former vice-presidents, governors, senators and congressmen, housewives, steelworkers, university professors, a convict, and a comedian.

But these apparent differences are insignificant compared to the characteristics the movements have in common. Most importantly, third parties are expressions of discontent with the major parties and their candidates. They are an explicit and deliberate rejection of the two dominant parties. Hence it is possible to formulate a general theory of third party voting that explains why John Anderson netted 6.6 percent of the vote in 1980, George Wallace 13.5 percent in 1968, and James Weaver 3.3 percent in 1880, as well as why minor parties performed so dismally in years like 1868, 1940, and 1960.

Historically, there have been distinct eras of third party strength: good years for third parties appear together, as do bad ones. Between 1864 and 1872, for instance, minor parties never polled as much as 1 percent of the presidential popular vote. Third parties also barely averaged 1 percent in the five elections immediately following World War II. Yet, in all but one presidential election from 1848 to 1860 and 1904 to 1924, third parties lured over 5 percent of the popular vote away from the major parties; during these years an average of 8.1 percent of the electorate joined third party causes.[1] These periods of major party vitality and frailty suggest that it is more than the peculiarities of a particular election that prompt voters to abandon the major parties; more systemic forces are at work.

In recent years the United States seems to have entered another period of major party breakdown and third party strength. Whereas minor parties averaged only .6 percent of the presidential vote in the 1952 to 1964 elections, 5.1 percent of the electorate deserted the major parties between 1968 and 1980.[2] At the same time, there has also been a significant increase in the number of presidential candidates running. Prior to 1968, only once (in 1932) did as many as seven minor party candidates poll votes in more than one state. Between 1900 and 1964 only five candidates, on average, did so. However, in 1968, eight third party candidates attracted votes in more than one state, nine emerged in 1972, and eleven in both 1976 and 1980. (The candidates and their vote totals are listed in Appendix A.) Never before have so many third party

---

[1] This is the median.
[2] These are also medians.

presidential candidates run and polled votes; not since the 1920s has third party voting been, on average, as high as in recent years. What explains this recent upswing in the number of candidates and voters abandoning the major parties? Why have they not stayed on to do battle within the Democratic or Republican parties?

Is third party voting primarily a reaction to one's political, social, and economic environment, or are changes in support for minor parties related to shifts in the composition of the electorate? The first alternative implies that citizens are deliberative—they respond to real world conditions. Changes (either accidental or intentional) in the electoral setting affect outcomes. On the other hand, if swings away from the major parties stem from shifts in the kinds of voters who comprise the electorate, the implication is that people are relatively steadfast in their decisions, and that election results vary (as do their political consequences) not so much because citizens act differently under different circumstances as because the composition of the electorate has changed. Major parties are relatively powerless to stem this sort of defection.

Although the factors that influence voting for major party candidates have been extensively explored, the standard theories of American voting behavior have had little to say about third party support. Most focus on how voters choose *between* the Democrat and the Republican, or *between* the incumbent and his challenger. These theories may be less applicable in a multi-candidate election in which voters must choose *among* three or more names. Moreover, the standard theories may not provide very powerful empirical explanations of third party support. For example, since less than one-tenth of one percent of the 1980 electorate identified with a minor party,[3] partisanship—a central variable in many theories of voting— is of little help in accounting for the size of John Anderson's backing (Campbell et al. 1960). Similarly, theories of voting that see elections as referenda on the performance of the party

---

[3] Center for Political Studies (hereafter abbreviated CPS) 1980 National Election Study.

in power cannot explain why unhappy voters defect to the second party in some years, but to a third or fourth in others (Fiorina 1981).

The impact of third parties on American politics extends far beyond their capacity to attract votes. Minor parties, historically, have been a source of important policy innovations. Women's suffrage, the graduated income tax, and the direct election of senators, to name a few, were all issues that third parties espoused first. As Fred Haynes has argued, third parties in the nineteenth century "were pioneers in the conversion of American politics from almost exclusive attention to constitutional and governmental matters to the vital needs of the people" (1916, p. 470). Why do some policy innovations originate outside the two-party system? What is implied here about the ability of the major parties to cope with new political issues?

Once a third party attracts substantial backing, one or both of the major parties, anxious to win over those supporters, seize the minor party's ideas as their own. Observed historian John Hicks:

> Let a third party once demonstrate that votes are to be made by adopting a certain demand, then one or the other of the older parties can be trusted to absorb the new doctrine. Ultimately, if the demand has merit, it will probably be translated into law or practice by the major party that has taken it up. . . . The chronic supporter of third party tickets need not worry, therefore, when he is told, as he surely will be told, that he is "throwing away his vote." [A] glance through American history would seem to indicate that his kind of vote is after all probably the most powerful vote that has ever been cast. (1933, pp. 26-27)

Thus the power of third parties lies in their capacity to affect the content and range of political discourse, and ultimately public policy, by raising issues and options that the two major parties have ignored. In so doing, they not only promote their cause but affect the very character of the two-party system.

When a third party compels a major party to adopt policies it otherwise may not have, it stimulates a redrawing of the political battle lines and a reshuffling of the major party coalitions (Burnham 1970, ch. 1). To the extent that the third parties are able to alter the political agenda and the distribution of major party support, they are an important political force. Understanding this source of change in the major parties and in American public policy requires that one discern the causes of third party voting.

In short, minor parties perform many of the same functions in American politics that parties and other political institutions more generally do: they "link people to government" (Sartori 1976, p. 25). Third parties are one of many vehicles people use to express their concerns. Like the major parties, third parties aggregate citizens' preferences into a political force and try to influence what governmental leaders do.

Finally, third parties are an important outlet for political discontent. When the major parties fail to do their jobs, voters can register their disapproval by throwing their support to a minor party. Although regarded as an extreme step in the American context, it is nevertheless a rather mild form of protest that does little to threaten the political regime. As such, third parties have been thought of as "safety valves for discontent" (Ranney and Kendall 1951, p. 455). People who feel ignored by the major parties but are unwilling to abandon their goals can, through an independent campaign, pursue their cause yet still retain their allegiance to the political system.

Before proceeding, we should clarify what we mean by a "major party" and a "minor party." In a given election, we shall call a political party "major" if it runs candidates for local, state, and federal offices in a majority of the states and if prior to the contest the party holds one of the two largest blocs of seats in the House of Representatives. A party's label in a specific year obviously cannot be based on its performance in that election, for what is important is how the voters perceived the party *before* they went to the polls. Thus, even if the Progressive Party had captured both the presidency and the House in 1912, it would not have altered the fact that on election day the voters did not regard it as one of the major parties.

By this definition, the Democrats became a major party in 1832; the Whigs attained that status in 1836 and were replaced in 1854 by the Republicans, who captured a plurality of the seats in the House of Representatives in that year's elections. Since then the Democrats and the Republicans have retained their major party standing.

We shall call all other presidential contenders "third party" candidates. We use this term interchangeably with "minor party," "independent," and "non-major party" candidates. There are admittedly differences between minor parties that run candidates for other offices and persist for several elections and independent candidacies that rise and fall in a single race for the presidency. As we discuss later in more detail, important third parties of the nineteenth century were largely of the first type, whereas those of the twentieth century have been predominantly of the independent genre. Nevertheless, these differences, like others mentioned previously, are dwarfed by the commonalities the movements share. Most prominently, they are all expressions of dissatisfaction with the major parties.[4]

Our analysis of the causes of third party voting in presidential elections relies on several kinds of data. We draw heavily upon historical accounts of each movement. We also analyze aggregate political, economic, and demographic data for presidential contests from 1840 on to explain fluctuations in third party support since then. Finally, we turn to survey data from presidential elections beginning in 1952 to isolate better what motivates people to abandon the major parties.

We start with the 1840 election because it was not until that year that the two-party system, as we would recognize it today, had taken final form. As McCormick noted, by the 1840s "two party alignments had been established throughout

[4] We also have found little that consistently and clearly distinguishes candidates who do not adopt a party label (like John Anderson in 1980) from those who do (like George Wallace in 1968).

the nation and . . . within each region—and in most states—
these parties were balanced and competitive" (1966, p. 342).
By 1840 the Whig and Democratic parties were contesting both
state and national elections. "There was a nationalization of
political identities. Voters everywhere thought of themselves
as either Whigs or Democrats" (p. 342). National issues dominated presidential politics by 1840, and many "modern" characteristics of a campaign—nominating conventions, formal
party platforms, party organizations, rallies, banners, and slo-
gans—had appeared (Chambers 1967, pp. 11-14; Shade 1981).
In addition, white male suffrage was nearly universal, and
all states, except South Carolina, chose presidential electors
by popular vote. Finally, because printed ballots had replaced
voice voting, election records became more complete in 1840.

The first question that we address is why American voters
have remained so loyal to the two major parties. In chapter
2 we identify three types of constraints—barriers, handicaps,
and major party strategies—that inhibit third party voting.
The major parties intentionally erect some of these hurdles;
others are a by-product of the formal structure of the electoral
system and two centuries of tradition. These constraints are
so formidable that only the most serious breakdowns of the
two major parties produce significant levels of third party
support. We illustrate how these forces have worked against
third parties by examining in chapters 3 and 4 some of the
more important third party movements to emerge since 1840.
As we shall see, politicians have always viewed third parties
as a path of last resort. Although many parties at first seem
as though they might displace one of the major parties, or at
least establish themselves as permanent forces, only one—
the Republican Party—has actually been able to do so.

A case-by-case analysis reveals that near the turn of the
century third parties changed in fundamental ways. These
changes parallel transformations that occurred within the major parties as well. Third parties of the nineteenth century
were, as a rule, true political parties. They held conventions,
had contested nominations, ran candidates for local offices,
won elections, and had relatively long lives. Important third

parties of the twentieth century, in contrast, have generally been little more than candidacies of individuals. These movements, described in chapter 4, have rarely survived without their founders. Voters were attracted to the magnetic personalities of these men at least as much as to the causes they represented.

Examination of the more successful movements suggests a number of common determinants of third party support. We develop a general theory in chapter 5 arguing that third party voting is motivated by three factors: major party deterioration, attractive third party candidates who present a viable alternative to the major party nominees, and an influx of voters with no loyalty to the two major parties. Third party voting is also constrained by citizen allegiance to the political system and by structural barriers that make it difficult for people to cast a third party ballot. We test the theory in chapter 6.

As will become apparent, a third party's relative success depends in part on who heads its ticket. In general, the greater the third party candidate's political prestige, the more votes he will attract. Since prominent candidates have a large impact on the level of minor party support, we must explain why they abandon the major parties. This is the focus of chapter 7.

We conclude by reflecting on what our findings indicate about major party vitality. Is the occasional breakdown of the two-party system unavoidable? Are there limits to the ability of the major parties to prevent defections? What do our findings imply about the strengths and weaknesses of the American two-party system?

PART I

CHAPTER 2

CONSTRAINTS ON
THIRD PARTIES

To UNDERSTAND the significance of a third party vote, one must first recognize how difficult an act it is to undertake. A host of barriers, disadvantages, and strategies block the path of would-be third party supporters. So formidable are these hurdles that third party voting occurs only under the most extreme conditions. The constraints we describe in this chapter ensure that third parties will never be on equal footing with the two major parties and help explain why a third party vote signifies something very different from a vote for either the Democrats or Republicans.

The two major parties, in Schattschneider's words, "monopolize power" (1942, p. 68). They are able to do so via three routes. First, barriers—powerful constitutional, legal, and administrative provisions—bias the electoral system against minor party challenges and discourage candidates and voters from abandoning the major parties. Third party movements are further handicapped because they have fewer resources, suffer from poorer press coverage, usually run weaker, less qualified candidates, and do not share the legitimacy of the major parties. Citizens do not accord minor party candidates the same status as the Democratic and Republican nominees; they see third party challengers as standing outside the American two-party system. These handicaps, by and large a side-effect of the way the electoral system is set up, raise the cost of third party voting. A third party vote, therefore, does not merely signify the selection of one of three equally attractive options; it is an extraordinary act that requires the voter to reject explicitly the major parties.

Finally, just as the Democrats and Republicans try to win votes from each other, they also pursue minor party supporters. By coopting third party issue positions, and pursuing other more devious political strategies, the major parties win over third party voters and delegitimize third party candidacies. Although the United States Constitution does not even mention political parties, through these barriers, handicaps, and political strategies the Democrats and Republicans have attained a privileged position in American politics.

BARRIERS

The rules that govern elections in the United States are far from neutral. They form barriers that block the emergence and discourage the growth of more than two parties. These biases help ensure that the Democrats and Republicans retain their position of dominance. The founding fathers created some of these barriers; the two major parties have helped erect others.

Constitutional Biases

The single-member-district plurality system governing most American elections discourages the emergence, growth, and survival of third parties. Under this arrangement, parties compete for an individual office—say, a Senate seat—and the candidate who obtains the most votes wins. The only way for a party to receive any immediate rewards (other than psychic ones) is for it to gain a plurality of the votes. Unlike a proportional representation system where 20 percent of the votes usually yields some seats in the legislature, in a single-member-district plurality system a party can receive 20 percent of the votes in every state and yet not win a single seat. Because citizens know third parties have very little chance of winning, they prefer not to waste their votes on them. Small parties become discouraged and either drop out or join with another party. At the same time, the system encourages the two major parties to try to absorb minor parties or prevent them from flourishing in the first place.[1]

---

[1] See Schattschneider 1942, p. 75; Duverger 1954, p. 217; Downs 1957, p. 124; Key 1964, p. 208; and Riker 1982, pp. 753-66. Of the 107 nations Rae

The presidential selection system is a peculiar variant of the single-member-district plurality method and hence poses similar problems for third parties. The Electoral College tallies the number of times each candidate wins one of the fifty-one single-member-district plurality contests held in the fifty states and the District of Columbia, weighting each outcome by the state's electoral votes. A candidate who comes in second or third in a particular state does not win a single electoral vote regardless of his percentage of the popular vote. Short of winning the election, the only way a minor party can hope to gain any power is to secure enough electoral votes to throw the election into the House of Representatives.[2]

The Electoral College system is particularly harsh in its discrimination against nationally based third parties that fall short of a popular vote plurality in every state. John Anderson, for instance, did not capture a single electoral vote in 1980, though he polled 6.6 percent of the popular vote. The Electoral College does favor regionally based third party candidates who are strong enough in particular states to gain pluralities. For example, in 1948, States' Rights nominee Strom Thurmond obtained 7.3 percent of the Electoral College vote with only 2.4 percent of the national popular vote.

Contrary to popular belief, most current proposals for eliminating the Electoral College would not benefit third parties. The most widely supported plan calls for the direct popular election of the president with a runoff if no candidate receives 40 percent of the votes cast. But as long as a president can be elected with less than an absolute majority of the popular vote, the plan would, for all practical purposes, work like a single-member-district plurality system. To prevent either the Democrats or Republicans from collecting 40 percent of the vote, minor parties would obviously have to poll at least 20 percent. This has happened only three times since 1840. Any

studies, 90 percent fit the maxim: "plurality formulae cause two-party systems" (1971, p. 93). The exceptions are countries where a minor party's strength is concentrated in a single region (Schattschneider 1942, p. 75; Rae 1971, p. 95).

[2] Only twice in nearly two hundred years (1800 and 1824) has the House decided an election, and in neither instance were policy concessions granted to the third place candidate, nor was he included in a coalition government.

direct vote system that allows a party to win with less than a full majority of the popular vote would hinder third parties, though the larger the plurality required to elect a president, the lower the barrier becomes.[3]

The single-member-district plurality system not only explains two-party dominance, it also ensures short lives for third parties that do appear. If they are to survive, political parties must offer tangible benefits to their supporters. Of the forty-five different minor parties or independent candidates that have received presidential popular votes in more than one state since 1840, 58 percent ran just once; 87 percent ran in three or fewer elections (table 2.1).[4] Even George Wallace—who as an independent in 1968 won 13.5 percent of the popular vote, 46 electoral votes, and had a relatively well-oiled organization in place—ran for the Democratic Party nomination in 1972 and vowed, both before he was shot in May and again at the July Convention, to work within that party.

Third party voters must be willing to support candidates who they know have no chance of winning. Moreover, because third parties wither so quickly, there is little opportunity for voters to grow accustomed to backing them or for this cycle of discouragement to be broken. The single-member-district plurality system is the single largest barrier to third party vitality.

[3] Other systems would be more generous to third parties. A direct popular election system with a runoff if no candidate received a *majority* of the votes cast would provide minor parties an opportunity, between rounds, to trade support for concessions. Under this arrangement, in a close election, a minor party might maneuver into a position of influence with relatively few votes. Alternatively, if the U.S. Congress elected the president by a majority vote, minor parties able to obtain seats in the House could bargain with other parties to form a majority coalition. On only five occasions since 1840 has over 10 percent of the House had minor party affiliations.

[4] All five parties (11 percent) that ran five or more times are, with the exception of the Prohibition Party, ideological parties of the left—Socialist Labor, Socialist, Communist, and Socialist Workers—that seem to live on benefits unrelated to electoral outcomes. Additionally, all five seem to be concerned chiefly with education—a goal substantially different from that of other minor parties. Able to satisfy this more limited ambition, they find it easier to survive (Olson 1965, ch. 1; Wilson 1973, ch. 3).

TABLE 2.1
Longevity of Third Parties in Presidential Elections, 1840-1980

Number of Elections in Which the Same Third Party (or Independent Candidate) Has Run for President	Percentage of Parties[a] (N = 45)	Cumulative Percentage
1 Election	58	58
2 Elections	16	74
3 Elections	13	87
4 Elections	2	89
5 or More Elections	11	100

SOURCE: Congressional Quarterly, *Guide to U.S. Elections* (Washington, D.C.: Congressional Quarterly, Inc., 1976); *Guide to 1976 Elections* (Washington, D.C.: Congressional Quarterly, Inc., 1977); Clerk of the House of Representatives, *Statistics of the Presidential and Congressional Election of November 4, 1980* (Washington, D.C.: U.S. Government Printing Office, 1981).

[a] Only parties or candidates receiving popular votes in more than one state appear in this table.

Ballot Access Restrictions

The Democrats and Republicans have constructed a maze of cumbersome regulations and procedures that make it difficult for minor parties and independent candidates to gain a spot on the general election ballot. Whereas major party candidates automatically appear on the ballot, third parties must petition state election officials to be listed. A candidate whose name does not appear is obviously disadvantaged: voters are not cued when they enter the polling booth; it is difficult and at times embarrassing for a voter to cast a write-in ballot.

Ballot access was not a problem for third parties in the nineteenth century, because there were no ballots as we now know them. Prior to about 1890, the political parties, not the states, prepared and distributed election ballots (or "tickets," as they were called), listing only their own candidates. Party workers peddled their ballots, usually of a distinct color and shape, at polling stations on election day. The voter would choose one of the tickets and drop it in the ballot box—an act not commonly performed in secret. Poll watchers, of course, could easily identify how the citizen voted. The voter, unless he scratched names off the party slate and substituted new ones, or combined portions of two or more ballots, was forced to support a party's entire ticket.

This all changed when states adopted the Australian ballot. Under the new system, each state now prepared an "official" ballot listing all the party slates, and voters could mark it secretly. It was both more difficult for parties to intimidate citizens and easier for voters to split their tickets (Rusk 1970).

However, this shift to the Australian method generated an obvious question: which parties should be listed on the official ballot? To keep the list of candidates relatively short, states had to restrict some candidates' access to the new ballot. Laws soon emerged making it difficult for non-major parties to appear. Half the ballots cast in 1892 were governed by these access laws; by 1900 nearly 90 percent of the votes cast were subject to such restrictions (figure 2.1).[5]

Because the states determine their own ballot access laws, minor party candidates wishing to place their names before the voters must overcome fifty-one different sets of bureaucratic hurdles. This is an arduous task for third party contenders, even well-financed ones. Petitions must be circulated within a specific time period that varies from state to state. They can be distributed only between early June and early August in California, for instance, and between August 1 and September 1 in Indiana. Filing deadlines also vary by state, and many occur relatively early in the election cycle—before the major parties have held their conventions. Five deadlines

---

[5] Although most states instituted access limitations when they changed to the Australian ballot, eighteen states postponed adopting these rules. Six were 1892 strongholds of Populist candidate James Weaver (Alabama, Kansas, Minnesota, Nebraska, South Dakota, and Wyoming), where presumably the motivation for the delay was to maintain easy ballot access for him. The remaining states had no need for formal ballot access restrictions because they had strong party organizations that could deter third party voting (Maryland, Massachusetts, Pennsylvania, Rhode Island, and Connecticut) or were one-party states where third party activity would have been of little threat (Georgia, Louisiana, North Carolina, South Carolina, Virginia, and Oklahoma).

FIGURE 2.1
Adoption of Australian Ballot and Third Party Ballot Access
Restrictions, 1840-1980

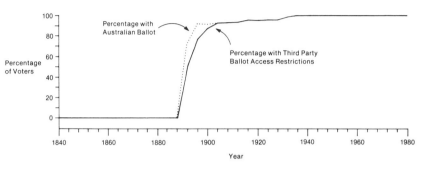

SOURCE: Arthur C. Ludington, *American Ballot Laws: 1888-1910* (Albany: New York State Library, 1911), and state election codes.

had already passed by the time John Anderson announced his candidacy on April 24, 1980 (Ohio, Maryland, New Mexico, Maine, and Kentucky). The remaining deadlines were scattered between May and late September. This lack of a uniform petition period or filing deadline means that a third party or independent candidate cannot mount a nationwide effort; instead, he must hold fifty-one different drives at different times during the campaign.

The number of signatures a candidate must gather varies from 25 people (Tennessee) to 5 percent of the state's registered voters (Montana, Oklahoma, and others). A candidate needed over 100,000 signers to qualify in California in 1980 and 57,500 to make the Georgia ballot. To qualify for all fifty-one ballots in 1980, each third party presidential challenger had to gather over 1.2 million signatures (Cook 1980a, p. 1315).

Other provisions define which voters are eligible to sign a candidate's petition. West Virginia forbids petitioners from voting in its primary; New York and Nebraska disqualify signatures of citizens who have already participated in a primary. Some states also have onerous provisions for validating signatures. Citizens in South Carolina must record both their precinct and voter registration numbers—exotic bits of information that few people know. New Hampshire requires that signatures be certified. Some states also impose complicated procedures on the distribution of signatures. Petitions must be collected by magisterial districts in West Virginia—a designation with which even most politicians are unfamiliar. New York requires candidates to obtain a specified number of signatures in each county.

Nine states in 1980 had either a sore loser law prohibiting a candidate who ran in the state's primary (but lost the nomination) from running in the general election or a disaffiliation statute forbidding independent candidates from belonging to a political party.

Since their introduction, every state has made at least one change in its ballot access laws.[6] Because nearly all third parties are short-lived, the requirements governing initial access are the pertinent ones. The hostile and suspicious political climate surrounding the two world wars prompted many restrictions on ballot access (American Civil Liberties Union 1943; Bone 1943, p. 524; Schmidt 1960, pp. 31, 125). Between Theodore Roosevelt's run in 1912 and Robert LaFollette's 1924 candidacy, ten states significantly increased the number of signatures required to qualify a candidate; some of these instituted restrictions for the first time. Only one state, Nevada, reduced the number of signatures needed. Although in the years preceding World War II states did not further boost the number of signatures required for a candidate to appear on

---

[6] Some states made it easier for minor parties, once they secured a ballot spot, to remain on the ballot in subsequent elections. Fifteen states added provisions allowing votes cast for a party in a previous election to qualify it for a ballot position: Alabama, Arkansas, California, Connecticut, Delaware, Georgia, Michigan, Montana, Nebraska, New Hampshire, North Dakota, South Dakota, Virginia, Wisconsin, and Wyoming (Ludington 1911; Durbin 1980). Four states reduced the number of votes needed: Idaho, Indiana, Louisiana, and Washington. Eleven increased the requirement: Illinois, Kansas, Maine, Maryland, Minnesota, Nevada, New Jersey, Ohio, Rhode Island, Tennessee, and Vermont. This provision can help the smallest of parties: Ellen McCormack's Right-to-Life Party polled over 50,000 votes in the 1978 New York gubernatorial election, so it automatically gained a spot on the state's 1980 general election ballot.

the ballot, they instituted filing fees, changed filing deadlines, and shortened the length of the petitioning period (*Columbia Law Review* 1937; *Yale Law Journal* 1948). The laws were more strictly enforced. In addition, by 1942, nineteen states had barred from their ballots (by legislation or election officials' rulings) Communists or parties that advocated the overthrow of the government by force or violence (Bone 1943, p. 526).

Recent court decisions have reversed this trend. As a result of the lawsuits initiated by George Wallace in 1968, Eugene McCarthy in 1976, and John Anderson in 1980, ballot access laws are now as lenient as they have ever been in this century. Even Libertarian Ed Clark was able to gain a spot on all fifty-one ballots in 1980.[7]

Despite these changes, which for the most part have been at the margins, it is still no easy task for third party candidates to win access to the ballot. All twentieth-century third party presidential candidates have had to struggle to obtain positions on the ballot. LaFollette found in 1924 that the laws were "almost unsuperable obstacles to a new party" (MacKay 1947, p. 179). He was forced to run under a variety of labels: "Progressive," "Independent," "Independent-Progressive," and "Socialist." Such a predicament can only contribute to voter

---

[7] Relaxation began with *William v. Rhodes* (393 U.S. 23 [1968]). Here the Supreme Court struck down Ohio's requirement that George Wallace both gather 433,100 signatures (10 percent of the votes cast in its last gubernatorial election) by February 7, 1968, some nine months before the general election, and be nominated by a political party that met Ohio's elaborate organizational requirements (Wiseheart 1969).

As a result of the eighteen suits the McCarthy campaign filed in 1976, the courts ruled more access laws unconstitutional. Laws that required petitioners to gather signatures in excess of 5 percent of the eligible electorate tended to be invalidated (Neuborne and Eisenberg 1980, p. 57). Other rulings struck down petition periods and filing deadlines that "a reasonably diligent candidate" could not meet.

The Anderson campaign's 1980 litigation successfully overturned additional requirements. (*Anderson v. Babb* [E.D. N.C. August 21, 1980]; *Anderson v. Celebrezze* [S.D. Ohio July 18, 1980]; *Anderson v. Hooper* [D. N.M. July 8, 1980]; *Anderson v. Mills* [E.D. Ky. August 14, 1980]; *Anderson v. Morris* [D. Md. August 6, 1980]; and *Anderson v. Quinn* [D. Maine August 11, 1980].) The Supreme Court again invalidated Ohio's statute, this time because of its March 20 filing deadline; Anderson won similar victories in Maryland, New Mexico, Maine, and Kentucky.

confusion and the general perception that third parties are temporary and makeshift, not deserving of equal consideration. William Lemke succeeded in getting his Union Party on the ballot in only thirty-four states in 1936 (Tull 1965, p. 167; Bennett 1969, p. 212). He failed to secure a spot in populous states like New York, where Father Charles Coughlin's National Union for Social Justice had a large following; California, home of Townsendism; and Louisiana, stronghold of the Share Our Wealth movement (Leuchtenburg 1971, p. 2843). Like LaFollette, Lemke could not always run under his own party name: he was forced to run as the "Royal Oak Party" candidate in Ohio and Pennsylvania, the "Third Party" challenger in Michigan, and the "Union Progressive Party" nominee in Illinois. In 1948 Henry Wallace not only confronted provisions that denied Communists a spot on the ballot but encountered capricious administration of other access laws as well (Schmidt 1960, pp. 124-52). George Wallace qualified for every ballot except the one in the predominantly black District of Columbia, but he was forced to run under six different party labels. Eugene McCarthy secured a spot on only twenty-nine state ballots; fifteen of these required court battles to win his position. (He won three additional suits after the election.) McCarthy did not appear on the ballot in crucial states like New York and California. John Anderson won positions on all fifty-one November ballots but only after a costly effort. The campaign spent more than half of the $7.3 million it raised between April and September on petition drives and legal fees (Whittle 1980, p. 2834). While the major parties prepare media ads, buy television time, and plan campaign strategy, third party candidates devote their scarce resources to getting on the ballot.

Although it is clear that, relative to the Democrats and Republicans, ballot access laws discriminate against independent challengers, we are less certain whether this bias is greater than the one that existed prior to the 1890s when the parties themselves prepared the ballots. Obviously, in one sense, the earlier arrangement was less onerous for third parties. They simply printed their own tickets; there was no maze of legal procedures. But, at the same time, the unofficial ballot system disadvantaged third parties in ways that were ameliorated with the adoption of the Australian ballot. First, under the old system, it was difficult for citizens to vote a split ticket since each ballot listed only a single party's slate of candidates. This in effect required voters to abandon their party for every office at stake in the election, even if they were attracted to only the third party's presidential nominee. Compared to an arrangement where split-ticket voting is easier, this probably reduced the likelihood of third party voting. Second, since a bolt to a third party was a public act, the cost of betraying longstanding loyalties was high (Woodward 1951, p. 244; Rusk 1968, pp. 128-30). Moreover, under the unofficial ballot system, a party needed organization and resources to print its tickets and distribute them on election day. But organization and resources are two commodities that third parties have always lacked. The shift to the official ballot eliminated these costs; the ballots were now printed and distributed at public expense. It is not clear that the official ballot adversely affected third parties more than the system it replaced. Nonetheless, these new restrictions still constitute a bias.

Campaign Finance Laws

The 1974 Federal Election Campaign Act (FECA) is the most recent instance of the major parties adopting a "reform" that freezes out third party challengers. Under the law, the Federal Elections Commission (FEC) provides the major party presidential nominees a lump sum ($29.4 million in 1980) for their campaigns. On top of this, the Democratic and Republican National Committees can raise and spend as much as they need to pay for legal and accounting expenses incurred in complying with the act. State and local party committees can raise and spend an unlimited amount on voter registration, get-out-the-vote drives, and other volunteer activities. "Independent" committees can also spend freely on behalf of the major parties.

Third parties, on the other hand, are eligible to receive

public funds only *after* the November election, and then only if they appear on the ballot in at least ten states and obtain at least 5 percent of the national popular vote. The exact amount a candidate receives increases with his total vote (assuming the initial ten state provision is met).[8] Given these requirements, only 10 of the 148 minor party candidates (7 percent) that have emerged in more than one state since 1840 would have qualified for retroactive public financing. Although third party candidates are denied the benefits of the pre-election subsidy, they must still comply with the FECA rules on disclosure of campaign contributions and are bound by the ceilings of $1,000 per election from individuals and $5,000 from political action committees.

Because the FECA mentioned only "minor party" candidates, "independent" Eugene McCarthy had to petition the FEC in 1976 to extend its coverage to him. Had a favorable ruling been received, and had McCarthy stayed above 5 percent in the polls, he may have had an easier time attracting contributions and securing loans. But the FEC took six long weeks, until mid-October, to rule against McCarthy on a straight party vote: Republican commissioners supported McCarthy, Democrats opposed him. (It was widely believed at the time that McCarthy would have taken more votes from Carter than from Ford.) John Anderson succeeded in 1980 where McCarthy failed. In early September, by a 5-1 vote, the FEC ruled that Anderson was the functional equivalent of a third party and that he would receive post-election funding if he cleared the appropriate vote and ballot hurdles.[9]

The FECA is a major party protection act. Democrats and Republicans receive their funds before the election, minor parties after. During the primaries, when name recognition is built and legitimacy established, contenders for a major

---

[8] In 1980, 5 percent of the vote would have yielded a $3.1 million post-election subsidy, 10 percent a $6.5 million subsidy, and 15 percent $10.4 million.

[9] Although Anderson had hoped to borrow against his anticipated federal funding, banks, fearing that their loans would be declared illegal campaign contributions if Anderson defaulted, were not forthcoming.

party's nomination receive matching federal funds; minor parties, which do not hold primaries, receive none. During the general election, major party candidates are freed from time-consuming and costly fund-raising activities; minor parties are not. National party committees may accept individual contributions of up to $20,000; independent candidates cannot. In short, this law ensures a large gap between the financial resources available to major and minor parties.

HANDICAPS

Most of the other constraints that third parties confront are consequences of the structure of the electoral system. Independent candidates are disadvantaged: they have fewer resources, receive poorer press coverage, are usually less qualified, and are not seen as legitimate contenders. Although these handicaps do not result from formal rules that discriminate against minor parties, they have a similar impact: they make voting for a third party an act requiring unusual energy, persistence, or desperation.

Campaign Resources

Without resources, an American political party's struggle is grim indeed. And, as a rule, third party candidates have had fewer resources than the major parties. This was true long before the Federal Election Campaign Act. The major parties grossly outspent Abolitionists in 1840, Free Soilers in 1848, and Populists in 1892 (Morgan 1971, p. 1728; Sewell 1976, pp. 75, 167). Even the most successful minor party challengers amass only a fraction of the resources available to their Democratic and Republican opponents. Former President Theodore Roosevelt, the best financed third party candidate on record, spent only 60 percent of the average major party total in 1912; George Wallace spent 39 percent and John Anderson only 49 percent when they ran (table 2.2).[10] Few minor party

[10] Even Teddy Roosevelt would have been no better off than other third party contenders were it not for George W. Perkins (a partner in the banking

TABLE 2.2

Campaign Expenditures by Minor Presidential Parties, 1908-1980

Year	Minor Party	Minor Party Expenditures	Average of Major Party Expenditures	Minor Party as Percentage of Major Party
1908	Socialist	$ 95,504	$ 1,147,430	8.3
1912	Progressive	665,420	1,103,199	60.3
	Socialist	71,598		6.5
1924	Progressive	236,963	2,564,659	9.2
1948	Progressive	1,133,863	2,431,815	46.6
	States' Rights	163,442		6.7
1952	Socialist Labor	88,018	5,820,775	1.5
1956	Socialist Labor	22,727	6,442,677	.4
1960	Socialist Labor	66,170	9,962,500	.7
	National States' Rights	4,269		a
1964	Socialist Labor	59,344	12,391,500	.5
	National States' Rights	41,964		.3
	Socialist Workers	2,570		a
1968	American Independent	7,223,000	18,498,000	39.0
	National States' Rights	24,727		a
	Socialist Labor	80,130		a
	Socialist Workers	40,481		a
1972	American Independent	710,000	41,289,000	1.7
	Communist	173,600		.4
	Socialist Workers	118,000		.3
	Socialist Labor	114,000		.3
	Christian National Crusade	93,000		.2
	People's	40,539		.1
	Prohibition	37,000		.1
	Libertarian	17,000		a
	Conservative	6,000		a
	Flying Tigers	977		a
1976	Communist	504,710	21,973,856	2.3
	Eugene McCarthy	442,491		2.0
	Libertarian	387,429		1.8
	American	187,815		.9
	U.S. Labor	180,653		.8

TABLE 2.2 (*cont.*)

Year	Minor Party	Minor Party Expenditures	Average of Major Party Expenditures	Minor Party as Percentage of Major Party
	Socialist Workers	151,648		.7
	Socialist Labor	59,820		.3
	American Independent	44,488		.2
1980	John B. Anderson	15,040,669	29,040,183	48.7
	Libertarian	3,210,758		10.4
	Communist	194,774		.6
	Socialist Workers	186,252		.6
	Right to Life	83,412		.3
	Workers' World	40,310		.1
	Socialist	36,059		.1
	Citizens	23,408		.1
	American Independent	13,931		[a]
	American	13,716		[a]
	Statesman	812		[a]

SOURCE: *Historical Statistics of the United States, Colonial Times to 1970*, p. 1081; Alexander Heard, *The Costs of Democracy* (Chapel Hill: University of North Carolina Press, 1960), p. 54; Herbert Alexander, *Financing the 1960 Election; Financing the 1964 Election; Financing the 1968 Election; Financing the 1972 Election; Financing the 1976 Election.* The 1980 statistics are provided by the Federal Elections Commission.

[a] Less than .1 percent.

candidates achieve anything near even these levels of spending: LaFollette in 1924 only spent 9 percent of the average major party total, and Thurmond only 7 percent in 1948. Almost every other minor party candidate was outspent by at least 50 to 1.

This disparity in resources means that third parties are significantly disadvantaged, if not crippled. Their ability to rent technical expertise, gather political intelligence, and campaign—especially through the media—is obviously restricted.

firm of J. P. Morgan), Frank Munsey (owner of five newspapers), and a few other wealthy benefactors who contributed the lion's share of his campaign chest (Mowry 1946, p. 288).

Moreover, because major parties do not have to allocate a huge proportion of their campaign chest to ballot access drives the way third parties do, the disparity in real available resources is greater than the simple proportions reported in table 2.2. After the ballot drives and court battles, Eugene McCarthy had only $100,000 left for media advertising in 1976 ($137,651 in 1980 dollars) (Cook 1980a, p. 1316). The 1980 Anderson campaign could not even afford to conduct polls—an essential weapon in a modern political arsenal. Staff were let go or went unpaid, little media time could be purchased, and campaign trips were cancelled (Weaver 1980a, p. B12; Weaver 1980b, p. D22; Peterson 1980a, pp. A1, A4).

The McCarthy and Anderson experiences are not unique: all third party and independent candidates have been strapped for campaign funds. The 1936 Lemke campaign, despite the backing of the National Union for Social Justice and Townsend Movement, was constantly plagued by financial problems. By mid-summer the Union Party had raised only $20,000 ($121,462 in 1980 dollars) (Bennett 1969, p. 211). LaFollette experienced similar problems, raising most of his money in one-dollar contributions (LaFollette and LaFollette 1953, p. 124). The campaign was in such dismal financial shape that it could not afford to send its cross-country rail campaign farther west then St. Louis (MacKay 1947, p. 156).

This scarcity of resources means that third parties are able to purchase only a fraction of the political advertising bought by the Democrats and Republicans (table 2.3). Even in 1968, George Wallace, the best financed of recent third party contenders, was able to secure only one-sixth of the radio and television time the major parties bought. In most years the situation is much worse: minor parties, on average, acquire one-twentieth of the television and radio time the major parties do.

Money, although certainly the most important campaign resource, is obviously not the only one. Elite support and a well-oiled, experienced party or candidate organization have always been essential. Here too the major parties are advantaged. As Haynes noted in 1924: "Party machinery has be-

TABLE 2.3
Media Expenditures by Minor Parties, 1956-1972

	Radio			Television		
Year	Minor Party Expenditures	Major Party Expenditures	Minor Parties as Percentage of Major Parties	Minor Party Expenditures	Major Party Expenditures	Minor Parties as Percentage of Major Parties
1956	$ 164,000	$ 3,019,000	5.4	$ 152,000	$ 6,484,000	2.3
1960	225,000	3,918,000	5.7	206,000	9,846,000	2.1
1964	209,000	6,899,000	3.0	350,000	17,146,000	2.0
1968	970,000	12,346,000	7.9	1,480,000	25,607,000	5.8
1972	1,577,000	11,933,000	13.2	1,515,000	23,052,000	6.6

SOURCE: U.S. Federal Communications Commission, *Report on Political Broadcasting* April 1961, July 1965, August 1969, March 1971, March 1973; U.S. Clerk of the House, *1956 General Election Campaigns* (85th Congress, 1st Session).

come so complex and requires so much technical skill in its manipulation that there seems less and less chance of its overthrow or seizure by inexperienced workers. It almost seems as though the Republican and Democratic parties must go on indefinitely" (p. 156).

It is easy to see why Haynes reached this conclusion. Few minor parties can compete with the major party organizations. The Liberty Party was "hopelessly outmatched by Whigs and Democrats in organization, experience, financial resources and political savvy," as was the "haphazard" Free Soil campaign eight years later (Sewell 1976, pp. 75, 166). William Lemke's total lack of a regular political organization contributed to his poor showing in 1936 (Tull 1965, p. 167; Bennett 1969, p. 241). Similar problems gripped Henry Wallace in 1948 (Schmidt 1960, pp. 92-123).

There are several reasons why these organizations flounder. Because third parties are short-lived, they have little time to build an electoral apparatus. Moreover, unlike the major parties, most presidential third parties do not run slates of congressional, state, and local candidates, so they have no other campaign organizations to draw upon. And since few third parties win federal, state, or local elections, the party lacks patronage—an important political resource through the late nineteenth and early twentieth centuries.

Some of these organizational problems would be alleviated if minor parties were able to persuade elected officials to join their independent cause. But they rarely can. Even strong Progressives like Senators William Borah and George Norris did not campaign for LaFollette, fearing Republican reprisals. Former President Theodore Roosevelt, who had the best opportunity for victory of any third party candidate, was unable to maintain his elite support. Most officials who had rallied behind his selection as the Republican nominee, including seven of the eight governors who originally advocated his candidacy, did not abandon the Republican Party (Mowry 1971, p. 2151). William Lemke could not attract the support of progressive or farm state politicians from either side of the aisle (Bennett 1969, p. 205), and few liberal politicians backed

Henry Wallace in 1948 (Schmidt 1960, pp. 37-39, 64-67). Only a handful of officeholders came out on behalf of George Wallace's 1968 presidential bid. Even when John Anderson's level of support in the polls stood at 20 percent, he had trouble finding a running mate, finally settling on former Wisconsin Governor Patrick Lucey.

Despite the many changes in presidential campaigns over the years, the need for superior resources and a strong and effective grassroots organization remains. Few if any major party candidates have won without them. Few if any minor party candidates have had them.

Media Coverage

Media coverage is also an essential component of a successful modern campaign. It supplies legitimacy and generates name recognition, both indispensible in attracting votes. But there is a huge disparity between the amount of coverage the media give minor parties and the attention they devote to the Democrats and Republicans. In 1980 the leading newspapers and weekly news magazines gave Reagan and Carter about ten times more coverage than *all eleven* third party and independent candidates combined.[11] This disparity showed up in network television news as well: between January and September the CBS Evening News devoted 6 hours, 10 minutes of coverage to Carter, 3 hours, 9 minutes to Reagan, and 1 hour, 46 minutes to Anderson (Leiser 1980).

Despite this imbalance, the media did treat Anderson relatively favorably in the opening months of his independent campaign. *Time* praised Anderson's intellect, his skills, and

[11] From the *New York Times, Washington Post, Christian Science Monitor, Newsweek, Time,* and *U.S. News and World Report* we collected 18.01 pounds of clippings on Carter and Reagan and 1.77 pounds on all the other 1980 presidential candidates.

This imbalance in media coverage is not new. Newspapers in 1840 barely mentioned that an abolitionist party had been formed (Nash 1959, p. 30). The press also devoted little attention to LaFollette in 1924 or to Henry Wallace in 1948 (MacKay 1947, p. 213; Schmidt 1960, pp. 90-91, 229-31; Yarnell 1974, pp. 47-49).

his willingness to confront issues. *Newsweek* pointed out that Anderson's intellectual and oratorical skills had long been acknowledged "even by House foes." They called his 26 percent support in the California Poll a "close third" and his 22 percent standing in New York a "competitive third" (Goldman 1980, pp. 28-38). *Time's* headline read: "Despite Problems, Anderson's Campaign is Starting to Move" (Warner 1980, p. 21). The reports were upbeat.

But the media's tendency to focus on the horserace soon brought stories highlighting the hopelessness of Anderson's cause. They no longer viewed Anderson as a serious challenger, but a "certain loser" (Lewis 1980). On the front page of the September 26 *Washington Star*, Jack Germond and Jules Witcover (1980) concluded: "With some exceptions, Anderson's leading supporters and advisors have abandoned their dream of winning the election. . . . This does not suggest that Anderson's backers are throwing in their cards, but only that they now see the rest of the campaign as a case of playing out their hands against essentially hopeless odds." A similar obituary appeared in the following day's *New York Times* where Warren Weaver, Jr., pronounced: "The independent candidate no longer has a serious chance of winning." The same day CBS reported that the Anderson campaign was "sputtering," and on September 28 David Broder, in the *Washington Post*, tossed in the final spade of dirt when he called the candidacy a fiasco and concluded it was going nowhere. From that point on, the press focused almost exclusively on Anderson's decline in the polls, his money problems, and his inability to gain endorsements. By the end of the campaign Anderson was no longer the star orator he was in June, but "fuzzy," "too preachy," "humorless," and "highflown" (Stacks 1980, p. 52).

This sort of coverage is understandable. We doubt that the media intentionally tried to undermine Anderson's cause. Nonetheless, the media can affect voters' perceptions by concentrating on who will win instead of what the candidates are saying. The de facto result benefits the major parties. We cannot unravel how much the media's treatment of Anderson caused his drop in standing or merely reflected it. But the fact remains that in the final crucial weeks of the campaign, voters saw little of Anderson in the press (not to mention Ed Clark, Barry Commoner, or John Rarick), and what little they did see was about Anderson the loser.

Televised presidential debates also exclude third party candidates. Only Nixon and Kennedy debated in 1960; only Ford and Carter appeared in 1976.[12] Although Anderson did debate Reagan in September 1980, Carter's unwillingness to participate delegitimized Anderson's candidacy and, along with ABC's simultaneous airing of the film "The Orient Express," contributed to a much smaller viewing audience than in 1960, 1976, or in the Carter-Reagan confrontation a week before the 1980 election.[13]

The primary reason third party candidates receive so little coverage is that broadcasters and publishers do not think they warrant attention. Nearly two out of three newspaper editors thought that their readers had little interest in third party candidates in 1980 (Bass 1982, p. 12). As James M. Perry of the *Wall Street Journal* put it:

> We base [our decision] on the simple proposition that readers don't want to waste their time on someone who won't have a role in the campaign. We're not going to run a page-one spread on a fringe candidate. We don't have a multiparty system. Until we do, nobody's going to cover these candidates. (Bass 1982, p. 11)

[12] Congress allowed broadcasters to freeze the minor party candidates out of the 1960 debates by temporarily suspending the "equal-time requirement" (Section 315a) of the Federal Communications Act that requires broadcasters who provide time to a legally qualified candidate for any public office to "afford equal opportunities" to all other candidates for the same office. The networks, to avoid the equal-time provision entirely, covered the 1976 and 1980 League of Women Voters debates as "news events." The FCC and the courts sustained this action, which minor parties naturally challenged (Alexander 1979, p. 441).

[13] Forty-four percent of the electorate viewed the Anderson-Reagan debate compared to 79 percent who saw the debates in 1960, 72 percent in 1976, and 83 percent who watched Reagan and Carter do battle in 1980 (CPS 1960 National Election Study; CBS/*New York Times* Poll, September 23-25, 1980, and October 25-27, 1980).

Marshall Field, publisher of the Chicago *Sun Times*, echoed this sentiment: "The country is run by a two-party system and those candidates 'chosen by the people' are the ones who deserve serious consideration" (McCarthy 1980, p. 149).[14]

The press does more than simply ignore minor party candidates; at times they are overtly hostile towards them. Metropolitan newspapers routinely attacked the Populists (Goodwyn 1978, p. 210). The press committed two sins against the Progressives of 1924: one of omission (lack of coverage), and the other of commission (the distorted reporting of Progressive issues and activities, sometimes accidental, sometimes intentional) (MacKay 1947, p. 211). The same scenario unfolded in 1948. The few stories that did appear on Henry Wallace focused on his Communist affiliations (Schmidt 1960, pp. 90-91, 229-31; Yarnell 1974, pp. 47-49; *Time*, 1948a, p. 16). To discourage support for Henry Wallace, newspapers in New Haven, Pittsburgh, Boston, Milwaukee, and Cleveland published the names, addresses, and occupations of people who signed his ballot petitions (Schmidt 1960, pp. 133-34).

In the past, minor parties have tried to overcome the media's neglect and abuse by relying on their own tabloids to get their messages across. The Union Party had the *Townsend National Weekly* with a circulation of 300,000; the Prohibitionists had several periodicals such as the *Voice*, which began in 1884 and rose to a circulation of 700,000 by 1888. In addition to his own publishing house, Socialist candidate Eugene Debs could rely on over three hundred English and foreign language newspapers and magazines with a combined circulation exceeding two million (Greer 1949, p. 271; Bennett 1969, p. 171; Storms 1972, p. 13; Weinstein, 1967, pp. 84-102). But unlike television, radio, or non-party newspapers, party publications allow a candidate to communicate only with the already faithful; they are ineffective at reaching non-supporters.

---

[14] The slim coverage the press gives to third party candidates may also be due to minor parties' inability to get their messages out as effectively as the Democrats and Republicans can. Three out of four daily newspaper editors claim that they received fewer press releases from third party candidates in 1980 than from the Reagan and Carter camps. Third party press releases were also less complete (Bass 1982, pp. 16-17).

Although the media are the voter's primary source of information about politics, neither print nor electronic journalists do much to alleviate the voters' dearth of information about third party candidates. The little that voters do learn about these candidates helps convince them that their cause is hopeless. When voters support third party candidates, they do so in spite of, not because of, the media's coverage of their campaigns.

Unqualified, Unknown Candidates

In every presidential election, a portion of the electorate makes their voting decision on the basis, not of issues or parties, but on who the candidates are. Thus another reason third parties generally do so poorly is that they run weak candidates who lack political experience and the credentials to be credible presidential contenders. While it is difficult, particularly in a historical perspective, to assess how voters perceive a candidate's capacity to perform as president, we may reasonably assume that one cue voters rely on is whether the candidate has had prior experience in an important office (like governor, U.S. senator, or member of the House of Representatives). All other things being equal, voters probably view candidates without these credentials as less qualified.

There is a striking difference between the political backgrounds of major and minor party candidates (table 2.4). Nearly all (97.2 percent) of the 72 major party presidential nominees between 1840 and 1980 had held the post of president, vice-president, U.S. senator, congressman, governor, military general, or cabinet secretary. Less than 20 percent of the minor party candidates had attained these positions.

By now the reason for this disparity should be clear. The biases against third parties created by the single-member-district plurality system and ballot access restrictions, as well as their disadvantages in organization, resources, and media coverage, all effectively discourage qualified candidates from running under a third party label. Well-known, prestigious candidates know that a third party effort will be hopeless and

TABLE 2.4

Political Experience of Major and Minor Party Candidates, 1840-1980

Highest Position Attained	Major Party Candidates	Minor Party Candidates[a]
Governor, U.S. Congressman, U.S. Senator, Vice-President, President	88.8%	17.6%
Military General	5.6	1.4
Cabinet Secretary	2.8	0
None of the above	2.8[b]	81.1
Total	100.0%	100.1%
(N)	(72)	(148)

[a] Minor party and independent candidates who ran for president and received popular votes in more than one state.

[b] Alton Parker, Democratic candidate for President in 1904, was Chief Justice of the New York Court of Appeals; Wendell Wilkie, Republican candidate in 1940, was a utility executive.

can end their political careers. Only extraordinary circumstances will push established politicians (and voters) into a third party camp.

The political obscurity of most minor party candidates, their inability to publicize themselves as major party contenders can, and their neglect by the media mean that many voters simply do not have information on these candidates. An unknown candidate is obviously unlikely to win many votes. Only 3 percent of the 1980 electorate claimed they did not know enough about Jimmy Carter to have an opinion about him; 18 percent said the same about Ronald Reagan. Yet 28 percent of the electorate had no information about John Anderson, 77 percent knew nothing about Ed Clark, and 85 percent knew nothing about Barry Commoner (CBS/*New York Times* Poll, October 1980). This disparity is even more striking among vice-presidential candidates: 15 percent of the electorate had not heard of Walter Mondale, 28 percent had never heard of George Bush, but 78 percent had never heard of Anderson's running mate Patrick Lucey (*Los Angeles Times Poll*, no. 35, September 2-7, 1980).[15]

Negative Attitudes Toward Third Parties

Third party candidates also do poorly because most people think they will do poorly. The prophecy that a candidate cannot win is self-fulfilling: money is harder to raise, political support becomes more difficult to attract, media attention dwindles, and people are unwilling to waste their votes. Few citizens ever think that third party candidates—even strong ones—can win. Only 4.3 percent of the electorate believed George Wallace stood a chance in 1968 (CPS 1968 National Election Study). At the height of John Anderson's standing in the polls, fewer than one in five citizens thought he had a "good chance" to win the presidency; in October less than 1 percent of the electorate believed he would be the winner (NBC/AP Poll, May 1980; CPS 1980 National Election Study). Not only was it clear that Anderson would lose, but two-thirds of the electorate thought he would lose big, trailing far behind Reagan and Carter.

Being perceived as a sure loser costs a candidate votes, though it is hard to say exactly how many. Anderson's 1980 pre-election support was 9 points higher when pollsters asked people how they would vote if Anderson had a "real chance of winning" (*Los Angeles Times Poll*, no. 35, September 2-7, 1980; ABC/Harris Poll, October 3-6, 1980). Of voters who at one point considered casting ballots for Anderson, 45 percent cited as a reason for their switch his inability to win (CPS 1980 National Election Study).[16]

[15] This asymmetry has existed in other years. In 1976, 27 percent of the electorate did not have enough information to form an opinion of Eugene McCarthy, compared to 2 percent for Gerald Ford and 4 percent for Jimmy Carter (CPS 1976 National Election Study).

[16] Shanks and Palmquist (1981) note that primary voters are more likely to support a candidate who appears to be viable.

The electorate's pessimistic prognosis for Anderson stemmed, in part, from

One consequence of a pessimistic prognosis is that citizens will abandon third party candidates for strategic reasons (Brams, 1978, ch. 1; Riker 1982, pp. 762-64). As one Anderson supporter put it, "If at the time of the election a vote for Anderson would cut into Carter's lead, and let Reagan win, I'd probably vote for Carter" (Roberts 1980, p. D22). Of the voters who considered casting ballots for Anderson but did not, over half feared that if they voted for him it would help elect their least preferred choice (CPS 1980 National Election Study). Major parties, of course, play on this fear.

A second prevalent belief is that the two-party system is a sacred arrangement—as American an institution as the Congress, the Super Bowl, or M*A*S*H. Third party candidates are seen as disrupters of the *American* two-party system. Thus minor parties do not start out on an equal footing with the Democrats and Republicans; they must first establish their legitimacy—something the voters do not demand of the major parties. This two-party sentiment, of course, reinforces itself: minor parties do poorly because they lack legitimacy, their poor showing further legitimates the two-party norm, causing third parties to do poorly, and so on.

Few citizens want to modify the electoral system to aid third parties. A mere 2 percent of the 1976 electorate suggested that the conduct of political campaigns should be changed to give more attention to third parties; just 2 percent thought that the presidential debates should be changed to include third party contenders (American Institute of Public Opinion [AIPO], no. 962, November 8, 1976). Only 3 percent of the 1980 electorate were in favor of more attention being paid to third parties; less than 1 percent expressed this opinion in 1972 (*Gallup Opinion Index*, no. 183, p. 60).

---

his low poll standing widely reported by the press. Of those who claimed to know Anderson's position in the polls, 99 percent correctly identified him as being in third place in the trial heats (CPS 1980 National Election Study). Yet even the 41 percent of the electorate that did not know where Anderson stood in the trial heats overwhelmingly predicted that he would lose. There are two possible explanations: either voters learned of Anderson's likely fate from the media—in particular, from non-poll related stories—or there is a standing belief that third party candidates cannot win. Both are probably correct.

While nearly all Americans (85 percent) have leanings or outright allegiance to one of the two major parties, less than one in a hundred identify with a minor party (the rest being independent or apolitical) (CPS 1980 National Election Study). If partisanship is a lens through which people interpret politics and evaluate candidates (Campbell et al. 1960), then few voters see the world in ways supportive of minor parties. Even though early in the campaign citizens may flirt with minor party candidates, by election day the pull of partisanship, the inevitable "he can't win—it's a wasted vote" argument, and the wearing off of the third party novelty bring voters home to the major parties. Third party support fades as the election approaches. This pattern of declining support has been apparent since the advent of survey data (figure 2.2). Strom Thurmond, whose regionally concentrated support in 1948 gave him a clear chance of carrying states in the deep South, is the only exception.

FIGURE 2.2

Decline in Voter Support for Third Party Candidates, 1924-1980

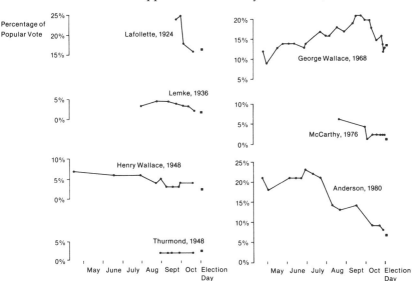

Major party loyalties and hostile community reactions often make it tough for voters to support a third party (Gaither 1977, pp. 26-29; Sombart 1976, p. 40). C. Vann Woodward described the difficulties Southern Populists faced:

> Changing one's party in the South of the nineties involved more than changing one's mind. It might involve a falling-off of clients, the loss of a job, of credit at the store, or of one's welcome at church. It could split families, and it might even call into question one's loyalty to his race and his people. An Alabamian who had "voted for Democratic candidates for forty years" wrote after breaking with the old party that he had "never performed a more painful duty." A Virginian declared after taking the same step that "It is like cutting off the right hand or putting out the right eye." (1951, p. 244)

The Lynds observed a similar phenomenon in *Middletown*:

> In 1924 it was considered such "bad business" to vote for the third party that no one of the business group confessed publicly either before or after the election to adherence to this ticket. "If we could discover the three people who disgraced our district by voting for La-Follette," declared one business-class woman vehemently, "we'd certainly make it hot for them!" (Schmidt 1960, p. 243)

Parties of the left suffered still harsher repression in the first half of this century. The Socialist Party's opposition to U.S. entry into World War I brought it endless abuse that continued through the postwar Red Scare. The mass hysteria was fueled by memories of Socialist Party opposition to the war, fear of a spreading Bolshevik Revolution, and the belief that Germany (and hence German-Americans) controlled the Bolshevik movement (because of the separate peace the Soviet Union reached with Germany in 1918). Labor unrest and riots spread, the newly formed American Communist Party became more visible, and as war prosperity waned, "the assumption that the country was under serious attack by the

Reds found wide acceptance" (Murray 1955, p. 16). Socialist leaders were prosecuted under the Espionage and the Sedition Acts of 1918. Local chambers of commerce maintained "their fight for 'Americanism' breaking up radical meetings, terrorizing Party members and supporters" (Weinstein 1967, p. 235).

The Red Scare helped neutralize parties of the left. Eugene Debs, who in 1912 had polled 6.0 percent of the presidential vote, drew only 3.4 percent in 1920 when he ran from the Atlanta cell where he had been imprisoned for sedition. The party organization survived in only seven states (Weinstein 1967, p. 235).

MAJOR PARTY STRATEGIES

The American presidential election system not only discourages third party candidates from running but provides an incentive for the major parties to squelch third party competition. The strategies the Democrats and Republicans employ are, of course, the same ones they use against each other, but because minor parties are handicapped, they are less able to fend off these attacks.

Cooptation

Minor parties often advocate policies not embraced by the major parties. Frequently, the major parties respond rationally to this signal that there are disgruntled voters and adopt the third parties' positions as their own. Often these new positions can be accommodated with relatively little discomfort to the party. Indeed, a major party's very survival depends on its ability to build a broad, heterogeneous coalition. Only third parties with the most extreme beliefs or narrowest of constituencies are immune from these raids.[17]

As we shall see in detail in the next two chapters, the major

[17] The longevity of the five ideological parties—Prohibition, Socialist, Socialist Labor, Socialist Workers, and Communist—can be attributed in part to their extreme stands and narrow bases of support.

parties successfully coopt third party votes through a variety of methods—campaign rhetoric, policy proposals and actions, political appointments and patronage. It is ironic that third parties bring about their own demise by the very support they attract. Although adopting their issue clearly steals the thunder from third parties, this is how minor parties have their impact on public policy. Third parties usually lose the battle but, through cooptation, often win the war.

Delegitimizing Tactics

The major parties also undermine third parties by delegitimizing them. It is common for major party candidates to argue that a third party vote is wasted, or that third party challengers are "fringe" candidates who stand outside the bounds of acceptable political discourse. As President Truman argued before a Los Angeles audience in 1948: "The simple fact is that the [Progressive] third party cannot achieve peace, because it is powerless. It cannot achieve better conditions at home, because it is powerless. . . . I say to those disturbed liberals who have been sitting uncertainly on the outskirts of the third party: think again. Don't waste your vote" (Ross 1968, p. 189). The major parties also try to undermine third party challengers by raising fear that a "constitutional crisis" would result from an Electoral College deadlock. This cry is heard whenever it looks as if a third party will capture some electoral votes, as in 1912, 1924, 1948, and 1968 (Hicks 1960, p. 101; Burner 1971, pp. 2485-86).

The major parties have employed a full array of dirty tricks against independent challengers. Populist speakers in 1892 spent a good part of the campaign contending with hecklers and dodging rocks, rotten eggs, and tomatoes, all courtesy of the major parties (Morgan 1971, p. 1727). The Omaha *Tribune*, which endorsed LaFollette in 1924, changed its mind and threw its support to Coolidge after receiving $10,000 in advertising from the Republican National Committee (MacKay 1947, p. 191).

The Nixon White House employed a host of devious tactics to sabotage George Wallace. As Watergate confessions later revealed, Nixon strategists contributed $400,000 to Wallace's 1970 gubernatorial primary opponent (Hersh 1973, p. 1; Rosenbaum, 1973, p. 1). They also leaked a story about an IRS investigation of Wallace's brother (Shanahan 1974, p. 1) and sent federal registrars into Alabama to sign up blacks. The Committee to Reelect the President paid a California Republican official $10,000 in 1971 to purge names from the state's American Independent Party rolls (Franklin 1973, p. 27).

On several occasions John Anderson's 1980 campaign was subjected to Democratic pranks. Carter forces tried to disrupt Anderson advance men (Peterson 1980b, p. A2), and administration officials distributed anonymous derogatory campaign literature to discredit Anderson's independent challenge (Associated Press 1980, p. 30).

The major parties also do not sit idly by as third party candidates battle state election laws. Instead, they actively fight to prevent minor parties from securing spots on the ballot. As Robert Neumann of the Democratic National Committee candidly boasted in June 1980: "We don't know how much it's going to cost [to keep Anderson off November ballots] but we'll probably spend what it takes" (Associated Press 1980, p. 30).[18]

Anderson's treatment was not unique. The major parties mounted comparable assaults against William Lemke in 1936, Henry Wallace in 1948, and Eugene McCarthy in 1976 (Tull 1965, p. 131; Schmidt 1960, pp. 151-52; Schram 1977, p. 286). The New York Democratic Committee alone spent over $50,000 successfully battling to keep McCarthy off its state ballot (Alexander 1976, p. 440). Lemke was unable to run under his Union Party label in Pennsylvania in 1936 because the state Democratic chairman had already registered that name to undercut Lemke support. As a result, Lemke was forced to run on the "Royal Oak" ticket (Tull, 1965, p. 131).

[18] Although on the June 10, 1980, MacNeil/Lehrer Report Neumann denied the charge, it was widely reported that the DNC had put aside $250,000 for this effort. The strategy centered on DNC-backed challenges to Anderson in fifteen states and help from friendly state election officials. For example, see Roberts 1980; Cook 1980b, p. 2378; Schram 1980, p. A1.

Conclusions

There are powerful constraints against third party voting in America. Barriers like the single-member-district plurality electoral system discourage minor parties from running and encourage major parties to coopt their policy positions and supporters. Ballot access restrictions make it difficult for third parties to get their names before voters and require candidates to devote huge sums to signature drives and court battles.

Limited resources, poor campaign organization, and a lack of elite support further handicap third parties. They are able to purchase only a small fraction of the advertising bought by the major parties, and to make matters worse, the media pay little attention to them. Minor party presidential candidates are likely to be inexperienced and less well known than their major party counterparts. The belief that a third party cannot win and that the two-party system is a sacred arrangement delegitimizes minor parties and discourages voters from supporting them. The two major parties play on these beliefs to subvert third party challengers.

All of these constraints, of course, are interrelated. The single-member-district plurality system discourages high caliber candidates from running outside a major party; if a weak candidate runs, he will attract few campaign resources, ensuring that most citizens will learn very little about him. This in turn reinforces the belief that the third party candidate cannot win, so citizens will not waste their votes on him. The weak electoral performance is self-perpetuating. People expect third parties to do poorly because they have always done poorly, so only weak candidates run—and the cycle continues.

Together these barriers, handicaps, and major party strategies raise the level of effort required for a voter to cast his ballot for an independent candidate. A citizen can vote for a major party candidate with scarcely a moment's thought or energy. But to support a third party challenger, a voter must awaken from the political slumber in which he ordinarily lies, actively seek out information on a contest whose outcome he cannot affect, reject the socialization of his political system, ignore the ridicule and abuse of his friends and neighbors, and accept the fact that when the ballots are counted, his vote will never be in the winner's column. Such levels of energy are witnessed only rarely in American politics.

THIRD PARTIES OF THE
NINETEENTH CENTURY

ALTHOUGH third parties are generally thought of as ephemeral, they were remarkably durable in the nineteenth century. Except for the Southern Democrats, every minor party of this era persisted in one form or another for at least two elections. Why did these parties emerge and endure? Who were their candidates and supporters? What were their relationships to the major parties?

Most nineteenth-century third parties functioned as complete political organizations. They were broad-based coalitions; often their supporters' only common bond was opposition to a particular party, policy, or candidate. They held contentious nominating conventions, entered state and local races, and recruited experienced candidates. Their existence depended on no single personality, and they survived long enough to build up party loyalty among their supporters.

Our survey of the Liberty, Free Soil, Know-Nothing, Constitutional Union, Southern Democrat, Greenback, People's, and Prohibition parties demonstrates how much these seemingly different movements had in common. Although they addressed a wide range of issues, there was great similarity in their strategies, goals, and organizational structures, as well as the hardships they suffered. Third party leaders all had great misgivings about their chosen paths, doing everything possible to work within the major parties before deciding to bolt. For the most part, they sought to displace one of the major parties, for they recognized that through third parties they would have only limited impact.

The commonalities that emerge from our survey indicate that it is indeed appropriate to fashion a single unifying explanation of minor party support. We later draw upon this historical evidence to develop a general theory of third party voting.

LIBERTY PARTY

The Liberty Party, an outgrowth of the American Anti-Slavery Society, was the first political party dedicated to the abolition of slavery. Its formation in 1840 precipitated a massive split among abolitionists, for many of them firmly believed that they would be more politically influential if they remained within the major parties. In fact, when the New York Anti-Slavery Society selected former Kentucky and Alabama state legislator (and onetime slaveowner) James G. Birney as its presidential candidate in 1839, Birney declined the nomination, preferring to see if the Whigs would choose a candidate sympathetic to their cause (Nash 1959, p. 27). But following the Whigs' selection of slavery supporter William H. Harrison of Virginia, the abolitionists, this time calling themselves the National Anti-Slavery Convention for Independent Nominations, again turned to Birney, who now accepted. The Liberty Party was born. The platform was relatively moderate: although the party called for the elimination of slavery in federally administered areas and the prohibition of inter-state slave trade, it did not regard slavery within a state as a matter over which the federal government had authority (Dillon 1974, p. 131).

The Liberty cause was plagued by a variety of problems. Whigs and Democrats virtually ignored the slavery issue in 1840 and "newspapers barely mentioned that an abolitionist party had been formed" (Nash 1959, p. 30). Even abolitionists contributed little support to the new party; many considered banking and tariff issues to be at least as important, while others hesitated to introduce the "moral" question of slavery into the "secular" arena of politics (Dillon 1974, p. 147). The party also suffered from severe organizational difficulties, and they printed too few election ballots, leaving some locales with none at all (Hesseltine 1962, p. 34).

In the end, the party attracted only about 7,000 votes (.3

percent) even though at least 70,000 voters belonged to abolitionist societies. Birney ran best in Massachusetts and New
Hampshire, where he won over 1 percent of the ballots. Most
anti-slavery advocates voted as they had traditionally and the
Whigs, who ran a well-packaged though vacuous campaign,
captured the White House for the first time (Chambers 1971).

In the next election, the Liberty Party did not wait to see
whom the major parties would nominate. In August of 1843
they again selected Birney and once more focused solely on
the non-extension issue. The dispute over the annexation of
Texas in 1844, adamantly opposed by anti-slavery forces, had
split both major parties. The Democrats denied former President Martin Van Buren their party's nomination because he
opposed the Texas treaty. The two major party nominees—
slaveowners James K. Polk and Henry Clay—had virtually
indistinguishable views on this issue. The Whigs, to whom
most anti-slavery voters were tied, warned those tempted to
stray from the fold that doing so would throw the election to
Democrat Polk, who was even more pro-slavery than Clay.
Clay equivocated on both Texas and slavery, and countered
Northern abolitionist defection by spreading rumors about
Birney (Blue 1973, p. 5). The Liberty Party was also frustrated
by Northern politicians' efforts to absorb the movement. As
party leader Salmon P. Chase lamented: "As fast as we can
bring public sentiment right the other parties will approach
our ground and keep sufficiently close to it to prevent any
great accession to our numbers" (Sundquist 1973, p. 47).

The 1844 Liberty Party tally remained small—slightly over
2.3 percent—but its 15,812 votes in New York gave that state's
36 electoral votes, and the election, to Polk.[1] The party ran
strongest in New England, where it polled an average of
nearly 6 percent. The Whigs blamed their loss entirely on the
Liberty Party; the abolitionists had antagonized the major
party most sympathetic to their cause (Rayback 1970, p. 99).

Following the election, the Liberty Party split into three

[1] Polk carried New York by only 5,106 votes. Sundquist cites estimates that
75 to 90 percent of the Liberty Party votes would have gone to the Whigs
(1973, p. 47).

factions: some leaders, especially Chase, sought to create a new party with a more moderate view on abolition and tried to forge coalitions with Northern anti-extensionists; New York philanthropist Gerrit Smith's faction wanted to include other issues in the party's platform; while a third group preferred to continue emphasizing only the anti-slavery position (Blue 1973, pp. 7-15).

The 1848 meeting of the Liberty Party selected Chase-backed New Hampshire Senator John Hale as its nominee; he accepted reluctantly two months later. Smith's faction split off to form the Liberty League, allowing Chase to lead the party into a coalition with other opposition forces.

Free Soil Party

The result of Chase's efforts to create a new party with a moderate position on abolition and with an appeal to a broader political constituency was the Free Soil Party. Launched in 1848, it was essentially a cross between the abolitionist Liberty Party and factions that had split off from both major parties for a host of different reasons. The Free Soil Party only went so far as to oppose the extension of slavery into newly acquired territories; to cull the support of Democrats and Whigs, it did not advocate action against states where slavery already existed.

The driving force behind the party was President Polk's plan to purchase land from Mexico. The proposal antagonized anti-extensionists, for it was generally presumed that slavery would be permitted in the new territory. In response, a group of Northern Democrats introduced in 1846 the Wilmot Proviso to outlaw slavery in the acquired territory. Because it would have mandated only anti-extension, not abolition, the Proviso proved to be the perfect ground for uniting Libertymen and rebellious Democrats and Whigs (Hesseltine 1962, p. 39). It also produced an irreparable breach in the ranks of the Democrats. Legislatures in Southern states vowed to fight any presidential candidate not unequivocally opposed to it. Although Congress voted down the Proviso in 1847, it was to become the key issue in the following year's presidential campaign.

The Democratic Party had also begun to splinter over patronage. Polk had emerged from his 1844 victory obligated to Van Buren for his help in winning New York. Although Polk made some effort to return the favor, Van Buren forces did not feel sufficiently repaid. As a result, antagonized Van Buren supporters became more willing to desert the party over the anti-extension issue as evidenced by their support of the Wilmot Proviso (Blue 1973, pp. 24-27). New York Democrats split into two factions: the Hunkers, whose main concerns were party unity and victory (and thus were said to "hunker" for office), and the anti-extensionist Barnburners, named for their refusal to support Hunker nominees for state office. (They were, it was said, willing to burn down the barn to get rid of the rats.)

Meanwhile, the Whigs were also coming apart. In Massachusetts especially, where most Whigs opposed the annexation of Texas, the party split into the manufacturing interests, willing to appease the South (the Cotton Whigs), and those who viewed slavery as a moral issue and were thus unwilling to suppress the question (the Conscience Whigs). But since the Cotton Whigs controlled the party, the Conscience Whigs' anti-slavery efforts were severely hampered. When, at their 1847 convention, a motion to support only an anti-extensionist nominee was defeated, many Conscience Whigs began to consider alternative political avenues.

For both Barnburner Democrats and Conscience Whigs, the 1848 national conventions provided the final impetus for a third party. At Baltimore the Barnburner Democrats lost their battle for recognition as the legitimate delegates from New York and responded by walking out, refusing to vote for a presidential nominee. Lewis Cass, who opposed both the Wilmot Proviso and the Barnburners solely to ensure his nomination, emerged as the Democratic candidate. The platform said nothing about anti-extensionism. The Conscience Whigs suffered a similar defeat in Philadelphia, as their party nominated slaveowner Zachary Taylor and also ignored the extension question. That the Barnburners and Conscience Whigs held out as long as they did before bolting is testimony both to the strong bonds of party loyalty and to their belief that a third party route should be used only as a last resort (Blue 1973, pp. 46-53).

A series of anti-extensionist conventions followed. Barnburners met on June 22 and, after some discussion, chose Van Buren as their candidate. Although Van Buren had refused past offers, he accepted this nomination, seeing it as an opportunity to punish the Hunkers. Meanwhile, all three factions (Barnburners, Conscience Whigs, and Libertymen) looked forward to a free soil convention to be held in August. Van Buren wanted to seek the backing of Conscience Whigs and Libertymen; his Barnburner supporters agreed, but they insisted that Van Buren head the coalition ticket. This was a problem: Van Buren had supported slavery in the past. Only his opposition to the annexation of Texas made him remotely tolerable to the other factions. Libertymen were skeptical of the alliance, for they feared it would dilute their commitment to abolition (Sewell 1976, pp. 152-53). Moreover, the party had already chosen its own candidate: New Hampshire Senator John Hale.

That the participants at the August convention had little in common was clear. Some Barnburners attended because they wanted revenge against the Hunkers; others saw the effort as a means of pushing the Wilmot Proviso or, more generally, ending Southern dominance of the Democratic Party. A plethora of anti-slavery forces, ranging from abolitionists to anti-extensionists, attended. Although each faction arrived with its own favorite candidate, after several days of clever backroom bargaining they struck a deal that left nearly everyone happy. Barnburners primarily wanted Van Buren; they were less concerned about the platform, which they thus used to pacify Libertymen and Whigs. The only real unifying force was the Proviso, which the platform unequivocally endorsed. Unlike the Liberty platform of 1844, however, it flatly rejected the federal government's power to intrude in the slavery question. Moreover, it failed to denounce the three-fifths clause and the Fugitive Slave Act. This was not an abolitionists' platform. But it was not the platform of a single-issue party either. Not only did it call for the discouragement of slavery, but it also championed cheap postage, trimming the bureaucracy, the election of civil officials, and a homestead law to provide grants to settlers. "In general, the new party emphasized the needs and interests of free, white labor" (Dillon 1974, p. 168). Van Buren won the nomination on the first ballot, defeating Liberty candidate Hale.

As a vote-getting machine, the Free Soil Party encountered a variety of difficulties. Because it formed only three months before the election, it was unable to generate "an apparatus as formal or as thorough as those of its Whig and Democratic rivals" (Hamilton 1971, p. 872). The party had virtually no local organization. It also had difficulty convincing anti-extensionists that siding with the new party would improve the Proviso's chances of passage. Many anti-extensionist leaders refused to desert the major parties. Even free Northern blacks could not be won over (Blue 1973, pp. 105-20). Meanwhile, Northern Whigs and Democrats actively courted Free Soil supporters. The Democrats played up Cass's Northern background and argued that popular sovereignty alone would guarantee that the territories would remain free. Whigs like Tom Corwin proclaimed that Taylor would not veto the Proviso (Sewell 1976, pp. 167-69).

Van Buren attracted just over 10 percent of the vote in November, though it is not commonly believed that he contributed to Taylor's victory. He ran best in Vermont, Massachusetts, New York, and Wisconsin, where he gathered over a quarter of the popular vote. In Vermont, Massachusetts, and New York he finished ahead of Cass.

The outcome disillusioned many Free Soilers, giving the major parties a chance to coax defectors back to the fold. In some states, like Illinois and Vermont, the Democratic Party's tactic was to adopt the Free Soil position outright. In others, New York and Michigan among them, Free Soilers formed compromise coalitions. Barnburner Democrats fashioned a truce with their Hunker rivals after it became clear that the split had caused both factions to suffer devastating losses in New York. So desperate for a reconciliation were the Barn-burners that they did not even hold out for a pledge of support for the Wilmot Proviso. Without the Barnburners, the Free Soil Party had little with which to continue (Blue 1973, pp. 152-60).

Left with only Whigs and former Liberty Party abolitionists, the Free Soil Party had little impact on the 1852 presidential election. The Compromise of 1850, which admitted California as a free state and allowed Utah and New Mexico to decide the issue for themselves, was seen as the "final settlement" of the slavery question. Both Democrat Franklin Pierce and Whig Winfield Scott endorsed the Compromise and thus kept slavery from becoming an issue in the campaign. The Free Soil Party, now dominated by Libertymen, selected their for-mer nominee John P. Hale, who reluctantly agreed to head the doomed ticket. The platform was more anti-slavery than it had been in 1848, attacking the Compromise of 1850 as "inadequate to the settlement of the questions for which they are claimed to be the adjustment" (Blue 1973, p. 243). Hale polled just under 5 percent of the vote nationwide, again doing best in Massachusetts, Vermont, and Wisconsin. (The Free Soil vote fell to 5 percent in New York as a result of the Barnburners' truce with the Hunkers.)

The passage of the Kansas-Nebraska Act in 1854 proved that the Free Soilers had been right about the inadequacy of the Compromise of 1850. The Act overturned the 1820 Mis-souri Compromise (which prohibited slavery in the Louisiana Purchase north of the 36th parallel) and destroyed the long-held belief that the slavery question had been settled. Slavery was once again an issue, but even Free Soilers recognized that their party was neither vital enough nor broad enough to defend the abolitionists' cause. Following the passage of the Kansas-Nebraska Act, anti-slavery forces throughout the North came together to form the Republican Party. Included in their ranks were former Free Soilers, Libertymen, Whigs, and a few Democrats. That very year the party captured a majority of seats in the House of Representatives.

The reemergence of the slavery issue, however, precipitated the death of the Whig Party. There was simply no way of reconciling the differences between pro-slavery Southerners and anti-slavery Northerners. Pro-slavery forces quickly found the Democrats more to their liking, while anti-extensionists became either Free Soilers or Republicans. Only those Whigs unpolarized by the slavery issue remained in the party. Displaced by the Republicans as a major party, old Whigs carried on for two more elections in the form of the Know-Nothing and Constitutional Union parties.

KNOW-NOTHING (AMERICAN) PARTY

Severe economic adversity in Europe drove record numbers of immigrants to the United States in the late 1840s and early 1850s. The blacklash spurred by their arrival was almost immediate: secret nativist societies and clubs sprang up throughout the North, where most immigrants settled. The clubs did not originally intend to enter politics directly, but following the election of Democrat Franklin Pierce in 1852, for which immigrant voters were largely blamed (or credited), the New York-based Order of the Star Spangled Banner began to build a nativist coalition to nominate candidates for public office.

Although the two were not always separable, the party seemed more intense in its hatred of Catholics than foreigners. It welcomed foreign-born Protestants into the order, but "every Know-Nothing firmly believed that Papists should be barred from every office in the national, state, and local governments and, if possible, driven back to the priest-ridden lands from whence they had come" (Billington 1933, p. 386). This antipathy towards Catholics was in fact the party's sole basis for unity; the sectional divisions that plagued the nation as a whole were equally prevalent within the party.

The movement grew quickly. In addition to its anti-Catholic stance, the party's secret rituals and greetings attracted members. Their refusal to divulge any relevant information to outsiders led Horace Greeley to dub them the "Know-Nothing Party." Its candidates were remarkably successful in the 1854 election, especially in Massachusetts, Delaware, and Pennsylvania. The governor, the entire state senate, and all but two state representatives in Massachusetts were party members. A year later the Know-Nothings won control of state legislatures in Rhode Island, New Hampshire, Connecticut, Maryland, and Kentucky, and came close in nearly a dozen other states.

Three factors account for the Know-Nothings' quick success (Billington 1933). First, the party was born at a time of major party decay. Because in some states a dozen parties jockeyed for support, Know-Nothing candidates were able to win many elections without electoral majorities. Second, the slavery issue had by this time produced a Southern, pro-slavery Democratic Party and a Northern, anti-slavery Republican Party. Many voters who were neutral on the slavery issue were attracted by the Know-Nothings' strong commitment to preserving the Union. Finally, there was intense anti-immigrant sentiment. Some people feared that European governments were intentionally dumping their unproductive citizens on the United States to weaken the nation. When working-class wages failed to keep pace with price rises, natives blamed surplus cheap foreign labor (Lipset and Raab 1970, p. 53). Whigs and Republicans also feared the immigrants' increasing political power, which, it was widely believed, Democratic bosses were able to manipulate (Foner 1970, p. 230).

By 1856, however, the party's fortunes had begun to wane. It had been unable to implement any of its anti-Catholic or anti-immigrant schemes. Although Know-Nothings held enough seats to control the balance of power in Congress, they could not convince their major party colleagues to support proposals for a twenty-one-year naturalization period and a ban on the immigration of all "foreign paupers, criminals, idiots, lunatics, insane, and blind persons" (Billington 1933, p. 411).

More important in the party's decline was the reopening of the slavery question with the passage in 1854 of the Kansas-Nebraska Act. Clearly the slavery question had not been settled by the Compromise of 1850. Slavery was once again the most important issue facing the nation, and aggressive advocates on both sides pursued their uncompromising solutions. Sectional strife was unavoidable. "The Know-Nothing Party, built on a basis of union and nationalism, could no more survive these sectional forces than the union itself" (Billington 1933, p. 423). Northern Know-Nothings took up the anti-slavery cause and, as a result, alienated their Southern supporters. Northern nativists joined the newly formed Republican Party, leaving much of the Know-Nothings' apparatus in the hands of ex-Whigs more devoted to preservation of the Union than the harassment of Catholics (Foner 1970, 240).

The Kansas-Nebraska Act also fractured the Whig Party. Led by former President Millard Fillmore, the "Silver Grey" faction, comprised of Northern commercial interests and Southern Whigs, tried to take control of what they saw as a growing Know-Nothing Party. Fillmore's goal was to transform the party from a nativist organization into an anti-Democratic, pro-Union party (Nichols and Klein 1971, p. 1014).

At their 1856 convention, however, the slavery issue split the Know-Nothings. Anti-slavery delegates bolted when Southern delegates tabled a motion that the party nominate only a candidate who supported the prohibition of slavery north of 36° 30'. The convention, now largely in the hands of Southerners, selected Fillmore as its nominee, signalling the party had abandoned its anti-immigrant, anti-Catholic roots. Fillmore was clearly no nativist and in fact had just been granted an audience with the Pope when he was notified of his nomination. He barely mentioned nativism in the campaign, stressing instead his pro-Union and anti-Democratic stands.

Fillmore collected 21.5 percent of the vote, the vast majority of which came from Southern states where the Republicans did not run a ticket. He carried only Maryland's 8 electoral votes. Support in New England, where anti-Catholic sentiment had led to the party's creation, was low. Northern nativists, more opposed to slavery than to immigration, cast their lot with the Republicans. The new party adopted none of their anti-immigrant, anti-Catholic positions.

CONSTITUTIONAL UNION PARTY

When the slavery issue tore the Know-Nothing Party apart, Northern party members turned to the anti-slavery Republican Party, while in border and Southern states former Know-Nothing supporters and the remnants of the Whigs joined forces to form the Constitutional Union Party. It was a party that would have wished away the slavery dispute. Backers felt that the only way to combat the growing sectionalism threatening to destroy the nation was to sidestep the slavery issue. But the Unionists, living in a world long gone, did not understand the intensity of the dispute. A majority of the delegates to their May 1860 convention "were or appeared to be venerable gentlemen representing a generation of almost forgotten politicians; most of them had retired from public life involuntarily rather than by choice" (Nash 1959, p. 89). The gathering was most notable for its evasion of controversial issues. The central plank of the 200-word platform called for support of "the Constitution of the country, the Union of the States, and the enforcement of the laws." In the words of one journalist, "I had heard a great deal of virtuous twaddle in public speeches within a few weeks, but the essence of the article was uncorked" by the delegates at this gathering (Nash 1959, p. 89). Few parties, major or minor, have ever been so intent on avoiding the issues.

The convention selected as its nominee former Tennessee Senator John Bell, who had entered politics as a Democrat, but later switched his allegiance to the Whigs.

For all practical purposes, there were two separate elections conducted in 1860—one in the North, between Republican Abraham Lincoln and Democrat Stephen Douglas, and another in the South, between Bell and Southern Democrat John Breckenridge. Lincoln did not even distribute ballots in nine Southern states. Bell polled 12.6 percent of the vote nationwide, carrying Kentucky, Tennessee, and Virginia's 39 electoral votes. His base of support was nearly identical to that of Know-Nothing Millard Fillmore four years earlier.[2] Despite this relatively strong performance, the party finished in fourth place. Its supporters, primarily Southerners, had no effect on the outcome.

SOUTHERN DEMOCRATS

For five consecutive presidential elections since 1840, the slavery issue had produced a third party. None of these minor parties, however, acted on behalf of pro-slavery forces. Presumably, slaveholder interests were being adequately represented by one of the major parties. By 1860 Southern Democrats no longer felt this was true.

The many slavery battles of the 1850s—over the Fugitive Slave Act, the Ostend Manifesto, the Kansas-Nebraska Act, and the Kansas Constitution—had eroded Northern support for the Democratic Party. By 1859 Northern Democrats had little power to oppose Southerners in Congress (Potter 1976, pp. 325-26). Yet Northern Democrats retained control of their party's conventions since voter support did not determine delegate apportionment.

Southern congressional Democrats spent little time worrying about party unity; the defense of slavery was their primary goal. No proposal was too outrageous. After an unsuccessful effort to repeal the prohibition against the African slave trade, they tried to promote a slave code that would protect slavery in territories under federal jurisdiction. Their chief concern was not with the contents of the proposal itself; instead, they sought to create a "doctrinal test to impose upon the [Northern] Douglas Democrats in the national convention which was less than three months away" (Potter 1976, p. 403).

The stage was set for a fierce battle at the April 1860 Democratic convention. Alabama Democrats instructed their delegates to withdraw if the party failed to include the slave code

[2] CUP = −2.69 + .96(KNP); R^2 = .65; where CUP is the percent of the state presidential vote cast for the Constitutional Union Party in 1860 and KNP is the percent of the state vote cast for the Know-Nothing Party in 1856.

in its platform. Seven other Southern state delegations resolved to walk out if Northern Democrat Stephen Douglas was nominated.[3] Douglas controlled just over one-half of the delegates—enough to determine the platform and hence prevent the inclusion of the slave code, but short of the two-thirds needed for nomination. There seemed to be little room for compromise: Southern Democrats felt the U.S. Supreme Court's Dred Scott decision had made their demand for a slave code a reasonable one and were prepared to withdraw if it were not adopted; Northwestern delegates vowed to do the same if it were included (Potter 1976, p. 408).

Days of debate failed to produce a compromise, and on the sixth day the question came to a vote. Delegates were to choose between a slave code plank and one that left to the Supreme Court the question of slavery in the territories. When the convention adopted the latter, the Alabama, Mississippi, Louisiana, South Carolina, Florida, Texas, Georgia, and parts of the Delaware and Arkansas delegations withdrew in protest, leaving the remaining delegates to select a nominee. Douglas forces assumed the South's withdrawal would reduce the number of votes needed to reach a two-thirds majority, but the convention chair ruled that two-thirds of the original number of delegates was still required. For fifty-seven ballots Douglas's support hovered around fifty percent—not even enough to have nominated him had he needed the support of only two-thirds of the delegates present. On the tenth day of the convention, the delegates decided to reconvene in Baltimore on June 18.

---

[3] Douglas had led the opponents of the Kansas Lecompton Constitution, which allegedly allowed the state's residents to vote on whether to permit slavery. (In fact, it guaranteed slaveowners the right to keep slaves already in the state, as well as all the descendants of those slaves.) Over the course of two referenda, one boycotted by the anti-slavery forces, the other by pro-slavery men, it was evident that Kansas residents disapproved of the constitution. Democratic President James Buchanan nonetheless proposed to admit the state into the Union with its pro-slavery constitution. Led by Douglas, House Republicans and Northern Democrats blocked the move. "The audacity of [Douglas's] unprecedented challenge astounded the slave power and created a party breach that was never repaired" (Binkley 1961, p. 200).

During the recess Douglas backers assembled new Alabama, Georgia, and Louisiana delegations to replace those
that had walked out of the April gathering. However, both
the new and old delegates appeared in Baltimore, demanding
accreditation. Now in control, Douglas forces awarded most
of the contested seats to the new delegations. In response,
Virginia, North Carolina, Tennessee, and parts of six other
contingents walked out. But again Douglas was unable to
muster the necessary two-thirds. After the second ballot, the
convention simply declared him its unanimous choice.

The following day, Southern delegates met to nominate
Vice-President John C. Breckinridge as their own standard
bearer and to adopt the slave code as part of their platform.
The Breckinridge Democrats battled with the Constitutional
Union Party for Southern votes, while Douglas and Republican Abraham Lincoln fought for Northern support. In an
effort to prevent a Lincoln majority in the Electoral College,
Southern Democrats formed fusion tickets with Bell and
Douglas forces in states where it appeared Lincoln could be
beaten. If the election could be thrown into the House, Breckinridge stood a chance of winning: Southern Democrats controlled 13 of 32 state congressional delegations, while Lincoln
held 15. It seemed unlikely that Lincoln would win over the
additional two state delegations needed for a majority, leaving
Breckinridge in a strong position.

But the strategy was for naught. Even if all the Douglas,
Breckinridge, and Bell votes were combined, they still would
not have prevented Lincoln's election: he carried 18 states,
15 by a majority. Those 15 alone ensured his Electoral College
victory even though he polled just under 40 percent of the
national popular vote. Breckinridge collected 18 percent of
the vote, won eleven Southern states, and finished second
with 72 electoral votes. His support was concentrated in the
rural South. Commercial interests in larger cities, uncom-
fortable with talk of secession, were less supportive. The
Southern Democrat ran best in counties with the fewest slaves:
landowners retained their historic ties to the Whigs (now in
the guise of the Constitutional Union Party), while the less

wealthy continued to vote for the Democrats (Potter 1976, pp. 443-45).

By 1864 there was, of course, no need for a Southern Democratic Party. The Civil War had settled the slavery question once and for all. Third parties that owed their existence to that issue vanished. But the Civil War left in its wake economic problems that would soon spawn new defections from the major parties.

GREENBACK PARTY

Prior to the 1870s, although farmers had always been a potentially powerful political force, they had never formed independent political organizations. But increased reliance on rail transportation, coupled with the railroads' exorbitant rates for shipping goods to market, prompted farmers to organize clubs known as granges. Since the federal government had granted the railroads huge tracts of land and subsidized rail operation, many farmers felt that the government should exercise at least some control over the rates railroads could levy (Fine 1928, pp. 57-58). As discontent with rail rate practices grew, the farmers mobilized.

Illinois led the movement, passing a law in 1871 that allowed a governor's board of commissioners to set maximum rail rates. Two years later, when the chief justice of the Illinois Supreme Court set the law aside, farmers mobilized to block his reelection. They also entered "anti-monopoly" candidates in 66 counties, 53 of whom won.

In an effort to defeat Republicans, grangers in many states formed alliances with the Democrats, attacking banking, railroad, manufacturing, land, and grain monopolies. Although in 1873 fusion tickets won prominent state offices in Wisconsin, Minnesota, Kansas, Iowa, and California, the success was short-lived; by 1876 the anti-monopoly movement had nearly evaporated. Laws regulating railroads were repealed because of railroad intimidation and poor service, or because the laws did not work well. Moreover, "railroad regulation had proved too narrow an issue on which to build a party" (Sundquist 1973, p. 98).

A new issue soon emerged. Western and Southern farmers' concern over the shortage of capital spurred a belief that greenbacks (legal tender not backed by specie) should again be issued, as they had been during the Civil War.[4] The Panic of 1873 gave further impetus to the greenback cause. Reckless railroad speculation and a European depression produced a burgeoning imbalance of trade that contributed to the failure of the powerful banking house of Jay Cooke and Company. One firm after another collapsed; trading on the stock market ground to a halt for ten days.

> Soon the panic lengthened into a depression. Industrial plants shut down, railway construction declined sharply, and over half the railroads defaulted on their bonds. Long bread lines began to appear in the larger cities—there was no notion of public relief—and tramps swarmed the countryside. Commercial failures increased to almost 6,000 in 1874, almost 8,000 in 1875, and over 9,000 in 1876. (Morison and Commager, Vol. II, 1962, p. 72)

In response to the increased demand for greenbacks, Congress passed the Inflation Bill of 1874. President Grant promptly vetoed the measure. His action produced massive splits in the Republican Party in several Midwest states, leading to resounding Democratic victories in that year's midterm election.

Following the setbacks in their bid to battle the railroads, many of the anti-monopoly parties disappeared. But in two states where the movement had been strongest—Illinois and Indiana—greenbackers took over these independent parties (Hesseltine 1962, p. 52). From these bases of support, they

---

[4] The National Labor Union, a group of trade assemblies, first floated this idea in 1867. The Union made an aborted run for the presidency in 1872 under the banner of the Labor Reform Party, but ran into serious difficulties when their presidential and vice-presidential nominees withdrew at the behest, some charged, of the major parties (Haynes 1916, p. 99). The Union threw its support to Charles O'Conor of New York, already the nominee of the Straight-Out Democrats; he polled less than .3 percent of the vote.

organized in 1876 the first National Greenback Party convention, selecting 85-year-old New York philanthropist Peter Cooper as their standard bearer. The platform called for "a United States note, issued directly by the Government, and convertible on demand into United States obligations" to serve "the necessities of the people whose industries are prostrated, whose labor is deprived of its just reward by a ruinous policy which the Republican and Democratic parties refuse to change."

But Cooper was hardly an enthusiastic candidate. Two weeks after being nominated, he voiced optimism that the party's currency goals could still be achieved through the major parties (Fine 1928, p. 62). Farmers, no longer battling the railroads, were not drawn to the Greenback cause. Cooper polled just .9 percent of the vote; only in Illinois, Iowa, and Kansas did he attract over 3 percent. Most of these votes came from Republicans (Haynes 1916, p. 119). It was an inauspicious start.

But the depression continued, generating still more suffering among farmers and laborers. The Greenback's ranks began to swell with citizens united in their demand for paper money. Workers saw the party as a means of rescuing industry and recreating jobs; to farmers it was a way to raise the price of farm goods and to ease their debts. Greenbackers and labor groups began to cooperate: "In all the states where they were organized, the Labor Reformers and Greenbacks were really two branches of the same party which was gradually being formed in the country to deal with the industrial and economic problems that the old parties were all too slow in taking up" (Haynes 1919, p. 121). The 1878 Greenback Party platform, which called for a shorter work week, government labor bureaus, and restrictions on contract prison labor and immigration, reflected the increased emphasis on labor demands produced by the fusion (Pollard 1962, p. 52). In that year's midterm election, the National Party (as it was then called) attracted over a million votes and captured 14 congressional seats. Much of this support, however, went to candidates who ran on fusion tickets with one of the major parties. The party ran best in the Midwest.

The Greenbackers nominated Congressman James B. Weaver to head their 1880 ticket. The platform, though radical for its time, proposed reforms that are today regarded as common features of American industrial society:

> all money to be issued and its volume controlled by the National Government, an eight hour work day, enforcement of a sanitary code in industrial establishments, curtailment of child labor, the establishment of a Bureau of Labor Statistics, the regulation of interstate commercial facilities by Congress or an agency of its designation, a graduated income tax, the ballot for women, and equal voting rights for Negroes. (Dinnerstein 1971, p. 1505)

Even though "on the major problems of the day—the industrial transformation and its polar effects of enormous wealth and acute poverty—the major parties had nothing to say," the Greenbacks were still unable to make major electoral inroads (Dinnerstein 1971, p. 1506). The depression's end, which the Republicans claimed to have brought about with their hard money policy, cut into Greenback support and left the labor–farmer coalition in shambles. Weaver attracted only 3.3 percent of the November vote. His strongest support, like Cooper's, came from the Midwest: he polled over 8 percent in Iowa, Kansas, Michigan, and Missouri. Greenback hopes of replacing one of the major parties were dashed. Following the election, many supporters returned to the major party fold. Most became Democrats, contributing to that party's overwhelming victories in 1882 (Haynes 1916, p. 145).

But by May of 1884 a new Anti-Monopoly Party had organized, demanding essentially the same reforms the Greenbacks had been advocating for years. It chose former Massachusetts Greenback Governor Benjamin Butler as its nominee, and shortly thereafter the Greenback Party nominated him as well. Yet it was not until August, after he had served as a delegate to the Democratic convention, that Butler accepted the nomination.

Although he started late, Butler campaigned vigorously, advocating that all opposition elements unite into a "People's

Party." The major parties again had little to say on the important issues of the day. "Both parties had not come to grips over economic issues. Both sides had ignored or touched lightly on such matters as labor unrest, farmer problems, public land policies, railroad regulation, the growth of monopolies and even tariff reform" (Roseboom and Eckes 1979, p. 107). But the economy was still strong, and despite a platform aimed at labor, the Greenback Party found its support coming primarily from farmers. Butler polled but 1.7 percent of the vote. Only in Kansas, Massachusetts, and Michigan did he capture over 3 percent.

The Greenback movement was effectively dead, though an offshoot—the Union Labor Party—surfaced in 1888. At the Union Labor Party convention, attended by former Greenbackers, Grangers, and Anti-Monopolists, the Greenback Party was officially dissolved. The Union Labor Party nominee, Alston Streeter, polled just 1.3 percent of the vote, finishing in fourth place behind the Prohibition Party candidate. "The labor parties had gone up like skyrockets and were now no more. The grangers, the greenbackers, the anti-monopolists, the third-party men, all were now without a home. The People's Party that soon arose [would be] like a shelter sent from heaven" (Fine 1928, p. 22).

PEOPLE'S PARTY (POPULISTS)

When agricultural hardship returned in the late 1880s, farmers resumed their independent politics. The People's Party marked the last in a succession of minor parties which, while focusing on slightly different issues, tapped the same reservoir of anti-industrial, pro-farmer/labor sentiment. "The independent parties which began to appear in the early seventies had come to be relatively permanent features of American political life though under changing names" (Haynes 1916, p. 221). Each transformation broadened the movement's appeal and added new ideas to its agenda (Sundquist 1973, p. 108).

The conditions that produced the Populist movement grew out of the post-Civil War settlement of the West. Much of the impetus for western migration came from the railroads, eager for customers who would take advantage of their vast holdings. Massive advertising campaigns drew settlers with prophecies of quick and easy wealth. Immigrants especially were lured to the West. In the wake of the Panic of 1873, promises of the easy life were effective. Between 1870 and 1880, the population of Kansas rose 173 percent; Nebraska, 268 percent; and the Dakota territory, 853 percent (Hicks 1961, p. 16). Unusual amounts of rainfall and rich harvests in the early 1880s contributed to the sense of bounty.

Families who migrated westward generally had little capital and thus had to rely on loans from Eastern banks. To boost their profits, mortgage companies encouraged farmers to borrow far more than they actually needed. "It was inevitable that this avalanche of credit, which far outran the real needs of the situation, should tempt the new West to extravagance, overinvestment, and speculation" (Hicks 1961, p. 23). As a result, land values skyrocketed, a trend that continued until 1887, when the near decade of abundant rainfall abruptly ended. Land values plummeted, ushering in a period of deflation.

Southern farmers faced a somewhat different plight. The collapse after the Civil War of the Southern banking system left little capital. Consequently farmers were forced to turn to local merchants, who advanced them the goods they needed in exchange for a lien on their future crop. It was a horribly oppressive system.

The effect of the crop liens was to establish a condition of peonage throughout the cotton South. The farmer who gave a lien of his crop delivered himself over to the tender mercies of the merchant who held the mortgage. He must submit to the closest scrutiny of all his purchases, and he might buy only what the merchant chose to sell him. He was permitted to trade with no other merchant except for cash, and in most cases his supply of cash was too meager to be worth mentioning. He must pay whatever prices the merchant chose to ask. He must market his crop through the merchant he owed until the entire debt was satisfied, and only then had he any right to determine the time and methods of its disposal. If his crop failed to cancel his debt, as was the case with great regularity, he must remain for another year—perhaps indefinitely—in bondage to the same merchant, or else by removing to a new neighborhood and renting a new farm became a fugitive from the law. Estimates differ, but probably three-fourths to nine-tenths of the farmers of the cotton South were ensnared to a greater or less degree by the crop-lien system. (Hicks 1961, pp. 43-44)

These problems might have been manageable were it not for the almost steady decline in commodity prices between 1870 and 1897. Some blamed overproduction for this state of affairs, but farmers pointed to the high profits pocketed by railroads and grain elevator operators. Putting their monopolies to good use, railroads were able to exact virtually whatever fees they chose to; elevator operators set arbitrary prices and cheated farmers when grading the crop. Low prices made it impossible for a farmer to pay off his debt. "The conviction grew on him that there was something essentially wicked and vicious about the system that made this possible" (Hicks 1961, p. 83). Conspiracy theories were commonplace. Farmers accused bankers of manipulating the money supply to bring about a scarcity of funds and causing the dollar to appreciate. To the farmer in debt, nothing could have been worse.

As they had in earlier decades, farmers again saw expansion of the money supply as the solution to their problems. What was needed, they felt, was an elastic currency that would allow more money to be placed into circulation as necessary. A number of farm organizations, particularly the National Farmers' Alliance (also known as the Northern Alliance) and the National Farmers' Alliance and Industrial Union (the Southern Alliance), actively expounded this view. The Northern Alliance, founded in 1880, grew first in Kansas, Nebraska, Iowa, and Minnesota, states beset by drought. The Southern Alliance, started in Texas in the mid-1870s to help ranchers round up stray animals and to protect against horse thieves, merged with the Louisiana Farmers' Union in 1887. By 1890 the Southern Alliance claimed about one million members; its northern counterpart had about two hundred thousand followers (Haynes 1916, pp. 234-35). The two Alliances tried, unsuccessfully, to unite in 1889.

With time, both Alliances fashioned distinctive political strategies. In the one-party South, the Alliance tried to capture the existing Democratic Party machinery. In this way, it ran no risk of splitting the white vote and allowing blacks to come to power. Northern Alliance members, on the other hand, saw a third party as their best hope, for efforts to work through the existing two parties had been discouraging (Hicks 1961, chap. 5). Conditions in 1890 were ripe for a political push, as drought in the West added to the problems of deflation, mortgage debt, and crop failure. Alliance-backed candidates won three gubernatorial, three senatorial, and fifty-two congressional races. They also captured seven state legislatures.

Despite the local victories, the disadvantages of the fragmented movement were apparent: Alliance forces were unable to enact desired legislation at the state level. What was needed, many Alliancemen believed, was "a national third party organization, which might supplement the state organizations and take the lead in securing national measures of reform that the states were powerless to effect" (Hicks 1961, p. 185).

The coalescing of the Alliances into a national movement paralleled the emergence of a catch-all scheme to solve the currency shortage. The "subtreasury" plan, as it came to be known, called for the government to warehouse non-perishable farm products while advancing farmers 80 percent of the value of the crop. "The farmers believed that through this subtreasury plan the volume of money would become adequate and elastic enough at harvest time and the rate of interest low enough to permit their moving their crops at a good profit" (Fine 1928, p. 76). The scheme's inflationary potential brought heavy criticism, and it was of course an easy target for those ready and willing to pin a "socialist" label on anything new. The subtreasury plan never stood a chance in Congress, and within a few years it was abandoned. Nevertheless, it helped publicize the farmers' desperate need for an expanded money supply.

Alliance leaders continued to build towards a national party convention to be held in 1892. As often happened throughout the nineteenth century, some quarters stubbornly resisted the idea of a third party. Southern Alliance leaders were especially slow to endorse the move; their strategy of capturing local Democratic Party machineries was still paying off. Only after they discovered that these local take-overs brought them few policy concessions from the national Democratic organization did the third party route appear more attractive.

Finally, in July of 1892, the People's Party convened its first national convention. Delegates endorsed government ownership of railroads, free coinage of silver, and a graduated income tax. In an effort to demonstrate that the People's Party was not merely another in a line of creations by professional third party men, several factions came to the convention hoping to nominate Judge Walter Gresham, a prominent Republican. But when Gresham prohibited his name from being considered, the convention had no choice but to select one of these professionals—former Greenback nominee James Weaver. Wrote the editor of *The Review of Reviews*:

If a man of Judge Gresham's record and standing could have been induced to leave his old party and assume the role of a Moses for the new movement, there would have been a great stirring up of dry bones. The People's party would have carried several states, and would have upset all calculations in a number of others. . . . As a matter of policy, Mr. Weaver's nomination was a mistake. A new party can only rise to strength by leading away masses of men from other parties. But the masses will not readily flock to new standards, except under the generalship of some trusted leader who goes with them. . . . But Mr. Weaver has belonged to the group of third party "come-outers" for so many years that his name is not one to conjure within either of the old camps. (Haynes 1916, pp. 262-64)

Weaver polled 8.5 percent of the November vote, winning majorities in Colorado, Idaho, Kansas, and Nevada, and over 40 percent in Nebraska, North Dakota, and Wyoming. Support for the Populists was particularly high in the newly admitted silver states. This was less the product of an attraction to the party as a whole than a reaction to the Populist free-silver plank. "Had the Populist program not included free coinage it could hardly have appealed seriously to any of the mountain states" (Hicks 1961, p. 268).

As with everything else, response to the party was different in the South. In only one Southern state—Alabama—did Weaver attract over 30 percent. His support came predominantly from rural areas. In the South, abandoning the Democrats meant splitting the white vote, so a switch to the Populists was painful. On the other hand, the Democrats' nomination of Grover Cleveland, whom Southern farmers viewed as an unrepentant tool of Eastern bankers conspiring to keep them poor, boosted Populist support. For a Southerner, it was far less difficult to back a third party candidate than a Republican.

The silver issue grew more pressing in the aftermath of the Panic of 1893, when the failure of the British banking firm Baring Brothers led to a drain on U.S. gold reserves. Money and credit became even more scarce and farm prices plummeted further. President Cleveland's indifference to suffering in the West and South only contributed to the regions' sense of desperation. His successful push to repeal the Sherman Silver Purchase Act of 1890—the only significant legislation ever passed on behalf of the silverites—focused still more attention on the issue.

To old-guard Populists, free silver was a reasonable goal, but still only a stop on the road to paper money. Populists took up the call largely because they saw it as the key to their eventual accession to major party status. However, it grew to be the issue they were most widely identified with.

The 1894 midterm elections brought mixed results for the Populists. Their vote total increased from 9.3 percent in 1892 to 11.2 percent, but because many Western fusion tickets had unraveled, the number of officials elected declined. The party, however, claimed a victory and, citing heavy Democratic losses, proclaimed itself the soon-to-be second party.

Within the Democratic Party, especially in the economically troubled South, the free-silver position gained wider acceptance. Western Democrats also became interested. Delegates from both regions met in June of 1895, committing themselves to working within the Democratic Party to enact free-silver legislation.

Meanwhile, some Populist leaders tried reducing the broad variety of issues to which the party was committed. "Keep the money question to the front. It is the only living issue before the people," the party chairman argued (Hicks 1961, p. 344). Some leaders were willing to join the Democrats to accomplish this goal. But such a step did not meet with universal approval. Southern Populists, who had in the past gained little from fusing with Democrats, opposed the idea. Moreover, free silver alone did not go far enough in meeting their needs for currency expansion.

The date of the party's national convention also became an important issue. Anti-fusionists wanted a February 1896 meeting so that the campaign could begin as soon as possible. But the convention was scheduled for July—after both major party gatherings—with the expectation that the Democrats and Republicans would continue to support a gold standard and push silverites straight into the ranks of the Populists. However, this strategy went awry when the Democrats endorsed free silver, condemned their own incumbent President Cleveland, and nominated Nebraskan William Jennings Bryan. Western Populists saw Bryan as one of their own and eagerly wanted to back him. Other Populists believed that doing so would only destroy their party. Fusionists controlled the

Populists' convention, however, and Bryan's nomination was ensured.[5]

The 1896 election marked the first time that the major parties had taken opposing stands on the currency issue:

> The economic rationale for the party system that had been displaced in midcentury by the issues of slavery, war, and reconstruction had reemerged at last. The major parties were again aligned on opposite sides of the genuine and crucial conflict of the day. In a country rent by economic depression, they appealed to the polarized electorate from opposing poles. (Sundquist 1973, p. 140)

There was simply no room left for the Populists.

The Bryan ticket went down to defeat, though Populist candidates for lower offices did quite well. Nevertheless, many Populists who had abandoned their cherished party for Bryan were discouraged by the results and found it easier to remain in the Democratic fold. Whatever hopes there may have been for rebuilding the party were further dashed by a marked improvement in the economy. Gold production skyrocketed and the currency shortage subsequently eased.

The party was dead, though Populist candidates ran in the

[5] The Democrats' nomination of Bryan left the party's gold supporters out of power for the first time. The defeated Gold Democrats (including the rebuked President Cleveland) split off to select their own nominee, Illinois Senator John Palmer. Their "National Democratic" Party platform called for the maintenance of the gold standard and limited use of tariffs. But since the party's position on money was not noticeably different from the Republicans', many Cleveland supporters saw little need for the new party and instead joined forces with Republican nominee William McKinley (Josephson 1963, p. 687).

It made little difference, even to the National Democrats' founders, whether disaffected Gold Democrats joined them or the Republicans. They had no thoughts of winning; their only goal was Bryan's defeat. Defections to either themselves or the Republicans would serve that cause. Many, in fact, worked for the National Democrats, then voted for McKinley (Stanwood 1898, p.561).

Thus it came as no great surprise when Palmer attracted less than 1 percent of the vote. He ran best (2.6 percent) in the Northeast, where most creditors lived. Support for the National Democrats was limited to those who opposed both Bryan's free-silver stance and McKinley's protectionist ways. Following the election, the coinage issue disappeared, and so too did the National Democrats.

next three presidential elections. Support, which came mostly from the South, never surpassed 1 percent. The forty-year sequence of minor parties rooted in the hardships of the farmer and laborer had finally come to an end. As the last of these, "Populism was the first modern political movement of practical importance in the United States to insist that the federal government had some responsibility for the common weal; indeed it was the first such movement to attack seriously the problems caused by industrialism" (Hofstadter 1955, p. 61). It was also the last important minor party to sustain a working national, state, and local organization over the course of several elections.

PROHIBITION PARTY

"Except in 1884 the Prohibition Party has never even slightly affected a national election and it had nearly nothing to do with the adoption of the Eighteenth Amendment; credit or blame for that accomplishment must go to the Anti-Saloon League" (Nash 1959, p. 146). The party nevertheless is noteworthy: having entered every presidential election since 1872, it is the longest-running third party in American history. It was also the first party to endorse a wide range of reforms, including women's suffrage, direct election of senators, an income tax, and child labor laws.

In its formative years, the Prohibition Party crossed paths with several other parties and social movements. Abolitionists and temperance advocates often united behind the same local candidates in the 1850s. Prohibitionists also sided with the nativist Know-Nothing Party against Irish and German immigrants who opposed temperance and against the major parties (who saw they had more to lose by offending immigrants than prohibitionists) (Gusfield 1963, pp. 54-57). The temperance and feminist movements were also closely linked. Suffrage leaders Susan B. Anthony, Elizabeth Cady Stanton, and Lucy Stone were all initially active in the temperance movement. The Prohibition Party was the first political party to accord equal status to women convention delegates and to endorse women's suffrage.

Several factors account for the party's formation in 1869. First, many states that had passed prohibition laws in the 1850s had since repealed them or had given up on their enforcement. Second, the Internal Revenue Act of 1862 both legitimized the liquor industry and gave the government a financial stake in maintaining liquor traffic. Third, with the formation of the United States Brewers' Association, liquor interests had increased their political influence. Finally, because the Civil War had resolved other, more pressing issues, temperance supporters could now devote far more attention to their cause (Colvin 1926, ch. 3). However, the party's strength did not grow as quickly as some had hoped. Many in the temperance movement resisted politics as a means of addressing this "moral" issue. Still others believed that the Republican Party would take up the cause, as it had done with abolition (Colvin 1926, ch. 5).

The Prohibition Party's initial forays into presidential politics were remarkably unsuccessful. Neither James Black in 1872, Green Clay Smith in 1876, nor Neal Dow four years later drew more than .1 percent of the vote. In all, the seventies was a decade of setbacks for the temperance movement: the liquor industry's political influence continued to grow, and more states repealed their prohibition laws.

As late as 1884, many prohibitionists still sought to achieve their goals through one of the major parties. To this end, the Prohibition Party delayed its convention until after the major parties held theirs, hoping that either the Democrats or Republicans would adopt the temperance position (Colvin 1926, p. 151). When the Democrats selected Grover Cleveland and the Republicans James G. Blaine, the Prohibitionists nominated John P. St. John, the most prominent man among them.[6] St. John's presidential campaign attracted over 147,000 votes (1.5 percent). His presence on the ticket was especially important in New York, where he polled 25,000 votes. Blaine's

[6] As Republican Governor of Kansas between 1878 and 1882, St. John made his state the first to pass a constitutional amendment imposing prohibition.

loss of New York by just over 1,000 votes cost him the election.[7]

Although the Prohibition Party continued to build support in subsequent elections, it also continued to have little influence over outcomes and public policy. Fears of large-scale defections led the major parties to make platform concessions, but the Democrats and Republicans soon learned that the number of temperance voters was small and that the ire of drinkers—particularly immigrant drinkers—was a greater political concern (Colvin 1926, ch. 10; Gusfield 1963, pp. 54-57). Clinton Fisk polled 2.2 percent of the 1888 popular vote and one-term Representative John Bidwell attracted nearly 2.3 percent in 1892, marking the party's strongest showing in its over one-hundred-year history. Despite these gains, prohibition laws still were not adopted.

The Prohibition Party continued to focus primarily on its one issue. The "narrow gaugers" who maintained control argued that the party stood no chance of success if it took on several cross-cutting divisive issues at once. At the 1896 convention, the party rebuffed free-silver forces who tried to add their plank to the platform. In protest, these "broad gaugers" split off to form the National Party, which attracted fewer than 20,000 votes.

The temperance movement's fortunes improved at the turn of the century. Between 1906 and 1912, seven states adopted prohibition laws. But these successes can be attributed to the efforts of the Anti-Saloon League and various church groups and to shifting social conditions, not to the Prohibition Party. "The rise of Prohibition strength owed a great deal to the sense of cultural change and prestige loss which accompanied both the defeat of the Populist movement and the increased urbanization and immigration of the twentieth century" (Gusfield 1963, p. 102). Rural residents felt that they were losing

---

[7] Even with St. John in the race, the Republicans' own bungling probably caused their loss. As Hirsch concludes, "there is wide concurrence in historical literature that Cleveland did not win the election of 1884. Blaine lost it. Any discussion of the contest revolves mainly around Blaine—his shortcomings, failings, mistakes, mishaps—for he is the central figure" (1971, p. 1581).

power to urban immigrants; drinking became more acceptable and commonplace. The population divided over temperance as rural native Protestants, spurred by their perceived declining status, pursued the issue with renewed vigor.

However, the prohibition movement and the Prohibition Party employed different political strategies: the Anti-Saloon League operated as a single-issue pressure group, while the party now took a broader view, adopting positions on tariffs, foreign policy, the civil service, social justice, and farm matters. The efforts of the Anti-Saloon League were what brought enactment of the Eighteenth Amendment in 1920, instituting nationwide prohibition. The League's success "taught the voter to remain in his old party and work there" (Colvin 1926, p. 380). With its view that individual candidates were more important than parties, the League helped bring about the Prohibition Party's decline. Support shrank from 1.9 percent for Sillas Swallow in 1904, to 1.4 percent for Eugene Chafin in 1912, to .7 percent for Aaron Sherman Watkins in 1920.

Even after the Eighteenth Amendment passed, the party continued attempts to rally prohibitionists under its roof. Evidently, few voters felt the need for this shelter: electoral support hovered under .2 percent. The repeal of the Amendment in 1933 produced no flood of votes either, and the party began to adopt conservative stands on a broader range of issues, including foreign policy, fluoridation, education, and government spending.

The party changed its name to National Statesman in 1980 as a way of signaling that its concerns extended beyond the seemingly long-closed issue of prohibition. Yet it polled only 7,100 votes that year, a showing that standard bearer Benjamin C. Bubar blamed on the change of name. As a result, the party plans to return to the Prohibition banner in 1984 (Smallwood 1983, p. 41).

CONCLUSIONS

Third parties of the nineteenth century were inextricably linked to the major parties. First, third parties in many ways resembled their major party counterparts: they ran candidates for lower offices, most held conventions to select their nominees, and there were often real fights over who would be the standard bearers. Like the major parties, they took stands on a wide range of issues to broaden their appeal. Third parties of this era were also relatively continuous. Every minor party, except the 1860 Southern Democrats, persisted in some form for at least two elections.

Second, leaders of these minor parties always tried to work within the major parties before they became independents. The political movements of this century pursued the third party route as a course of last resort. Only when attempts at alliance failed, or when a faction was unable to win policy concessions or capture a major party nomination, did politicians and voters organize independent parties. The reluctance of dissenters to form third parties is evident in the limited ability of new parties to attract prominent men as their standard bearers. Most of the minor party pioneers of this century were relative unknowns—James Birney, Peter Cooper, and James Black, for example. However, once a minor party had established itself, it was often able to entice more prominent candidates away from the major parties. Two former presidents—Van Buren and Fillmore—abandoned the major parties during this century, as did eight men who had served in the U.S. Congress or as a state's chief executive.

Third, many of the minor parties of the nineteenth century either grew into or out of the major parties. The Liberty Party was incorporated into the Free Soil Party, which in turn became part of the Republican Party. The Know-Nothing Party and the Constitutional Union Party both descended from the Whigs.

In sum, the minor parties of this era were not random phenomena totally disconnected from the political mainstream. They behaved like major parties, they drew from the major parties, and they evolved into or from major parties. In a system absent of constraints against minor parties, they might very well have achieved equal status with the major parties.

But third party movements found it extremely difficult to sustain themselves. After several elections, either the conditions that originally precipitated the parties' formation disappeared, or one of the major parties took up the third parties' cause. Since third parties always fell short of their goal of displacing a major party, their voters usually became discouraged and gave up. Third parties could distribute few instrumental benefits—either policy victories or patronage—making it difficult for them to maintain voters' allegiance.

The nineteenth-century pattern of third party development—parties formed, then picked their candidates—did not persist into the twentieth century. Candidates began to emerge before the movements, and third party politics began to revolve around individuals instead of parties. As we shall see in the next chapter, these changes parallel those taking place within the major parties.

CHAPTER 4

INDEPENDENTS OF THE TWENTIETH CENTURY

ALTHOUGH the third parties of the 1800s closely resembled the major parties, the same cannot be said for those of the twentieth century. The most prominent movements of the 1900s—Theodore Roosevelt's, Robert LaFollette's, and Henry Wallace's progressive parties, William Lemke's Union Party, Strom Thurmond's States' Rights Party, George Wallace's American Independent Party, Eugene McCarthy's Independent Party, and John Anderson's National Unity Campaign— are all more accurately labeled independent campaigns than political parties. None had any real organization distinct from the candidate's own following, and for most of them the "party" would not have existed without the candidate. Whereas men of stature in the nineteenth century bolted to a minor party only if it had some prior history, in the twentieth century prominent politicians were less hesitant to initiate an independent campaign. There were few efforts to build organizations with staying power, or ones that could operate effectively without their mentors. The most successful third parties of the twentieth century disappeared after a single election; they were not continuous like their nineteenth-century counterparts.

These changes had their parallels within the major parties, which also became more candidate-centered. Both the major and minor parties responded to an evolving environment: technology replaced organization as the crucial ingredient, with less reliance on a formal party apparatus.

THEODORE ROOSEVELT

Theodore Roosevelt's third party candidacy marked the first time a minor party challenge centered on a man rather than his cause. Every previous third party run began with a party, which in turn selected a nominee. But in 1912 Roosevelt was the party. Had he not run, it is unlikely there would have been a Progressive challenge that year.

This is not to say that Roosevelt did not represent a cause—he clearly did. People who had not profited from the new industrialism demanded their share of the wealth and viewed Roosevelt as their protector against the unbridled greed of the corporate barons. He was the first president to enforce the Sherman Anti-Trust Act effectively, and his threat to take over the coal industry if management was unable to reach a settlement with workers marked the first time a president had sided with organized labor. He also obtained legislation to check abuses by the railroads, meat packers, and the drug industry.

Roosevelt left office in 1909 confident that his hand-picked successor, William Howard Taft, would continue down this progressive path. But Taft disappointed progressives soon after his inauguration when he acquiesced to Senate protectionist demands for higher tariffs. His proposal to rescind railroad anti-trust laws and to seek railroad assistance in drafting new rules also raised the progressives' ire. The President and conservative congressional leaders, tiring of progressive complaints, "agreed that the measure should be passed without amendment and that anyone who opposed it should be treated as an enemy of the party" (Mowry 1946, p. 99). But when even non-progressive Republicans abandoned the bill, the measure failed.

Animosity between the factions intensified as Taft openly campaigned against progressive members of Congress in 1910. Progressives fought hard to retain their seats, organizing local clubs to counter those Taft had established. Although the attack failed—primary voters consistently rejected conservative candidates—it was a costly and destructive fight for the Republican Party.

In the midst of the 1910 campaign, Roosevelt returned from his year-long sojourn in Europe and Africa "thoroughly convinced that Taft, though sincere, had permitted reactionary forces to lead him into a position that had inevitably occasioned the revolt of the progressive faction" (Mowry 1946, p. 126). Taft had dismissed some Roosevelt cabinet officials whom he had pledged to retain, and there were reports that the White House was mistreating members of Roosevelt's family. What bothered the former President most, however, was not that Taft had betrayed the progressive cause, but that in the process he had weakened the Republican Party.

> Roosevelt's boundless contempt for the Democratic party unconsciously made him antagonistic to anything that might enfeeble Republicanism and thus enhance the possibility of a Democratic victory. Then too he was supremely proud of the fact that he had, seemingly through his own efforts, left the party in what had appeared to be an impregnable position. Now when he saw it in shambles, an artist's pride in his own creation was touched, and a sense of irritation grew against the man who, he reasoned, had destroyed it. (Mowry 1946, p. 131)

And so Roosevelt directed his efforts in 1910 to rebuilding party solidarity rather than electing progressives. His scheme for revitalizing the party was first to gain the confidence of progressives and then to address conservative concerns. But realization of the first goal made the second impossible. Moreover, Taft and Roosevelt were suspicious of one another, each interpreting the other's moves as personal attacks. In the election, the Democrats soundly thrashed Republicans of all stripes. Taft's party lost fifty-seven congressional seats, giving the Democrats control of the House for the first time in sixteen years. The Republicans also relinquished their hold on nine state legislatures, a turn of events that contributed to their loss of thirteen U.S. Senate seats.

In the aftermath of this disaster, Taft too set out to reunite the party, but progressives were determined that he not be renominated in 1912. Progressive members of Congress asserted their independence: forty-seven Representatives declared themselves unbound by the positions of the Republican caucus, and thirteen Senators demanded recognition as a separate minority of the Republican Party, entitled to their fair share of committee assignments. Prominent progressives organized the National Progressive Republican League.

Roosevelt, meanwhile, was predicting a Republican loss in 1912, regardless of who was nominated. He seemed willing to support Taft, anticipating that the President's defeat would leave the party no choice but to reorganize under Roosevelt's own direction. Through most of 1911 there was no indication that Rooselvelt himself was planning to run.

It was Taft's decision, late that October, to prosecute U.S. Steel under the Sherman Anti-Trust Act that finally brought Roosevelt into the race. As president, Roosevelt had in 1907 allowed U.S. Steel to purchase the ailing Tennessee Coal and Iron Company, ostensibly to prevent major bank failures that would have ensued had the company folded. The merger may or may not have been necessary, but it did eliminate a competitor of U.S. Steel. Taft's suit was a direct personal slap at Roosevelt: the implication "was that Roosevelt, in permitting the transaction, had been completely duped" (Mowry 1946, p. 191). Roosevelt's vociferous public defense had the effect of turning him into a candidate for the Republican nomination. As public support for Roosevelt's position grew, T.R. reevaluated his chance of success and permitted public efforts on his behalf. With hindsight, one may question the wisdom of the move. Had Roosevelt not entered the race, Taft surely would have been renominated and would have lost to the Democrats, leaving the Republicans with no one to turn to in 1916 but Roosevelt.

It was a bitter campaign. Taft captured Southern delegates by organizing state conventions before Roosevelt's forces were prepared. Since Roosevelt's strength lay with the voters, he fought to boost the number of states that would hold direct primaries, successfully convincing six states to join the six that already selected delegates in this manner. In these states Roosevelt was inordinately successful, winning 278 delegates to Taft's 48. Meanwhile, tempers ran so high at some state conventions that fist fights broke out. At the Michigan gathering, the party split into two separate meetings. Then "amid the wildest disorder and violence both conventions, from the same platform, simultaneously went through the motions of selecting two sets of delegates" (Mowry 1946, p. 232). The battle grew even more heated in Taft's native Ohio; Roosevelt's sizable primary victory there left the Republican nomination in doubt.

The Republican National Convention was the next battlefield. Neither Roosevelt nor Taft seemed to have enough honestly elected delegates to secure the nomination (DeWitt 1915, p. 80). The critical fight ensued over 254 contested seats. Which candidate deserved the seats remains an open question. But Taft, through his control of the Republican National Committee, ensured that the contested cases were decided in his favor. The Committee awarded all but 19 of the seats in question to the incumbent, giving Taft the majority he needed for renomination.

Faced with certain defeat, Roosevelt and his advisors met to review their options. For some months Roosevelt had considered abandoning the Republicans if party bosses stole from him the nomination that he perceived the masses so clearly wanted him to have. His advisers disagreed on what the next step should be: those whose own careers prevented them from bolting argued against a third party, while those who had nothing to lose supported the idea. To Roosevelt, it was a question of money: he would not run without it. When newspaper magnate Frank Munsey and U.S. Steel director George Perkins vowed to foot the bills, this last hurdle disappeared.

Roosevelt immediately informed the Republican convention of his decision to form a new party. As a result, most of his delegates refused to vote for a nominee. That night, Roosevelt supporters gathered to hear their candidate's call to arms.

Roosevelt's Progressive (Bull Moose) Party convened six weeks later. Its platform echoed earlier Greenback and Populist pledges, calling for the direct election of U.S. senators, direct primaries, women's suffrage, publication of campaign expenditures, regulation of interstate industry, a minimum wage, unemployment insurance, and old age pensions. There was a divisive battle over an anti-trust plank considered essential by most party leaders, but opposed by financial backer Perkins. In the end, the plank was deleted, antagonizing many supporters.

The movement quickly ran into other difficulties. The Democrats nominated Woodrow Wilson, appeasing most progressives in that party. Moreover, many Roosevelt supporters balked at the third party route; some backed Wilson instead.

For all practical purposes, the fall campaign was a battle only between Roosevelt and Wilson. Taft's defeat was certain. But in a contest between what people perceived to be two progressives, Roosevelt stood little chance. In the end, he polled 27.4 percent of the popular vote—more than any other third party candidate—and captured 88 votes in the Electoral College. If his only goal was to defeat Taft, he succeeded: the President finished third with a mere 23.2 percent and 8 electoral votes. Roosevelt's strength was largely urban. Agricultural regions, bastions of third party strength in the past, did not support "Roosevelt's paternalistic philosophy of government. . . . A high protective tariff, the regulation of industrial monopolies, the long list of labor reforms, offered little to the farmer" (Mowry 1946, p. 280).

The returns demonstrated that the Progressives were a party in name only. Its appeal was limited to its presidential candidate; as a rule, candidates for local offices fared poorly. The Progressives constituted

> no committed ideological bloc whose political course was directed by what was necessary to advance a program; they merely followed their leader where he led. Roosevelt's Progressive party remained in being, but when, in the 1914 midterm election, the Wilson administration showed a loss of support, it was the Republicans rather than the Progressives who benefited. It was evident that the public support given the Progressive party in 1912 had been Roosevelt's personal following, which did not

attach automatically to other candidates running as Progressives. (Sundquist 1973, p. 164)

As president, Wilson induced Congress to pass progressive legislation, including tariff reduction, a child-labor law, and creation of the Federal Trade Commission. Although he was a progressive in his own right, "there is little doubt that [Wilson] jumped on the progressive bandwagon because he was convinced that a Democratic victory in [1916] might well depend on the votes of social justice advocates" (Link and Leary 1971, p. 2269).

The Progressive Party machinery, hamstrung by infighting and a lack of money and patronage, decayed. Since the party had won only a handful of local offices, it was unable to provide many rewards to supporters. Frank Munsey withdrew his backing, leaving George Perkins as the party's sole financial patron. Perkins himself remained a source of controversy within the party. His opposition to the Sherman Anti-Trust Act, which had split the party's 1912 convention, was still nettlesome. (Western progressives considered the Act sacrosanct.) Many party leaders demanded that Perkins be ousted, but Roosevelt viewed Perkins's continued presence as essential and denounced this "advanced radical element." Roosevelt warned that if Perkins were banished, he too would go.

Yet, for all practical purposes, Roosevelt had by now given up on the Progressive Party as a vehicle for recapturing the White House. Only one Progressive was elected to the House in 1914 (down from 14 in 1912) and the party's national vote dipped below two million. Roosevelt focused on the European war. However, this interest increasingly estranged him from progressives, many of whom opposed U.S. involvement. Roosevelt soon found himself aligned with conservative corporate powers who bankrolled "patriotic" organizations dedicated to ending the nation's isolationism.

Since Roosevelt's top priority was Wilson's defeat, and this required a unified Republican Party, he fashioned a reconciliation of sorts with conservatives. Roosevelt hoped to extract concessions from the Republican Party in exchange for the progressives' return. Ideally, he wanted to capture both the Republican and Progressive nominations.

Republican leaders, however, were determined that Roosevelt not be nominated. In an effort to win back progressive support, they were willing to compromise on Charles Evans Hughes. Delegations from the two parties met to hammer out a solution, but progressives remained intractable. Minutes after the Republicans selected Hughes, the Progressives nominated Roosevelt. This time Roosevelt declined, realizing the futility of the venture. The Progressive Party disintegrated as a result: some members went to Hughes, others to Wilson. It was final testimony to the party's dependence upon Roosevelt. As one Roosevelt advisor later wrote:

> For all its legal status, the Progressive party cannot really be said to have been a political party at all. Rather, it was a faction, a split-off fragment of its mother star, the Republican party, which, like a meteor, flamed momentarily across the sky, only to fall and cool on the earth of solid fact. . . . The lesson taught by the Progressive incident seems to be the familiar one: that a party cannot be founded without a definite cause, or solely upon the personality of an individual. To survive the hardships of the initial years, a new party must be a party of ideas, not of men. If the Progressive party had framed an issue that was at the same time clear and of large actual consequence, it would not have died upon the defection of its leader. . . . The answer of the Progressives was, "Make Roosevelt president." And when it became clear that they could not do that, the Progressives disbanded and the country knew them no more. (Pinchot 1958, pp. 172, 226-27)

Socialist Parties

The history of the socialist movement in the United States has been marked by a string of spin-offs and split-ups. Four parties—Socialist Labor, Socialist, Socialist Workers, and

Communist—have demonstrated a remarkable staying power uncharacteristic of American third parties. They have survived because their goal—education—is so different from that of other parties. As a result, they have been able to endure even though they usually garner very few votes.

Although socialism as a political movement in the United States had its roots in the 1853 Workingmen's Alliance, it was not until 1877 that the Socialist Labor Party formed. It ran its first presidential candidate in 1892. The party, however, never attracted much support; its strength peaked in 1900 when Joseph Malloney polled nearly .3 percent of the presidential popular vote. The party still persists today (making it second to the Prohibition Party in minor party longevity), though not since 1924 has its nominee won as much as .1 percent.

In response to the Socialist Labor Party's doctrinal rigidity, a moderate faction split off in 1901 and, along with former American Railway Union President Eugene Debs's Socialist Democratic Party, established the Socialist Party. It was to be the most successful and the most ideologically flexible of the American socialist parties. In many respects it is appropriate to speak of the Socialist Party in the same breath as the Greenback or Populist parties: all were by-products of an economic transition that imbued in many Americans the feeling that they had been left behind. But whereas the Greenbackers and Populists advocated an increased role for government, Socialists saw collective ownership of the means of production and distribution as the solution.

An unofficial alliance between Social Laborites and the Social Democratic Party in 1900 had produced nearly 100,000 votes (.6 percent) for Debs. The formal merger in 1901 boosted their electoral strength considerably: the party attracted over 2.5 percent of the presidential vote in five consecutive contests. The charismatic Debs was the party's standard bearer in four of these campaigns (all but 1916). The party's strength peaked in 1912 when it captured 6 percent of the presidential ballots. Debs ran strongest in the West, attracting between 11 and 16 percent of the vote in Arizona, California, Idaho, Montana, Nevada, Oklahoma, and Washington. The party elected over 1,200 local officials, including 79 mayors. Despite this support, Debs maintained that his fundamental goal was not to win office, but "to teach social consciousness" (Weinstein 1967, p. 11).

The relatively high vote totals of these years are attributable to at least two bases of support. First, this marked the only period in which a socialist party tried to forge political coalitions with other social movements. The party was

> a coalition of regional groups that had different, even conflicting points of view. In this diversity lay the party's strength. By the mid-twentieth century standards of left-wing organization, such a conglomerate aggregation as this would have been impossible, but the prewar Socialists enjoyed relative success precisely because they were so catholic in their organization. (Shannon 1955, pp. 6-7)

In Oklahoma, party support was consistently high because of Socialist concern with farmers' problems. In the West, the party enjoyed similar support because it pushed Populist ideas that would benefit tenant farmers. And in the Far West, union miners and lumberjacks who espoused more radical notions supported the party.

European immigrants provided another base of Socialist Party support. Between 1900 and the outbreak of World War I, over twelve million people immigrated to the United States from Europe. Some had socialist allegiances at home, which made their transition to the American Socialist Party an easy one. In the early 1910s, Italians, Scandinavians, Hungarians, Germans, Poles, Lithuanians, and Russians, among others, formed foreign-language federations affiliated with the party. Yet their support turned out to be a mixed blessing. Since immigrants provided an inexpensive competitive labor supply that threatened union-won gains, the new arrivals themselves became a divisive force within the party.

The years surrounding World War I were trying ones for the movement. Socialists opposed President Wilson's preparedness program and argued that the United States should enter the war only if the public, through a national referendum, approved the action. These positions stimulated a wave of hostile attacks by government officials, the press, and the public. It became difficult, if not perilous, for the party's candidates to campaign for office. Under the Espionage Act, the Postmaster General seized Socialist publications sent through the mail. Party leaders, as well as rank-and-file members, were indicted and prosecuted. "Some [indictments] were designed to hamper party organization and activity as was the indictment of Victor Burger in the middle of his campaign for Senator in Wisconsin in March 1918. Others seemed aimed simply at terrifying and intimidating individuals" (Weinstein 1967, pp. 160-61). Vigilantes prevented Socialists from using meeting halls; night riders tarred and feathered Socialist speakers. Police in South Dakota, for instance, broke up the state party convention and forced some delegates out of town. By the war's end 1,500 of the more than 5,000 Socialist Party locals had been destroyed (Weinstein 1967, pp. 145-61). Debs nonetheless polled over 3.4 percent of the 1920 presidential vote, campaigning from the Atlanta prison cell where he was serving time for making an anti-war speech.

In disarray, the party joined a number of progressive groups in backing Robert LaFollette in 1924. Although there were disputes with labor unions over specific strategies and stances, the idea of building a broadly based party appealed to many Socialists. They were disappointed when unionists, unable to elect LaFollette, returned to the major party fold.

The Socialist Party that emerged from the LaFollette venture was markedly different from its earlier incarnation. Its new leader and six-time standard bearer Norman Thomas, a college-educated refugee from the ministry, reflected this change. Intellectuals replaced unionists, farmers, and immigrants; New York, where Socialists had enjoyed little support in the past, became the new base of power. Party backers were generally middle class and well educated rather than working class.

Although the Depression provided the party with a temporary resurgence—2.2 percent of the vote in 1932—Franklin Roosevelt's New Deal won back all but the most committed supporters. The 1936 Socialist vote fell to .4 percent—its lowest level since its founding. In some states the drop-off all but wiped out the party as a viable force: Thomas plunged from 20,067 to 1,373 votes in Iowa, from 63,299 to 11,325 votes in California, and from 25,476 to 2,872 votes in Minnesota. Thomas's explanation for the decline was unambiguous: "What cut the ground out pretty completely from under us . . . Roosevelt in a word. You don't need anything more" (Leuchtenburg 1971, p. 2845). Although the New Deal clearly did not implement the Socialist Party's platform, it nonetheless attracted former Socialists to the Democratic coalition. The New Deal was economically conservative, yet its rhetoric was much more radical and anti-business. "In part this radicalism sprang from disenchantment with the experience of collaboration with business. In part, too, no doubt, it was an opportunistic improvisation designed to neutralize the clamor on the left" (Schlesinger, 1960, p. 392). The Socialist Party last ran a national candidate in 1956.

In 1921, at the behest of the Soviet Union, left-wing groups that had split off from the Socialist Party two years earlier formed the Workers' (Communist) Party. Functioning largely as a mouthpiece for the Soviet Union, the party ran presidential candidates in each election between 1924 and 1940, and then resurfaced with a national ticket that has persisted since 1968. The Communist Party's support peaked in 1932 when it attracted nearly .3 percent of the presidential ballots. A Trotskyite faction broke off from the Communist Party in 1938 to form the Socialist Workers Party. The SWP has run a national candidate in every election since 1948, but none has captured over .1 percent of the popular vote.

With the exception of the Socialist Party, which enjoyed substantial local and national support over a number of elections, socialist parties have had little impact either on election outcomes, on the major parties, or on American public policy. They are noted most for their longevity, remarkable in light of the paucity of tangible electoral success. Aside from 1912, Socialists had their best showing in 1924 when, ironically, the candidate they supported did not even bear their party's name.

Robert LaFollette

Before 1924, a number of third parties had sought to forge a coalition between dissatisfied farmers and laborers, but the interests of the two groups never seemed quite compatible. Party leaders inevitably addressed themselves to the concerns of one group but not the other. Robert LaFollette's 1924 Progressive campaign succeeded where others had failed.

There are similarities between LaFollette's progressive movement and Theodore Roosevelt's. LaFollette, like Roosevelt, believed that government should protect citizens from the excesses of monied powers, and both sought to open up the electoral process as much as possible. Like Roosevelt, LaFollette personified his party; without him, there would not have been a 1924 Progressive campaign for president.

Yet it is equally important to recognize that the Progressive parties of 1912 and 1924 were by and large separate entities operating in very different political and economic contexts. Especially different was the economic health of workers and farmers. Agricultural prices were relatively high in 1912; real GNP per capita grew 4.1 percent that year. The 1924 election, on the other hand, followed the post-war depression: real GNP per capita had fallen 20 percent between 1918 and 1921. Although the economy rebounded in 1922 and 1923, GNP fell 2.2 percent in 1924. It was a period of Republican dominance in which laborers frequently lost out to corporate–government alliances. In 1922 a federal district court had ordered railroad workers to halt their strike against wage cuts. Union membership declined as more workers were laid off by the depression. Under President Coolidge, Treasury Secretary Andrew Mellon—the aluminum, oil, and banking magnate—pushed through enormous tax cuts for the wealthy. Big business had captured the federal government, and laborers and farmers were left out in the cold.

The farmers' misfortunes paralleled their predecessors' plight in the late 1800s. Agricultural prices more than doubled between 1915 and 1919, and farmers, confident of continued good fortune, invested heavily in machinery and built roads and schools. But prosperity gave way when agricultural prices collapsed. Foreign demand for farm goods fell, population growth slowed, and dietary habits changed, all while productivity rose. As a result, commodity prices had dropped 44 percent by 1921. Although other sectors of the economy began to recover the following year, farmers were left behind: in 1924 prices remained one-third lower than their 1920 levels.

Farmers found an outlet for their grievances in the Non-Partisan League. The movement formed in 1915 to fight for changes in tax laws, insurance and mortgage programs, and the running of mills, grain elevators, packing houses, and storage plants. Unlike earlier farm organizations, the League was explicitly a political group from its inception. However, it remained independent of both parties. The League's strategy was to enter and back favorable candidates in both parties' primaries. It elected a number of its candidates in 1916.

Four groups—the railroad brothermen, the Non-Partisan League, the Socialist Party, and the "Committee of Forty-Eight" (a group of progressives left hanging by Teddy Roosevelt's decision not to run in 1916)—came together in 1922 as the Conference for Progressive Political Action (CPPA). In that year's elections, six states sent CPPA-endorsed candidates to Congress. A total of 140 members of the new Congress were believed to be sympathetic to the CPPA cause (MacKay 1947, p. 67). In light of these encouraging results, the Conference met again in December to debate the idea of a 1924 third party run. Although the Socialists favored the move, the railroad brotherhood was reluctant to abandon the major parties, and farmers preferred the direct primary path. The plan went down to defeat.

But American progressives reconsidered the idea when they saw similar movements in other nations achieving success through third parties. The British Labor Party's displacement of the Liberals showed that a worker-socialist coalition could succeed. At the same time, Canadian farmers had banded together in the National Progressive Party to win stunning victories (MacKay 1947, p. 74; Lipset 1968). The CPPA agreed to meet on July 4, 1924, after both major party conventions, to name a presidential candidate. It was clear that the CPPA would pursue the third party route if both major parties failed to choose a progressive.

Only in the Democratic Party was there hope that an acceptable candidate would emerge. The Republicans overwhelmingly renominated Coolidge. But the Democrats were too busy bludgeoning each other to worry about attracting progressive support. After 103 grueling ballots, they finally settled on John W. Davis, a man of intelligence and integrity, but a man whose law firm served J. P. Morgan and other financial interests.

The Progressives gathered while the Democratic bloodbath was still underway. LaFollette was their only plausible choice. As governor from 1901 to 1905, he established a national reputation with his "Wisconsin Idea," which called for direct primaries, equalized corporate taxation, and railroad regulation. He continued to work for progressive causes when he joined the Senate in 1905 and campaigned vigorously for the 1912 Republican presidential nomination, until Roosevelt undercut him with his late entry into the race. Like Roosevelt, LaFollette abandoned the Republican Party that year, but supported Democrat Woodrow Wilson.

Although LaFollette wanted to run as an independent in 1924, he did not want to create a party organization until after the election. "A straight-out third party fight, he warned, would jeopardize the seats of many progressives in Congress who had won office through one of the major parties and who might be called upon to help choose a President should the election be thrown into the House" (Hicks 1960, p. 98). So rather than have the delegates select him, the CPPA national committee made the nomination. The Socialists reluctantly went along.

The convention's platform minced no words. The chief villain was monopoly. Delegates demanded public ownership of water power and railroads, protection of collective bargaining, direct primaries and elections, the approval of wars by referendum, and an end to the use of injunctions to resolve labor disputes. The platform gave special attention to the farmer's plight.

LaFollette picked up the American Federation of Labor endorsement, marking the first time in history the AFL officially backed a presidential candidate. However, the unions proved to be lethargic compatriots. As it became clear that LaFollette's chances of winning were slim, labor's commitment weakened. After all, unions had to stay on good terms with the major parties, which most certainly would remain in power. Promised financial support from organized labor never materialized.

The major parties, as they are prone to do, ignored each other and turned on LaFollette instead. Even though LaFollette had explicitly and publicly spurned the Communist Party, critics charged him with being a dangerous radical. LaFollette's proposal to empower Congress to overrule Supreme Court decisions made him an easy target for those wanting to portray him as out to destroy the American system.

The campaign suffered from the same problems that plague almost all independent candidates: LaFollette had difficulty getting on ballots, there was insufficient financial support, and he lacked a well-run organization. He was forced to run under four different party names, and the Republicans outspent him twenty to one. Without Progressive Party candidates running for lower offices, there were few experienced local politicians willing to promote the cause. "The movement, concentrating on capturing national office, overlooked a condition of American politics obvious to the most casual observer, namely, that the great national political machines are established upon sound, substantial, local structures" (MacKay 1947, p. 194). The Progressive Party was little more than LaFollette's own personal following. Moreover, LaFollette's unwillingness to develop a formal party organization upset the Socialists. The Socialists had no dreams of winning this election; they wanted to build for the future. This aim left them at odds with the nearsighted laborites, who could not think beyond an immediate victory.

Although LaFollette campaigned vigorously, his effort was not enough. He polled nearly 5 million votes—16.6 percent. About four out of five of these ballots were cast for LaFollette the Progressive; the rest were cast for LaFollette the Socialist and LaFollette the Farm–Laborite. MacKay estimates that over half of LaFollette's support came from farmers, and a fifth each from union members and socialists (1947, p. 221). He ran strongest in the West, garnering about 30 percent in the Pacific and Mountain states. He also carried 24 percent of the vote in the ten largest cities (Burner 1971, p. 2487). In the end, LaFollette won only Wisconsin's 13 electoral votes, although he finished second in all eleven Western and Southern states.

The Socialists played an important role in LaFollette's effort. He ran well in areas where they were well organized.

[The Socialists] had the local organizations which could provide the framework for the construction of the new party, and, moreover, unlike many promoters of a progressive party, whose enthusiasm exceeded their experience, they had a rich knowledge of how to conduct campaigns, in meeting the tactics of the old parties, in exchanging blow for blow in practical politics. The Socialists had their name on the ballots in almost all the states—a priceless heritage for the Progressives. (MacKay 1947, p. 55)

To committed progressives, the election results demonstrated the need for a party structure. They met almost immediately to try building one. But the unionists were tired of third party activity, and although they attended as a courtesy, they quickly withdrew their support. At the same time, most farmers had become pacified by rising commodity prices. The retreat of these forces left only the Socialists and a few diehard farmers to organize another effort. The meeting adjourned with these two groups unable to reach agreement on a strategy. LaFollette's death in June 1925 ended any last hope for a new party.

WILLIAM LEMKE

A third party again took up the farmer's cause in 1936. Disaffection with Franklin Roosevelt's presidency surfaced early in his first term. This was hardly unique to FDR. The difference, though, was that much of this opposition was spearheaded by three "social prophets"—Father Charles E. Coughlin, Reverend Gerald L. K. Smith, and Dr. Francis Townsend—whose leadership was more spiritual than political and whose strongest affiliations were religious, not partisan (Schlesinger 1960, p. 16). Because each drew his support from distinct issue and geographical constituencies, the threat of such an alliance caused great consternation in the Roosevelt administration (McCoy 1958, pp. 70-71).

Although the "radio priest" Father Coughlin had originally supported Roosevelt's programs, he split with the administration in early 1935 when it became apparent that the President would not adopt Coughlin's inflationary cure for the Depression. Coughlin claimed five million members in his National Union for Social Justice, a following concentrated largely in the Northeast, especially Massachusetts.

Reverend Gerald L. K. Smith was the self-proclaimed inheritor of Louisiana Senator Huey Long's Share Our Wealth movement, which commanded a largely Southern following. Long proposed that the government tax away all income over $1 million and all inheritances over $5 million, and that it provide every citizen with an initial stake of $5,000 and a $2,000 annual income. This plan would have distributed far more money than it would have brought in. Although it was "economic fantasy, it produced a response" (Schlesinger 1960, p. 63). By mid-1935 Reverend Smith, then Long's chief assistant, was claiming seven million followers. This was clearly an exaggeration, but Long was still someone to watch closely. He began to think of his organization as an alternative to the major parties. The New Deal, its leaders, and its administrators were Long's chief target, though he did not see the Republicans as providing a satisfactory alternative either. "When the New Deal blows up," he told a group of GOP Senators, "you old mossback Republicans need not think you'll get the country back. It won't go to you, and it won't go to those Democrats over there" (Schlesinger 1960, p. 243).

In anticipation of a Long independent run, the Democratic National Committee commissioned a poll in early 1935 to gauge his strength. Roosevelt political strategist James Farley reported that "to our surprise . . . [Long] might poll between 3,000,000 and 4,000,000 votes as the head of a third party" (Farley 1948, p. 51). The sounding showed that support would be drawn largely from Democratic ranks and that Long "might constitute a balance of power in the 1936 election" (Schlesinger 1960, p. 252). To avert defections, the White House persuaded politicians to disassociate themselves from Long's Share Our Wealth Society and excluded Long supporters from federal patronage. Whether these moves would have averted a Long candidacy will of course never be known—he was assassinated on September 10, 1935. Smith laid claim to his following, but a deal between Roosevelt and Louisiana politicians brought an end to the Share Our Wealth movement and left Smith looking for a new organization to lead.

Townsend's crusade on behalf of old-age pensions was thought to be the strongest of the three movements. Like the others, it sought only a single end—in this case, a monthly government payment of $200 to everyone over 60. While the Townsend movement cannot claim credit for initiating the social security debate, its apparent strength contributed to the passage of the Social Security Act of 1935. But this law still left millions of elderly without any assistance, and Townsend quickly gave up on Roosevelt, choosing instead to try to elect his followers to Congress. With a claimed membership of five million, the movement presented a clear danger. To combat it, the major parties launched a congressional investigation into the organization's finances. Although Townsend pointed to his $300 bank balance as proof of no wrongdoing, he was unable to stop the committee, whose only goal was to destroy his organization. Townsend finally refused to testify further, whereupon a man, who later introduced himself as Reverend

Smith, gently ushered him out of the hearing. The two quickly fashioned an alliance of sorts.

Meanwhile, Roosevelt's policies had also raised the ire of Republican Representative William Lemke of North Dakota. Lemke, who grew up on a farm, naturally took the concerns of farmers to heart. Farmers' economic problems, which began long before the Depression hit other sectors, had become particularly acute by the 1930s: between 1928 and 1932 farm prices fell nearly 75 percent. North Dakota was among the hardest hit states; at one point, nearly half its population was on relief.

To address the problem, Lemke developed two proposals— one concerned with bankruptcy, the other with debt. He approached Hoover first, but was turned away. Lemke then met with Roosevelt, and took the Democrat's response as an endorsement of his plans. The Congressman campaigned vigorously for FDR in 1932 and looked forward to playing a prominent role in shaping the new administration's farm policy. Roosevelt, however, had collected a group of economists for that purpose, and Lemke's inflexible personality alienated those advisors, severely limiting his influence.

Lemke found the administration's farm bills unacceptable. His alternative, the Frazier–Lemke Bankruptcy Act, would have allowed farmers to reduce their debt to a level comparable to the value of their property. All debts in excess of a farmer's property value would be cancelled. When he was unable to push his own plan out of committee, Lemke decided to try bypassing that hurdle. He embarked on a long speaking tour on behalf of the bill. His goal was to collect the 145 congressional signatures needed to discharge the bill out of committee, where it had stalled. Roosevelt openly lobbied against him, incurring Lemke's bitter enmity. The Congressman was nevertheless able to collect enough support to discharge the bill and see it through the House. Roosevelt, unwilling to alienate farmers, had no choice but to sign it. Lemke became the farmer's hero.

Lemke next turned attention to his bill that would allow

farmers to refinance their mortgages at lower rates.[1] The Roosevelt administration campaigned even harder against the refinance bill. Although Lemke was again able to collect enough signatures to bring it to the floor, it was attacked as inflationary. Even the American Federation of Labor came out against it after pressure from the President. When the measure was defeated, "Lemke knew that one man and one man alone had stood in his way—the man whom he, Lemke, felt that he had placed in the White House in 1932" (Blackorby 1963, p. 215).

Lemke welcomed an opportunity for revenge and saw a third party run both as a means of getting even with Roosevelt and as a way to develop a farmer–labor alliance that could capture the White House in 1940. Both goals, though, required a strong performance in 1936, and Lemke realized he needed help. He turned to Coughlin.

Coughlin, who had crusaded for the refinance bill, regarded its defeat as the last straw. Although the precise arrangement remains unknown, Lemke and Coughlin agreed to a third party presidential campaign to be headed by Lemke. Coughlin also began to negotiate with the Townsend–Smith alliance. A four-way coalition formed and three days later—July 19, 1936—Lemke declared his Union Party candidacy. The press, however, gave the story little play: American boxer Joe Louis had just defeated German Max Schmeling.

The party's platform, a rewrite of the tenets of the National Union for Social Justice, endorsed Lemke's agricultural proposals, but endorsed neither the Townsend plan nor Share Our Wealth. The platform reflected Coughlin's disdain for his partners, and as a result, Townsend and Smith were reluctant to campaign actively for Lemke. Townsend was suspicious of "rival mass leaders" and unenthusiastic about being closely tied to a losing candidate (Bennett 1969, p. 199).

In the end, the three prophets did little to help Lemke. Townsend, caring only about his pension plan, devoted most

[1] The Supreme Court slowed Lemke's efforts by ruling the bankruptcy measure unconstitutional, forcing Lemke to work for passage of a revised version.

of his time to denouncing Roosevelt, telling his supporters to vote for Republican Alf Landon if Lemke was not on their ballot. Coughlin's shrill rhetoric, apparent anti-Semitism, and anti-Roosevelt venom, brought widespread ciritcism.[2] He spoke less and less of Lemke, not even mentioning the candidate's name at his final pre-election rally. The party disassociated itself from Smith when he announced plans to "seize the government." Lemke attracted few other national political leaders to his crusade, and Midwest farmer labor alliances also refused to back him.

Roosevelt strategists feared that Lemke would draw votes mainly from the Democrats, particularly in the Northern plain states where the Union Party could poll enough votes to tip the balance to Landon.[3] The President countered the threat by strengthening the Democratic platform's farm planks and directly appealing for farm votes in several campaign speeches (Tull 1965, p. 130).

When the ballots were counted, Lemke attracted less than 2 percent of the vote. His support was concentrated in Massachusetts, Minnesota, Rhode Island, Oregon, and his home state of North Dakota. His backers' constituents failed to come through. Less than 2.5 percent of citizens over 55 years of age voted for him.[4] No more than 1 percent of those who favored compulsory old-age insurance backed Lemke.[5] Only 3.5 percent of farmers cast a Union Party ballot.[6]

In the aftermath of the election, Coughlin dissolved his organization, saying that his followers had shown him no loyalty. Lemke, who had once hoped to keep the party together for future elections, likewise disbanded his Union Party.

---

[2] In his outbursts, Coughlin attacked the Vatican and U.S. clerics, and claimed that Roosevelt was "anti-God" and "the dumbest man ever to occupy the White House."

[3] Their concern was bolstered by an American Institute of Public Opinion (AIPO) poll showing that 70 percent of Lemke's supporters voted for Roosevelt in 1932, while only 9 percent voted for Hoover.

[4] AIPO surveys, nos. 56, 57, and 60.

[5] AIPO survey, no. 56.

[6] AIPO surveys, nos. 56, 57, and 60.

Henry Wallace

When prosperity returned in 1948 after two years of post-war recession, citizens turned their attention to foreign policy issues.[7] Henry Wallace believed that President Truman's antagonism towards the Russians was leading the nation to war. This belief prompted Wallace to run for president as an independent.

Wallace had been a prominent figure in the Roosevelt administration. After eight years as Secretary of Agriculture, Wallace was picked by Roosevelt as his 1940 running mate. The President was looking for a liberal, and Wallace fit the bill. But Wallace was not well liked by party leaders, especially Southerners who were offended by his advocacy of civil rights. He was an active vice-president, continually speaking out on his post-war vision of worldwide democracy accomplished through a policy of internationalism linking all nations. On the domestic front, he chided professional anti-communists and spoke of "economic democracy," a concept critics quickly labeled as socialist.

Under pressure from Southern party leaders, Roosevelt watched quietly as the Democrats dropped Wallace from the 1944 ticket. In spite of this rejection, Wallace campaigned diligently for Roosevelt. In gratitude, the President offered him his choice of cabinet posts (except Secretary of State). Wallace opted for Commerce. After Roosevelt's death, Truman allowed Wallace to remain in office, though this was largely a Truman ploy to maintain labor union support for his administration (Blum 1973, p. 38).

Wallace's fundamental disagreement with Truman's foreign policy soon became apparent. Wallace believed in a strong United Nations and sensitivity to Soviet fears, while Truman held that military strength ensured national security. By 1946 Wallace had given up all hope of influencing Truman's foreign policy (Blum 1973, p. 45). Their rift came to a head when, in

[7] Forty-four percent of those polled in June 1948 thought foreign policy was the most important problem facing the nation (*Gallup Opinion Index*, No. 181, September 1980, p. 11).

a September speech, Wallace seemed to accept the notion of U.S. and Soviet spheres of influence. Commentators and politicians from all points on the political spectrum attacked the Secretary's position. Although the President had approved the address prior to its delivery, the uproar forced Truman to disavow it. Aware that there was an irreparable breach, Truman asked Wallace to resign.

Out of office, Wallace continued to criticize the administration. With encouragement from organizations like the International Longshoremen's and Warehousemen's Union and groups opposed to Truman's foreign policy, he began to consider a third party run for president.

Organized labor, a crucial element in the New Deal coalition, was also toying with the idea of a third party challenge in 1948. Some unionists planned to work closely with the Progressive Citizens of America (PCA), while others were drawn to the newly formed Americans for Democratic Action (ADA) and its pledge to remain vigilantly anti-Communist. When the issue of affiliation with the ADA or the PCA threatened to split the Congress of Industrial Organizations (CIO), its president, Phillip Murray, convinced the union to disassociate itself from both organizations. This action dried up a sizable source of support for what was to become Wallace's Progressive Party (Schmidt 1960, p. 29).

Truman's veto of the Taft–Hartley Act in June 1947 ended organized labor's flirtation with third parties. A. E. Whitney, who one year earlier had pledged his railway workers union's entire $47 million treasury to defeat Truman, now declared that Truman had been "vindicated in the eyes of labor." A third party, in his view, would be "suicidal" and "out of the question" (Schmidt 1960, p. 33; Yarnell 1974, p. 23).

The Progressive Citizens of America, first formed with the intention of working within the Democratic Party, figured prominently in Wallace's independent candidacy. Although in September of 1947 Wallace reaffirmed his commitment to the Democratic Party, the PCA National Executive endorsed Wallace three months later. An early deadline for placing his name on the California ballot forced Wallace to make a quick decision to become an independent. Wallace accepted PCA support in mid-December and formally announced his candidacy on December 29.

However, by this time only the American Labor Party and the Communist Party still stood fully behind Wallace. The liberal press condemned his campaign, saying it would lead to a Republican victory. The only bright spot came in February, when an ALP and Progressive Party nominee won a special congressional election against a Democratic opponent. Some observers took this as a sign of Truman's weakness in urban areas, and reports indicated that support for Wallace had grown in Michigan, Pennsylvania, Illinois, and California as a result (Berman 1970, p. 91).

In an effort to win over Wallace supporters, administration rhetoric grew more liberal. Truman proposed a 50 percent increase in social security benefits and an extension of coverage, as well as national health insurance, slum clearance, low rent housing, federal aid to education, increases in the minimum wage and in unemployment compensation (Page 1978, p. 70). The President advocated many of the liberal domestic policies that appeared as planks in the Progressive platform (Schmidt 1960, p. 224). In response to a growing concern that blacks would defect to Wallace because of his "freedom pledge," the President proposed a ten-point civil rights program that would, among other things, provide federal protection against lynching, ensure blacks the right to vote, and establish a Fair Employment Practices Commission (FEPC) to prevent discrimination in employment (Yarnell 1974, pp. 71-74).[8]

To undercut the Wallace peace plank, the President tried unsuccessfully to send Supreme Court Chief Justice Vinson to Moscow to "explore ways of peacefully ending the cold

---

[8] One would think that Truman advisors would have recognized the consternation these proposals would cause in the South. But, as strategist Clark Clifford advised, the South should be considered "safely Democratic" and could be "safely ignored." Clifford felt that winning crucial states like Ohio, Illinois, and New York, where blacks held the balance of power, was more important (Yarnell 1974, ch. 3). His forecast was of course wrong.

war with Russia and the Berlin Blockade" (Schmidt 1960, p. 225). But Wallace's espousal of peaceful coexistence lost much of its appeal in March anyway, when Communists overthrew Czechoslovakia's democratic coalition. Wallacites had regarded that nation as a shining example of the possibilities of Soviet–Western cooperation.

Wallace had little hope of winning the election. What he wanted instead was a strong show of support as a means of protesting Truman's policies. Ten percent of the vote was a bare minimum. But from a high mark in the polls of 11.5 percent in February, his support declined steadily. When the ballots were counted in November, Wallace had attracted less than 1.2 million votes (2.4 percent). Nearly half this total came from New York; only there and in California did he top 4 percent. His New York strength was due in large part to his strong Jewish support—over 15 percent cast Progressive ballots.[9] He also ran strongly among professionals and the well educated. Students were three times more likely to back Wallace than non-students.[10] Only .5 percent of voters who identified with one of the major parties defected to Wallace; 4.5 percent of the independents backed him. By November union families were no more likely to support Wallace than were non-union households.[11]

Wallace's Progressive Party marked the first time a third party had been launched because of foreign policy, and therein lay his problem: the economy was relatively healthy, reducing his ability to attract support from labor and farm groups. Moreover, Wallace advocated a soft line with the Soviet Union at a time when Communists were seen as anathema. That he had the support of the Communist Party was only viewed as proof of his complicity in their conspiracy, an inference that Truman and the hostile press played up.

[9] AIPO survey, no. 432.

[10] Delegates to the party's spring convention were predominantly young, one-third were women, and many were union members and professionals. Big names and famous faces were rare; it was a meeting of political novices (Schmidt 1960, pp. 181-83).

[11] AIPO surveys, nos. 432, 433, and 444K.

Following the election, the party, which had once hoped to be a long-term force on the political scene, disappeared. Some scholars have argued that Wallace was simply ahead of his time. "Indeed Wallace's fundamental trepidations about American policy, all of them prominent before he left office, had become by the early 1970s common criticisms of the history of the interceding years" (Blum 1973, p. 48).

STROM THURMOND

Truman's 1948 civil rights proposals naturally drew heavy fire from the South. The Mississippi Democratic executive committee resolved that delegates to the Democratic National Convention should walk out if Truman's civil rights program became part of the platform. At their March conference, Southern governors recommended that convention delegates be instructed to vote against Truman, and that presidential electors not vote for any candidate who supported civil rights. Other gatherings approved similar resolutions (Key 1949, pp. 331-32). Meeting in May in Jackson, Mississippi, states' rights advocates vowed that, despite their loyalty to the Democratic Party, they would not accept a nominee who supported civil rights.

When it became apparent that Truman had grossly underestimated Southern reaction to his civil rights proposals, he withheld formal introduction of the legislation and delayed action to end discrimination in federal employment and to integrate the armed forces (Kirkendall 1971, p. 3107). The administration hoped that sitting on the fence would appease both Southerners and Northern liberals.

But neither Truman nor Southern segregationists got their way at the July Democratic National Convention. Three Southern motions to weaken Truman's moderate civil rights plank failed. Moreover, a group of Midwestern delegates persuaded the convention to adopt an even more liberal plank than the one the administration had introduced. In response, half of the Alabama and the entire Mississippi delegation walked out as the presidential balloting began. "Their departure was accompanied by jeers and boos from Northern delegates. The atmosphere in the building became taut as remaining Southern delegates seethed in rage" (Lachicotte 1966, p. 42). Although nearly every Southern vote was cast for Georgia Senator Richard Russell, Truman won the nomination.

The disaffected Southerners met in Birmingham the following week to plan the Dixiecrat campaign. "The gathering consisted of the big brass of the Democratic party of Mississippi, of conservative leaders of Alabama, of Governor [Strom] Thurmond of South Carolina and his entourage, and a miscellaneous assortment of persons of no particular political importance from other states" (Key 1949, p. 335). No Southern congressmen or senators attended except those from Mississippi. The nominating process was remarkably slipshod. One report claimed that Arkansas Governor Ben Laney was offered the lead spot on the ticket and refused (Lachicotte 1966, p. 43); another said the same of former Alabama Governor Frank Dixon (Barnard 1974, p. 115). Thurmond was the next choice; he was given less than an hour to decide (Lachicotte 1966, p. 43). In his acceptance speech, Thurmond denounced Truman's civil rights program and bemoaned the South's declining political power, asking his followers to demonstrate that Southern votes were no longer "in the bag" for Democratic candidates.[12]

Thurmond's campaign never picked up much support from Southern Democratic leaders. Most remained committed to working within the party and were unwilling to jeopardize their own careers. However, their response differed from state to state. With the aid of sympathetic election officials in four states—Mississippi, Alabama, South Carolina, and Louisiana—the Dixiecrats were able to get Thurmond listed on the November ballot as the Democratic nominee.

By this point Truman could do little to win over States' Rights Party supporters except deemphasize civil rights in the

[12] Much of the South's power in the Democratic Party had been diluted in 1936 when the party abandoned the two-thirds majority needed for nomination in favor of a simple majority.

campaign. As support for Henry Wallace waned (it dropped from 7 percent in March to 3 percent in September [figure 2.2]), administration strategists grew increasingly comfortable downplaying civil rights. Truman devoted only one campaign speech (in Harlem) to this issue (Kirkendall 1971, pp. 3127-28). When in the South, he discussed economics.

Although the precipitating factor in the creation of the party was Southern opposition to Truman's civil rights program, the Dixiecrats were driven by other economic and political concerns as well. Southern conservatives had long objected to the attention many New Deal policies paid to cities, unions, progressives, and minorities. In some states, especially Alabama, these other issues were at least as important as civil rights (Barnard 1974, p. 97). "The leaders of the Dixiecrats, whatever their persuasion or chief concern, were generally men who had been outside the dominant faction in state and national politics since Franklin Roosevelt worked his revolution within the Democratic Party" (Barnard 1974, p. 100). It was more than a simple civil rights backlash; it was an effort to recapture their party.

That November, Thurmond collected 2.4 percent of the vote nationwide and 22.6 percent of the vote in the South. He captured the 38 electoral votes of the four states in which he was listed as the Democratic nominee.[13] As a rule, the Dixiecrats ran best among whites who lived in areas with the highest concentration of blacks (Heard 1952, p. 27).

Southern defections from the Democratic coalition in 1948 persuaded party leaders to soften their racial stand. Truman was unable to enact any of his civil rights proposals during his second term. By 1952 racial moderates (advocates of a position agreeable to Southern whites) had regained control of the Democratic convention, nominating Adlai Stevenson—a candidate acceptable to the South. To further entice Dixiecrats back into the Democratic column, Stevenson selected

[13] He also picked up the vote of one faithless elector from Tennessee. V. O. Key noted: "The chances are that Thurmond carried Alabama and Louisiana only because of the maneuvers that made him the 'Democratic' nominee in those states" (1949, p. 342).

Alabama Senator John J. Sparkman as his running mate. Stevenson did not stress racial issues in the campaign.

The Republicans also had a Dixiecrat strategy in 1952. Eisenhower spent more time campaigning in the South than had his Republican predecessors. He stressed his opposition to the FEPC and advocated making fair employment compliance voluntary. Eisenhower carried four Southern states in 1952; the rest returned to the Democratic fold.

George Wallace

As racial concerns grew more salient in the 1960s, they became increasingly associated with and even camouflaged by issues traveling under different names. To some, these new issues— "law and order" and "urban unrest"—were natural extensions of century-old racial disputes. To others, they were simply new ways of packaging old prejudices. In either case, these were the themes of former Alabama Governor George Wallace's 1968 independent presidential campaign.

Wallace established his national reputation in June 1963 when, as Governor, he blocked the doorway to the University of Alabama to bar two black students from entering. This purely symbolic gesture (the students enrolled the same day) drew nationwide attention to Wallace's opposition to federally mandated integration. Speaking invitations poured in from around the country.

Encouraged by this exposure, Wallace entered three Democratic primaries in 1964 to test his popularity outside the South. His campaign operated with almost no financial backing and confronted well-organized opposition. These disadvantages made his vote totals—34 percent in Wisconsin, 30 percent in Indiana, and 43 in Maryland—even more stunning. Wallace contemplated an independent run that year, but pulled back after Republicans nominated conservative Barry Goldwater. (Wallace's campaign contributions also dried up soon after Goldwater's selection [Carlson 1981, p. 40].)

Because Alabama law prevented consecutive gubernatorial terms, Wallace ran his wife Lurleen for the post in 1966, assuring voters he would be her top advisor. Soon after her victory George Wallace embarked upon his third party presidential campaign, declaring there was not "a dime's worth of difference" between the major parties. The American Independent Party, as he called it, grew around Wallace. It did not run candidates for other offices except in Oklahoma, where doing so was required to get on the ballot. The AIP had no succession plans.

Civil rights activities and four years of urban unrest had "hardened the lines of racial conflict," leaving a large audience receptive to Wallace's message (Broder 1971, p. 3716). And Wallace had a remarkable ability to get his message across to those who wanted to hear it. Noted a former Alabama senator, "He can use all the other issues—law and order, running your own schools, protecting property rights—and never mention race. But people will know he's telling them, 'A nigger's trying to get your job, trying to move into your neighborhood' " (Frady 1968, p. 6). Wallace seemed unconcerned with the charges of racism that followed him, believing racism to be the key to his success. Yet he attracted not only avowed racists, but also those who felt their position in American society was slipping as a result of the emergence of blacks as a prominent political and social force (Lipset and Raab 1970, p. 334). It was *change* that Wallace supporters feared, and blacks symbolized the change. Wallace also attacked government bureaucrats and other "pointy head" intellectuals.

When Wallace announced his candidacy in February 1968, 11 percent of the electorate said they would vote for him. By late summer his support had nearly doubled.

Both Republican Richard Nixon and Democrat Hubert Humphrey took steps to combat Wallace's apparent strength. To attract potential Wallace supporters, Nixon softened his stand on racial integration. In a private session with Southern Republican National Convention delegates, he advocated policies more tolerant of segregation; he also publicly advocated an end to the policy of cutting off federal funds from segregated schools (Page 1978, p. 143). "Nixon worked to create the impression of special sympathy for the South. In his tours of the region he embraced Southern cultural symbols and identified himself with leading Southern political figures—especially Senator Strom Thurmond of South Carolina" (who was now a Republican) (Page 1978, p. 144). Nationwide he advocated an alternative to mandatory school busing: "freedom of choice"—a scheme that would let parents decide where their children would go to school. Nixon's running mate, Spiro T. Agnew, an obscure governor from the border state of Maryland and a popular figure in the South, suppurated much of the rhetoric aimed at Wallace voters.

There was little that Hubert Humphrey, a vociferous civil rights advocate for over two decades, could do to appease Wallace supporters on racial issues. Instead, he tried to convince people that a vote for Wallace would be a vote for Nixon. Organized labor also helped Humphrey persuade blue-collar workers to remain loyal to the Democrats.

Even though Wallace campaigned in the North, his greatest chance of success remained in the deep South. If he could pick up 100 electoral votes in these states, he could stalemate the election and force a deal with either Nixon or Humphrey before balloting began in the House. But Wallace's poll support, which peaked at 23 percent in mid-September, began to slide. He lost ground primarily in the North where, counter to the expectations of Nixon's strategists, people were switching to the Democrats. Humphrey, who had emerged from the disastrously acrimonious Democratic convention with seemingly little chance of winning, was rapidly gaining strength.

In November Wallace polled nearly 10 million votes (13.5 percent). Although he ran best in the former Confederacy (capturing 34.3 percent of the popular vote), Nixon's Southern stragegy kept Wallace down to just 46 electoral votes. Of the fifteen Southern and Border states, Wallace carried but five (Alabama, Arkansas, Georgia, Louisiana, and Mississippi). Humphrey won only Texas, Maryland, and West Virginia; Nixon carried the rest. Nixon's move to the right was crucial in holding Wallace's support to a minimum in the South and in key Northern states like California, Illinois, Ohio, and New Jersey, where Nixon won by only a few points.

As a rule, whites toward the bottom of the socio-economic ladder were most likely to support Wallace. He enjoyed the backing of 20 percent of white unskilled workers, but only 5 percent of white professionals. Over 17 percent of those with less than a high school diploma voted for Wallace, compared to less than 5 percent of those with college degrees.[14] A disproportionate number of the young also voted for Wallace: 17 percent of whites who entered the electorate after 1960 voted for Wallace, compared to 9 percent of those who had been voting since the New Deal.[15]

He drew heavy support from those who felt most disaffected from the political parties and from the political system. Independents were twice as likely as party identifiers to vote for Wallace. The former governor polled about four times as many votes from people who on balance disliked the major parties or their nominees than he did from the less disgruntled. Citizens who saw no differences in the way the two major parties ran the country were 10 percent more likely to cast a Wallace ballot than those who saw some distinctions.[16]

Issues also mattered. Nearly 18 percent of whites who felt the federal government had become too powerful voted for Wallace, as did 20 percent of those strongly opposed to school integration and 38 percent of those who felt the appropriate means of dealing with urban unrest was to use all available force to suppress it.[17]

Once in office, Nixon continued to campaign for Wallace votes. Former Thurmond aide Harry Dent became Deputy Counsel to the President to keep a "Southern eye" on administration policies. The President ordered chief of staff H. R. Haldeman to "establish and enforce a policy in this admin-

[14] Crespi (1971, p. 124) found that when levels of education and income are examined simultaneously, differences in education continue to matter, whereas differences in income do not.
[15] AIPO surveys, nos. 771 and 772; CPS 1968 National Election Study.
[16] CPS 1968 National Election Study.
[17] CPS 1968 National Election Study.

istration that no statements are to be made by any official that might alienate the South" (Evans and Novak 1971, p. 145). The White House delayed the Johnson administration's fall 1969 school desegregation deadline. In June the Justice Department came out against extension of the Voting Rights Act of 1965. Furthermore, the administration watered down desegregation plans for twenty-one South Carolina school districts.

For the first time since *Brown* v. *Board of Education*, the government entered a major civil rights case arguing against desegregation. The Supreme Court's unanimous October 29 decision ordering desegregation "at once" created the confrontation Nixon had hoped for. Observed Evans and Novak, "now Richard Nixon, more than ten months as President, had fulfilled John Mitchell's formula. By reversing his own HEW and Justice Department officials, the President had been reversed by the Supreme Court and so had dramatized his Southern credentials" (1971, p. 156).

Nixon's initial choices for Abe Fortas's vacated seat on the Supreme Court also pleased Wallace's constituency. His first nominee, Clement F. Haynsworth, Jr. was not only a Southerner (from Thurmond's home state of South Carolina, no less), but a strict constructionist who had voted against desegregation while Chief Justice of the Fourth Circuit Federal Court. When the Senate rejected Haynsworth, Nixon submitted the name of G. Harrold Carswell, a federal judge from Tallahassee. Carswell's conservative civil rights record and, more important, his questionable qualifications as a jurist, led to his rejection as well. Despite these defeats, Nixon was once again able to reaffirm his Southern credentials.

When Wallace returned to the Democratic fold in 1972, the American Independent Party nominated California Representative John Schmitz to head its ticket. Schmitz won only 1.4 percent of the national popular vote and only 1.1 percent in the South. Nixon, meanwhile, captured 69.7 percent of the Southern vote (11 percent more than in the rest of the country). The President's "Southern strategy," with some help from George McGovern's candidacy, successfully brought Wallace voters into the Republican column in 1972.

After the election, the party split into two factions: the American Independent Party and the American Party. In 1976 the AIP nominated former Georgia Governor Lester Maddox, who won just .2 percent of the presidential vote; the American Party nominated farm magazine publisher Thomas Anderson, who also attracted a mere .2 percent. AIP candidate Congressman John Rarick polled less than .1 percent of the popular vote (41,246) in 1980; Percy Greaves, Jr., the American nominee, polled under 7,000 votes.

Eugene McCarthy

Quite likely, the most important feature of Eugene McCarthy's 1976 third party presidential campaign was his success in challenging state ballot access laws. McCarthy's eighteen lawsuits not only helped him secure spots on twenty-nine state ballots, but were also instrumental in making it easier for future third party candidates—particularly John Anderson and Libertarian Ed Clark in 1980—to place their names before the voters.

McCarthy's electoral appeal actually peaked in 1968. His anti–Vietnam war campaign drew 42 percent of the New Hampshire Democratic primary vote, contributing to President Lyndon Johnson's decision to abandon his bid for renomination. McCarthy lost the nomination to Johnson's heir apparent Hubert Humphrey, but succeeded with the help of other liberals in overturning the Democratic Party's unit rule and winning reforms in the delegate selection process. McCarthy flirted with a run for the 1972 nomination, but a sustained campaign never materialized.

McCarthy decided to run as an independent in 1976, entering no Democratic primaries that year. He claimed that the Democratic Party was so divided that it would produce a weakly worded platform and "the nominee won't be standing for anything very much" (*Congressional Quarterly Weekly Report* 1975, p. 164). In many respects, McCarthy's 1976 platform was an extension of the issues he had raised eight years earlier. Although Vietnam was no longer a concern, McCarthy continued to criticize American military and foreign policy, advocating a $20 to $30 billion cut in defense spending and recognition of Cuba and Vietnam (Vaden 1977, p. 17). He also continued to attack the "personalized presidency," advocating removal of the fence around the White House and replacing the rose garden with cabbage and squash patches as a way of reducing the mystique and trappings of the office (Jones 1975, p. 2283). On the domestic front, McCarthy supported a 35-hour work week as a way to reduce unemployment. He also backed curbs on both energy consumption and on the use of automobiles.

McCarthy campaigned hardest in Iowa, Colorado, Oregon, California, and in fifteen states in the Northeast and upper Midwest. He hoped to attract support from the huge number of voters who had no allegiance to either major party. Yet in November he polled only 756,631 votes, less than 1 percent of the total cast. He ran best in Oregon, where he polled nearly 4 percent. In only five other states did he tally over 2 percent. Voters under the age of 35 were three times more likely to support McCarthy than those over 35; students were four times more likely to vote for him than were other citizens. Liberals, the college-educated, and professionals were also slightly more likely to cast a McCarthy ballot. He made few inroads with the "independents," collecting slightly less than 2 percent of their votes.[18]

Without a vivid issue, hampered by ballot access laws and Federal Election Commission restrictions, and ignored by the media, McCarthy was never able to build much of a following. Since he intentionally refused to build a party structure, the only real legacies of his campaign are the ballot access laws he overturned.

JOHN ANDERSON

Every third party campaign discussed so far grew from either fervent attachment to a single cause, intense dislike of an

[18] AIPO survey, no. 962K; CPS 1976 National Election Study; CBS/*New York Times* Poll, November 2, 1976, and November 3-10, 1976.

incumbent president, or both. John Anderson's 1980 candidacy seems not to have fit this mold. He had no vivid, emotional issue like abolition, free silver, progressivism, or states' rights with which to rally his supporters. He did not accuse the incumbent president of treachery, as Teddy Roosevelt, William Lemke, and Strom Thurmond had done.

Many observers believe that the shockingly poor quality of the 1980 major party nominees prompted John Anderson to run. Jimmy Carter was a weak, indecisive chief executive who had presided over one of the nation's most humiliating foreign crises (the Iranian taking of American hostages) and the worst election-year economy since the Depression. His opponent, Ronald Reagan, was an aging conservative warhorse with a penchant for foolish statements and a reputation for inactivity. Although much of Anderson's support may have resulted from reactions to the major party candidates, Anderson's own motivations for running go back farther. In 1978 the New Right mounted a fierce primary challenge to his bid for a tenth term in Congress. He narrowly won the primary and went on to be reelected, but it was a bitter experience. Anderson knew he would be targeted again in 1980 and wanted no part of it. By mid-1978 supporters suggested that Anderson seek the Republican presidential nomination. "The idea appealed to Anderson. It would be a way to take the fight back to those in his party who opposed him, who said he should find another home" (Broder et al. 1980, p. 207). Anderson apparently had few delusions of winning, but appreciated the opportunity it would give him to speak out. He declared his candidacy on June 8, 1979.

Anderson quickly developed a reputation as a man willing to take stands not likely to ingratiate him with Republicans. He proposed a fifty cent per gallon gasoline tax to reduce consumption, which would be balanced by a 50 percent cut in the social security tax. He supported ratification of the SALT II treaty and advocated handgun control before a meeting of the New Hampshire Gun Owners club. At a debate for Republican candidates in Iowa, he criticized Reagan's economic program, remarking that the only way to balance the budget, cut taxes, and increase defense spending at the same time was "with mirrors." That debate brought Anderson national recognition.

Anderson drew favorable notices in the press and, perhaps more importantly, in Garry Trudeau's *Doonesbury* comic strip. He appeared on the popular comedy show "Saturday Night Live." Although for most of his career Anderson had been an unwavering conservative, he became a liberal hero of sorts. Recognizing that Anderson's strongest appeal was not to Republicans, his fundraiser Tom Mathews floated the idea of a third party campaign (Broder et al. 1980, p. 227). But Anderson, anticipating strong showings in the Massachusetts and Vermont primaries, continued to work for the Republican nomination. The Illinois primary, which Anderson lost to Reagan, ended the dream. By then it was clear that Carter and Reagan would be the major party nominees. And yet money was still coming in, and Anderson was still receiving favorable press. Anderson's advisors convinced him that the only way he could continue to speak out on issues was to make a third party run. His independent crusade began on April 24.

The campaign spent much of its time trying to establish its legitimacy. Like all third party candidates, Anderson had to convince people that he had a chance to win. President Carter, fearing he would be the chief victim of the challenge, attacked Anderson as a creation of the media and just another Republican. It was indeed Anderson's strategy to pick primarily on Carter. "If Carter collapses," one Anderson aide noted, "we hope to pick up the pieces" (Whittle 1980, p. 2834). Through late spring and early summer Anderson's support in the polls hovered around 20 percent. In New England he was polling twice that, running ahead of both Reagan and Carter.

His poll standings proved to be the key to his participation in the presidential debates, needed to establish his legitimacy. The League of Women Voters, which had sponsored the Ford–Carter debates in 1976, decided to invite Anderson to its September 1980 debate if the polls showed he had the support of at least 15 percent of the electorate. Anderson met this hurdle and received an invitation, but Carter, still fearing that any Anderson gain would come at his own expense, refused to participate. Despite Anderson's inclusion in the debate, his standing in the polls continued to decline. He was not invited to the second, crucial debate on October 28.

Anderson attracted 6.6 percent of the November vote. Even if all of Anderson's voters had gone to Carter (a 3:2 split would be more realistic) Carter would still not have won either a popular or electoral vote majority. Anderson ran best in New England (averaging 13.3 percent) and worst in the South (2.6 percent). His supporters tended to be young, well educated, and affluent: 14 percent of voters aged 18 to 24 backed Anderson, compared with less than 2 percent of those over 70; 28 percent of students and 11.5 percent of voters with college diplomas cast an Anderson ballot; over 12 percent of professionals and 10 percent of those with incomes in the top 5 percent of the nation supported Anderson. He ran marginally better among Democrats than Republicans (4.5 percent, as compared to 3.9 percent) and did well (13 percent) among those who did not care who won the election.[19]

In some ways, Anderson's ability to collect as many votes as he did is remarkable in light of his not having an emotional issue with which to cement his following. He had a number of novel ideas, but these were not the stuff of great political movements. Anderson flinched at suggestions that his support merely reflected dislike for Carter and Reagan, and many of his backers surely believed in him. Nevertheless, it is certainly true that most people would have never taken an interest in Anderson had they not been so unhappy with the major parties' candidates.

CONCLUSIONS

The important challenges of the nineteenth century came from relatively stable minor *parties*, whereas those of the twentieth century came from independent *candidates*. When prominent politicians abandoned the major parties in the 1800s, they cast

[19] AIPO surveys, nos. 1164G and 1165G; CPS 1980 National Election Study.

their lot primarily with established third parties; men of stature formed their own parties in the twentieth century.

Technological and political changes over the last century have lessened the need for political parties and have made it possible for both major and minor party candidates to run without the aid of a preexisting organization. In the nineteenth century, a party apparatus provided the only supply of resources and means of reaching the voters. However, the political party's monopoly over resources and expertise evaporated in the twentieth century. As a result, party outsiders like Jimmy Carter have been able to win nomination and election despite having only lukewarm support from their party's leaders. The technological and political changes that allowed Jimmy Carter to win the presidency also allowed men like George Wallace and John Anderson to make relatively successful independent challenges without preexisting organizations.

More efficient forms of transportation have provided recent candidates with mobility and have allowed them to reach voters more easily and directly, decreasing the need for a preexisting structure to rally support. The completion of the railroad system meant that third party candidates, like their major party counterparts, could embark on unprecedented national campaigns. Teddy Roosevelt, Eugene Debs, and Robert LaFollette were dynamic, mesmerizing speakers, and much of their support, no doubt, grew from their new-found ability to reach a larger number of voters in person. Airplanes, of course, further increased a candidate's mobility and direct access to the electorate.

The development of new forms of communication have had an even greater impact on a candidate's ability to reach voters without help from a political party. William Lemke, for example, drew support from followers of Father Coughlin, the "radio priest." Television helped convey George Wallace's symbolic rejection of integration at the University of Alabama. Third party candidates can use the new media to reach more voters at less cost than was ever before possible through a nineteenth-century party organization.

As the media have become more important, so too have media experts. The old campaign managers were experienced politicians who knew how to win votes. Expertise could be found only within the existing parties. But now public relations and image consultants are readily available for hire. Instead of needing to cultivate experience over a period of elections, a candidate can immediately buy the advice he needs. John Anderson did not have to build a party organization; he simply rented David Garth.

Finally, technological changes have allowed for increasingly sophisticated political strategies all without the aid of a political party. Little more than a computer, telephones, a postage meter, and a consultant are needed. Direct mail places a candidate in contact with potential supporters. Polls to gauge the pulse of the electorate have replaced the candidate's need for local party organizations.

In sum, technological innovations have permitted candidates to be increasingly free of political parties. Independent-minded politicians who were once unwilling to embark on third party campaigns without the help of an already existing locally based party can now take the plunge more readily.

Nineteenth-century minor parties enjoyed, on average, longer lifespans than their more recent counterparts. There are two explanations. First, in the 1800s it took several elections for parties to build organizations; they could not buy expertise as twentieth-century candidates can. Since it took parties time to build strength, voters and politicians were willing to stick with them as they grew. Voters in the nineteenth century expected less from parties' initial forays; they were confident that future efforts would be more successful. Second, third parties depended less upon individual personalities in the nineteenth century. There was no single person so essential to the Free Soilers, Greenbacks, or Populists that they would have vanished without him. This relationship is in marked contrast to the inability of more recent parties (Bull Moose, Union, and States' Rights, to name a few) to survive without their mentors.

Although few parties in either century lasted for more than

two elections, the prohibitionists and socialists created parties that endured for remarkably long periods of time. They took positions that the major parties could not easily accommodate; hence they were in no danger of being coopted. In addition, they made no effort to forge coalitions through compromise. As a result, ideological intensity was maintained. Finally, they avoided setting electoral goals for themselves and were thus spared disappointment when they failed to draw many votes.

As the last three chapters demonstrate, there are many similarities among what might at first glance appear to be dramatically different third party movements. It is evident that over the years voters have been bound to the major parties by a common set of ties and have been drawn to third parties by similar sorts of concerns. We now develop a general theory that draws upon these commonalities to account for the emergence and performance of third parties since 1840.

PART II

CHAPTER 5

A THEORY OF THIRD PARTY VOTING

DESPITE the two-party norm and the formidable hurdles that third parties confront, minor parties do manage to attract support in every election. As we have already seen, there is considerable variation in the level of third party voting. In some years independent candidates are unable to lure even .1 percent of the electorate to their causes, whereas in other contests over 10 percent of the public abandons the major parties. Why is third party voting so much higher in some years than in others? What prompts citizens to desert the major parties? What types of people are most likely to exit; what types are most likely to remain loyal?

In this chapter we build upon the examples analyzed in part I to formulate a general theory—one that accounts for not just an instance or two of third party strength, but for fluctuations in third party support over time. We shall argue that when certain motivations to vote for a minor party candidate are high, and the constraints against doing so are low, citizens will start down the third party path.[1] Although we rely heavily upon historical examples in specifying the theory, it is important to remember that regardless of how strong the evidence for a particular proposition may appear to be on the surface, a variable's impact on third party voting can only be assessed by evaluating its effect across time while simultaneously considering other, competing explanations. We defer to the next chapter these more precise estimates of the causes of third party support.

[1] Our thinking in this chapter is influenced by Hirschman (1970).

MOTIVATIONS FOR THIRD PARTY VOTING

Three motivations prompt people to vote for a third party. Citizens do so when they feel the major parties have deteriorated so much that they no longer function as they are supposed to, when an attractive third party candidate runs, or when they have acquired an allegiance to a third party itself.

Major Party Deterioration

The two-party tradition in this country is the product of an unspoken pact between the masses and their leaders. Citizens support the political system because politicians provide (or appear to provide) certain benefits. To compete for votes at election time, each party argues that its candidate is better able to manage the government, ensure economic vitality, and represent the preferences of the citizenry. Voters need only choose between the two parties; they cast their ballots for the candidate who seems most able to carry out the charge of office, or against the candidate who has betrayed their faith or who appears least capable of delivering on his promises— or both. It is a relatively easy decision: only two alternatives need be weighed, and when a party or candidate fails to live up to citizens' expectations, voters can simply cast their ballots for the other party in the next election.

But what do voters do when both parties deteriorate? Where do they go when they do not have faith in either candidate's capacity to govern, when neither nominee seems to represent their concerns, and when both parties appear incapable of providing prosperity? When the two political parties violate their implicit pact with the people, citizens can either sit out the election or abandon the major parties to support a third party alternative.

The third party route is a path of last resort. Although the opportunity for third party voting is always present (people can join a third party at any time), voters postpone this step until they are firmly convinced that further action within the major parties would prove fruitless. Because the cost of exit is high and the likelihood of achieving desired goals through third party activity is low, severe deterioration of the major parties must take place before significant third party activity occurs. Furthermore, since the minor party route is taken in desperation, people may not fully consider where this path will lead, only what it takes them away from. A third party vote is a vote *against* the major parties. Nevertheless, minor party voting is an instrumental act. Citizens who cast a third party ballot do so to advance the same policy goals they were precluded from achieving within the major parties.

ISSUE UNRESPONSIVENESS

Neglected Preferences: The positions of the major party nominees on the salient issues of the day can be one source of voter disaffection. The greater the distance between the positions of a citizen and the major party candidates, the higher the likelihood the citizen will vote for a third party (Downs 1957, ch. 8). As the proportion of voters who are distanced from the major party candidates grows, not only does the number of people who abandon the major parties go up, but so does the probability that third party candidates will emerge with positions that meet the concerns of estranged voters. Also, the more salient the issue over which citizens disagree with the major party candidates, the greater is the third party vote.

It is unlikely that at every election voters compare their positions to those of all the candidates, major and minor party contenders alike. In some years ten or more candidates run, and each has a distinctive position on one or more issues. Hence it would be hopelessly time-consuming and complicated for voters to gather information on all the candidates to choose the one who best approximates their own preferences. Instead, only when citizens feel a sufficient amount of distance between themselves and the major party nominees will they begin to contemplate a third party vote. Thus they need not gather information on all the third party choices in every election, nor must they judge which of the many candidates they are closest to. Indeed, given the paucity of information on most minor party contenders, it would be un-realistic to expect voters to do so. Only when voters feel estranged from the major party candidates will they seek out information on the other alternatives.

This decision rule implies, quite plainly, that people may fail to choose the candidate whose positions are closest to their own. However, it would be less sensible for voters to expend the energy needed to do so. Even if they wanted to, there is little guarantee that they could actually learn where all the minor party candidates stood on more than a few issues.

To illustrate these propositions, consider the following sit-uation: assume that on a particular issue dimension, say civil rights, the Republican candidate takes a middle-of-the-road position relative to the electorate, and the Democratic can-didate takes a position just left of center (as illustrated in figure 5.1a). If V_1 represents voters$_1$'s (very conservative) position on racial issues, then the distance between his position and even his most preferred major party candidate (the Repub-lican) is large. Similarly, a voter who has an extremely liberal position on this dimension (V_2) will also feel estranged from both major party candidates. Because these two voters are disaffected from the stands the major party nominees have taken, they might search for a third party alternative. If a minor party candidate emerges with a position that is closer to voter$_1$'s than is the Republican candidate's, voter$_1$ will be more likely to cast a third party ballot. His probability of abandoning the Republican Party increases with the salience of the issue. Likewise, voter$_2$ will prefer a third party candi-date whose position is closer to her own than is the Demo-cratic candidate's. The greater the distance between the voter and the nearest major party candidate, the more likely it is that the voter will look for a third party alternative, and that a minor party candidate will emerge with a position closer to the voter's than is the nearest major party candidate's—hence the greater the likelihood the voter will cast a third party ballot.

How much third party voting there is in the aggregate depends on the positions of the major and minor party candidates, the importance of the issue, *and* the distribution of the voters' preferences. If there were very few citizens like voter$_1$ and voter$_2$, then we would not expect much third party voting. Under this scenario there is a low probability that a third party candidate would emerge to meet the specific concerns of these few citizens. If a candidate should emerge, he would poll very few votes. Most citizens would not be estranged from the major party candidates; few would even consider voting for a third party alternative. This scenario is illustrated in figure 5.1b. Here the major party candidates' positions appear as they did in figure 5.1a. The height of the curve at each point on the dimension represents the proportion of the electorate who have a given position on the issue; the shaded area denotes voters who may feel estranged from the major party candidates on this issue and who would be likely, depending on the salience of the issue, to search for a minor party candidate whose position is closer to their own.

If we hold constant both the major party candidates' positions and the importance of the issue, but change the distribution of voter preferences to reflect a more conservative electorate (as in figure 5.1c), third party voting should increase since more citizens are now distanced from the major party candidates' positions. In this case, we would expect that a third party candidate would emerge to meet the concerns of the discontented on the right. By the same token, if we hold constant the distribution of preferences as they appear in figure 5.1c and merely change the positions of the major party candidates to those shown in figure 5.1d, then the amount of third party voting would decrease (assuming the importance of the issue remained unchanged).

Thus we expect that the greater the distance between the positions of the voter and the major party candidates, and the greater the salience of the issue, the higher the probability of third party voting. Note that it is impossible to formulate general aggregate propositions about the amount of third party voting without knowing *both* the distribution of voter preferences on the issues and the positions of the candidates.

FIGURE 5.1
Hypothetical Positions of Voters and Major Party
Candidates on Civil Rights

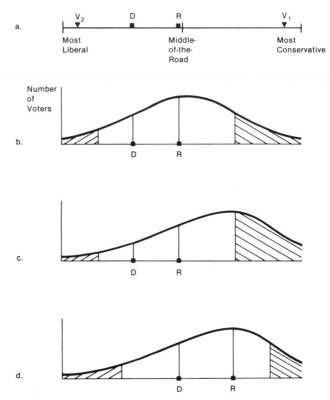

The shaded area represents voters who are closer to a third party
candidate than to a major party candidate.

Nevertheless, some third party voting is likely whenever there
exists an ideological hole unfilled by a major party candidate.

The 1948 and 1968 elections are two cases where it appears
that voters' estrangement from the major party candidates'
positions led many to support minor parties. Southerners
resented both Harry Truman's and Thomas Dewey's civil rights
policies. Truman's ten-point civil rights program would have,

among other things, provided federal protection against lynching, safeguarded the right to vote, and established a Fair Employment Practices Commission to prevent discrimination in employment. Dewey, although not as liberal as Truman, was a moderate on racial issues and just to the right of center on New Deal social welfare issues (Rosenstone 1983, appendix A). His positions on most issues were not that different from Truman's (Kirkendall 1971, p. 3133). Thus racial and New Deal social welfare conservatives stood a long distance from the major party nominees. Into this vacuum stepped the Dixiecrats. Thurmond strongly opposed the President's civil rights package, as well as his tax, labor, and economic policies. Most accounts of the 1948 election attribute Thurmond's support to this Southern disaffection with the major party candidates' racial and social welfare positions.

George Wallace's strength in 1968 can be understood in a similar way. Voters' estrangement from the major party candidates' positions, not only on race but also on civil unrest and the Vietnam War, seems to have spurred the campaign. As Converse and associates posit: "The Wallace candidacy was reacted to by the public as an issue candidacy" (1969, p. 265).

Both Nixon and Humphrey (the latter more fervently) supported existing civil rights laws on public accommodations and housing. Although both approved equal employment opportunities and supported *Brown* v. *Board of Education*, there were some differences (Page 1978, pp. 46-82). Humphrey spoke enthusiastically about past civil rights legislation while Nixon was more ambivalent about the existing laws. Nixon stood a bit to the right of center on civil rights; Humphrey was substantially to the left.

But the distance between Humphrey and Nixon is negligible compared to the space separating the two from George Wallace. Throughout his tenure as governor, Wallace battled federal authorities over civil rights: he resisted the integration of Alabama schools, tried to prevent civil rights demonstrations, and opposed the 1964 Civil Rights Act. During the 1968 campaign, Wallace advocated repealing both the Voting Rights

Act of 1965 and the 1968 open housing law while he continued to oppose federally ordered school integration. Voters' attitudes towards Wallace were strongly associated with their positions on civil rights (Converse et al. 1969).

Law and order—civil unrest in particular—was also a prominent issue in 1968. Here again, Nixon took the moderate stand and Humphrey the liberal one, leaving conservative voters without a candidate. Wallace filled this hole as well. His hardline law-and-order position was unambiguous: "When both national political parties say we've got to remove the causes of rioting, looting and burning, they're saying that these anarchists have a cause. . . . Poverty is not a cause for anarchy." In response to one newsman's question about his plan for stopping urban riots, Wallace bluntly stated that "people who riot ought to be bopped in the head," and that this treatment was "too easy" for some (*Congressional Quarterly Weekly Report* 1968, p. 2565).

With regard to the third issue, Vietnam, there was again little to distinguish Nixon's positions from those taken by Humphrey (Page and Brody 1972). Both candidates called for a gradual deescalation of the war and opposed rapid withdrawal, though their positions were fuzzy. Wallace was not much more specific about his Vietnam program than were the major party nominees, but his rhetoric—particularly that directed against anti-war protesters—was hawkish. His choice of former General Curtis LeMay as his running mate furthered that image.

In light of these circumstances, according to one observer, the 1968 election "demonstrated that millions of voters can be attracted to a third party when the two major parties are perceived as offering unsatisfactory alternatives on important issues" (Asher 1980, p. 189). Two questions remain, however: what is the marginal effect of issues in 1968 after other causes of third party voting are taken into account, and does estrangement from the major party candidates' positions explain third party voting *in general*?

Neglected Issues: Issues may affect third party voting by a second route. When voters have concerns they feel the major parties are neglecting, they may be more likely to support a third party alternative. The more prominent the unaddressed issue, the higher the probability of a third party vote.

This explanation of minor party support has surfaced sporadically. The major parties in 1840, for instance, simply avoided the abolition question that Liberty Party backers raised (Chambers 1971, p. 655; Sewell 1976, p. 84). Both Whigs and Democrats similarly refused to stake out unequivocal positions on the Wilmot Proviso in 1848.

The sixteen-year period between 1876 and 1892 was marked by an unwillingness of either major party to address the issues of currency deflation, debt, industrialization, and monopoly that had created such severe economic adversity for farmers (Burnham 1955, p. 131, Dinnerstein 1971, p. 1506). "The parties had not come to grips over economic issues. Both sides had ignored or touched lightly on such matters as labor unrest, farmer problems, public-land policies, railroad regulation, the growth of monopolies and even tariff reform" (Roseboom and Eckes 1979, p. 107). It was not until the 1896 Bryan–McKinley contest that the major party presidential candidates addressed these issues head on.

The unwillingness of the Democrats and Republicans to speak to these concerns, it is argued, led to disaffection with the major parties and contributed to Greenback and Populist strength in the closing decades of the nineteenth century:

> The postwar parties responded to new divisive, cross-cutting issues just as the prewar parties had—defensively. They evaded and straddled and postponed, just as the prewar Whigs and Democrats had evaded the demands of the abolitionists. And so the farmers in their zeal for a redress of grievances were driven to the recourse the abolitionists had found—third party action. The economic issues that became the dominant conflicts of society in the 1870s were fought for more than two decades not between the major parties, but between them, on one side, and a series of minor parties on the other. (Sundquist 1973, p. 94)

ECONOMIC PERFORMANCE

A poor economy is sure to promote voter disaffection with at least one of the major parties. While the incumbent party suffers at the polls during periods of economic decline (Kramer 1971; Tufte 1978; Fair 1978), a failing economy may also make voters more inclined to abandon the major parties altogether. They are likely to be so inclined especially if neither party appears capable of resolving the situation. People suffering economic adversity may turn to a third party either because they hope it will improve their lot or because periods of economic hardship signify to them a failure of the traditional parties to meet their obligation to keep the nation economically healthy. If either notion holds, minor party voting will be higher during economic downturns than during prosperous years.

Agricultural Adversity: On several occasions, economic adversity has led farmers down the third party path. After the Civil War, Southern farmers who relied on crop liens to purchase goods found themselves unable to meet their debts when farm prices fell precipitously (figure 5.2). Between 1865 and 1896 cotton dropped from 15¢ to 6¢ a pound. A bushel of wheat that sold for $1.07 in 1870 drew only 63¢ in 1894-1897; over the same period corn fell from 43¢ to 30¢ a bushel. Overall, agricultural prices fell 73 percent during these three decades. As C. F. Emerich noted at the time, the tumbling prices

> made more difficult the payment of interest charges and mortgage debts, increased the number of mortgage fore-closures, prolonged the period required for tenants to rise to land ownership, caused the expense for hired labor to be a greater drain upon the resources of the farm, made the inequitable burden imposed upon the farmer by the general property tax more difficult to carry, increased the strain of maintaining a higher standard of living and rendered less endurable the tyranny of railroad discriminations and the exactions of trusts. (Fine 1928, p. 74)

FIGURE 5.2
Wholesale Price Index for Farm Goods, 1840-1940

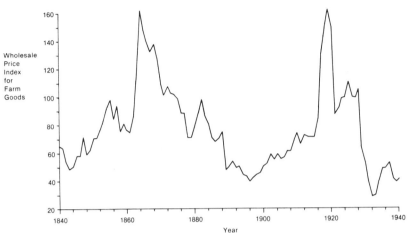

SOURCE: *Historical Statistics of the United States.*

By the closing decades of the century, farmers had also grown increasingly dependent on the business establishment for marketing their goods. Western and Southern farmers had to ship their crops to market by rail, and since the railroads held virtual monopolies, local freight rates were considerably higher than charges for longer hauls in the East. Grain farmers were also at the mercy of elevator owners who arbitrarily set prices and undergraded the farmers' crop.

Both Greenback and Populist Party fortunes seem to have sprung from the agricultural depression. The Greenback Party formed in Iowa in 1876—the year that state's wheat yield was poorest. Although the party drew only .9 percent of the 1876 national vote, when depression hit two years later it won over a million votes and captured fourteen congressional seats. Greenback Party fortunes fluctuated with the farm economy: "When prosperity returned in 1879 and provided work for the unemployed and better prices for the farmers, there was a recession from politics. . . . [T]he presidential elections of

1880, 1884 and 1888, therefore, marked the decline and end of the Greenback-labor agitation" (Fine 1928, p. 69). Greenback support fell from 3.3 percent in 1880 to 1.7 percent four years later; the party did not run a presidential candidate in 1888.

Farm prices remained fairly stable between 1879 and 1884, but when commodity prices tumbled again in 1889, third party activity resumed, this time in the form of the Populist Party. There is widespread consensus that the party was "born out of the economic tribulations suffered by the southern and western farmers" (Fine 1928, p. 72). Falling farm prices, growing mortgage debt, farm foreclosures, and massive crop failures resulting from the 1890 drought led to the Populist Party's birth. The 1892 agricultural depression brought the new party heavy support in that year's presidential election. But as with the Greenbacks two decades earlier, when crop prices rebounded after 1896 and farm prosperity returned, farmers retreated from the Populist cause.

Third party support seems to result more from long-term changes in farm prices than from short-term fluctuations. Farmers experienced declining prices in the years immediately following the Civil War, but it was not until the late 1870s, when prices reached pre-Civil War lows, that third party agitation appeared. In fact, the 1876 price drop that preceded the emergence of the Greenback Party was no more severe than the price downturn that occurred in most other postwar years. The year that the Populist Party was founded, 1890, was actually a year when farm prices rose in the short run.

There are several reasons why farmers would have turned to third parties only after long-term price declines. First, the prudent response to short-term adversity (if there was any political response at all) was to give the *other* major party a chance to govern, rather than to pursue the third party route immediately. Only after both major parties had tried and failed to alleviate the farmers' economic plight did farmers set out on a minor party course. Second, in the short run, farmers could refinance their debt (even if only through another round of crop-liens). But as prices declined over time, farmers' debt grew and the threat of foreclosure increased. Only then, in desperation, did they turn to the one peaceful political route remaining. Finally, farmers' third party activity drew from extensive socio-economic networks that took years to develop. The Greenback Party, for example, derived much of its strength from the Grange movement, which had been active for nearly ten years. These networks contributed greatly to activity on behalf of farmers' interests, much of which was funneled through third parties.

If this economic explanation of farmer support for third parties can be generalized, then we should expect loyalty to the major parties in the prosperous opening decades of the twentieth century and a return to third party voting in the early 1920s and 1930s when adversity again set in. Following World War I, farmers enjoyed the highest prices they had ever known, their income doubled in just four years, and they invested in machinery and more land—all bought on credit. But agricultural depression returned in 1920. Prices collapsed (by 1921 they had dropped 44 percent); farm income fell 40 percent. Between 1916 and 1920 a farmer needed 62 bushels of wheat to pay the yearly interest on a $2,000 mortgage. Five years later, 108 bushels were necessary to meet the same interest payment (Stedman and Stedman 1950, p. 86). When industrial prosperity returned in 1923, farmers' capacity to purchase manufactured goods fell further. As in the closing decades of the previous century, farmers were again caught with huge debts and a diminished ability to meet payments. Bankruptcies, which averaged 1.5 per 10,000 farms in 1905-1914, were sixty-five times more numerous during the 1920s. Again, those who suffered economic adversity turned to a third party—this time the Progressives.[2]

[2] The thesis that economic adversity leads farmers to third party activity has been advanced outside the American context as well. Lipset's account of the rise of third parties in Canada rests heavily on economic factors. Third party agitation began when the price of wheat fell in 1913 (1968, pp. 75-76). When Canadian farmers suffered from the same adversities that American farmers faced in the early 1920s, third party strength increased (pp. 78-83). As Lipset concluded: "In Saskatchewan the postwar depression precipitated the tremendous sweep of the Progressive Party in 1921" (p. 84). The depres-

General Economic Adversity: Although few segments of the population are as sensitive to price fluctuations as farmers are, it is reasonable to expect that economic duress among the electorate at large may also lead to third party voting. Average citizens, like farmers, may view economic downturns as a failure of the two major parties. Although some historians make this claim, the evidence bearing on it is mixed at best. The Liberty Party capitalized upon the 1837 depression and economic recovery after 1844 hurt its cause (Hesseltine 1957, p. 13). Support for the Communist Party allegedly grew, even among native-born Americans, during the depression of the early 1920s (Greer 1949, p. 187). The prosperity that prevailed in 1948 is said to have dimmed Henry Wallace's fortunes (Schmidt 1960, p. 242).

Despite these examples, there are striking instances where economic adversity did not lead to much third party activity. The most obvious example is 1932, when minor parties won less than 3 percent of the presidential vote. Third parties have also done well in prosperous years, polling, for instance, 13.9 percent in 1968, when real per capita disposable income rose 2.8 percent. In short, Herring's conclusion that "third parties are bred in prosperity as well as depression" seems appropriate (1965, p. 182).

UNACCEPTABLE MAJOR PARTY CANDIDATES

Because American elections are more battles between *candidates* than contests between *parties* or sets of *ideas*, who the candidates are has a sizable impact on how people vote. The more that citizens trust a candidate or perceive him as capable of performing well in office, the more votes he will attract (Kinder and Abelson 1981). This judgment has an impact over

sion of the 1930s boosted Cooperative Commonwealth Federation strength (pp. 204-205).

Agricultural depression in Germany has been cited as one cause of the growth of the Nazi party in the early 1930s (Lipset 1963, pp. 131-37; Heberle 1970; Cameron 1981). As Loomis and Beegle noted, "the manner in which the Nazis swept the farmer-peasant organizations of pre-Hitler Germany into the Nazi movement has parallels in the American Greenback, Farmer's Alliance, Populist and similar movements" (1946, p. 734).

and above the effect of the voters' estrangement from a nominee on the issues or their assessment of the relative ability of the candidates to manage the economy.

When voters perceive neither the Democratic nor the Republican candidate as capable of doing the job, they may have difficulty bringing themselves to vote for either person. A reasonable way out of this dilemma—particularly if people feel they must vote either to fulfill their citizen duty or to punish the candidates—is to pull a third party lever. Knowing that a minor party challenger has little or no chance of victory may eliminate the voters' need to worry much about whether or not the contender is well suited for office. Thus the third party candidate's own qualifications or personal characteristics may have little to do with the decision to vote for him. Voters may cast ballots not only *for* third party challengers but *against* the major party nominees. Many observers have cited voter displeasure with Ronald Reagan and Jimmy Carter as an important source of John Anderson's strength in 1980.

Attractive Third Party Alternatives

Although third party voting may be driven largely by displeasure with the major parties or their candidates, the quality of the available substitute probably also affects the likelihood that people will cast third party ballots. When citizens view a minor party candidate as legitimate—that is, when the candidate has attributes that resemble those of most major party nominees—voters are more likely to choose the third party alternative. The greater the legitimacy of the third party candidate, the higher is the probability that voters will cast their lot with him.

The quality most closely associated with candidate legitimacy is experience: a third party challenger who has held high public office is electorally advantaged. Widespread name recognition gives him a leg up over more obscure contenders. Earlier campaigns and tenure in office have sharpened his political skills, and he has probably built (or could restore) a well-oiled campaign organization staffed by loyal and experienced supporters. The extent to which a candidate can enjoy these advantages is of course dependent upon precisely what sort of electoral experience he has had. A congressman from Kansas has more political prestige (and hence is more advantaged) than a city councilman from Trona, California, but both have less status than a former president.

It is conceptually useful to divide minor party candidates into three groups. The first, which we call *nationally prestigious* third party candidates, includes current or former presidents and vice-presidents, as well as current or former U.S. senators, representatives, or governors who have run for president or vice-president within one of the major parties.[3] We call the remaining current or former senators, representatives, and governors (that is, those who did not run for a national office on a major party ticket) *prestigious* third party candidates. We refer to all other independent challengers, whether they be mayors or machinists, as *non-prestigious* third party candidates.

As a rule, nationally prestigious third party candidates attract more votes than do prestigious candidates, and both run ahead of non-prestigious contenders. Political elites, potential contributors, the media, and ultimately the voters view third party challengers who have held prominent elective office as more legitimate aspirants for the White House than those who have not. Current or former senators, congressmen, and governors have a pre-existing electoral base, political organization, and political experience. And, by virtue of having won at least one major election, they are as a group probably better candidates than people who have not held these offices; their track records indicate they have the qualities and skills that attract votes.

Nationally prestigious third party candidates have an even greater advantage—widespread name recognition. These candidates, having already run national campaigns, are likely to enjoy greater legitimacy and have more supporters who have voted for them and made contributions in the past. They are

[3] This includes both major party nominees *and* candidates who sought the nomination by entering primaries in at least one-fifth of the states in the Union.

also more apt to have a national organizational base. When George Wallace (a nationally prestigious candidate) ran in 1968, he drew heavily on the foundation laid by his 1964 run for the Democratic presidential nomination (Carlson 1981). Finally, information about nationally prestigious candidates is easier for the voter to come by. Three times more voters in 1980 recognized John Anderson (a nationally prestigious candidate) than either Ed Clark or Barry Commoner (both non-prestigious candidates).

Between 1840 and 1980 nationally prestigious candidates ran for president on third party tickets nine times; prestigious candidates ran on seventeen occasions. The vote distribution for each set of candidates is displayed in table 5.1. On average, nationally prestigious candidates attract 13.5 percent of the

TABLE 5.1
Vote for Non-Prestigious, Prestigious, and Nationally
Prestigious Third Party Presidential Candidates, 1840-1980

Popular Vote	Minor Party Candidate		
	Non-Prestigious Candidate	Prestigious Candidate[a]	Nationally Prestigious Candidate[b]
Less than 1%	87.7%	35.3%	11.1%
1-3%	9.8	41.2	11.1
3-6%	2.5	11.8	0
6-9%	0	5.9	11.1
Over 9%	0	5.9	66.6
Total	100.0%	100.1%	99.9%
(N)	(122)	(17)	(9)
Median vote	.5%	1.7%	13.5%

SOURCE: Congressional Quarterly, *Guide to U.S. Elections* (Washington, D.C.: Congressional Quarterly, Inc., 1976); *Guide to 1976 Elections* (Washington, D.C.: Congressional Quarterly, Inc., 1977); *Congressional Quarterly Weekly Report*, January 17, 1981, p. 138.

[a] John Hale, 1852; John Bell, 1860; Green Clay Smith, 1876; James Weaver, 1880; Benjamin Butler, John St. John, 1884; James Weaver, John Bidwell, 1892; John Palmer, 1896; Thomas Watson, 1904, 1908; J. Frank Hanly, 1916; William Lemke, 1936; Strom Thurmond, 1948; John Schmitz, 1972; Lester Maddox, 1976; John Rarick, 1980.

[b] Martin Van Buren, 1848; Millard Fillmore, 1856; John Breckinridge, 1860; Theodore Roosevelt, 1912; Robert LaFollette, 1924; Henry Wallace, 1948; George Wallace, 1968; Eugene McCarthy, 1976; John Anderson, 1980.

vote, prestigious candidates 1.7 percent, and non-prestigious candidates only about .5 percent. (These are medians.)

Another indication of the impact that prominent candidates have on third party voting is evidenced by observing how a minor party's presidential vote changes over time when a prestigious candidate either becomes its nominee or ceases to head the ticket. The Greenback Party vote, for instance, went from .9 percent in 1876 when (non-prestigious) Peter Cooper was its standard bearer to 3.3 percent in 1880 when (prestigious) James Weaver led the slate. The Free Soil Party's total dropped from 10.1 percent in 1848 when (nationally prestigious) former President Martin Van Buren ran to 4.9 percent four years later with (prestigious) U.S. Senator John Hale on the ballot. Similarly, the American Independent Party went from 13.5 percent in 1968 with (nationally prestigious) George Wallace heading it to 1.4 percent in 1972 with (prestigious) U.S. Representative John Schmitz as its leader.

Thus, the higher the quality of the third party candidate, the more attractive the independent alternative appears to voters. This obviously is not the voter's only consideration; other factors are surely at work. Nationally prestigious third party candidates have polled as little as .9 percent and as much as 27.4 percent of the presidential popular vote. Support for prestigious candidates has ranged from .1 to 12.6 percent, and several non-prestigious candidates have garnered over 3.0 percent of the vote. Furthermore, these numbers do not indicate whether prominent candidates themselves attract votes, or if they are merely adroit enough to run at the right times. A precise estimate of the impact of candidate quality on third party voting must be sensitive to other forces that may both cause prestigious candidates to run and also affect the amount of third party voting.

Third Party Loyalty

When a third party persists over a period of time, voters can develop an allegiance to it, just as they can become loyal to a major party. Even parties that seemingly disappear and then resurface under different names can count on some partisan attachment: Libertymen became Free Soilers, many Know-Nothing supporters went on to vote for the Constitutional Union Party, and Greenbackers later joined the Populist cause.

By the same token, immigrants who developed party loyalties in their home countries may feel attached to a like-minded party in the United States—especially immigrants from countries with viable socialist parties. Upon arrival in the United States, many found the Populist, Progressive, and Socialist parties to be the most attractive choices (Fine 1928, pp. 89-90; Shannon 1955, pp. 43-45; Weinstein 1967, p. 327).

If allegiance to a minor party develops, then the extent of third party voting will be related to previous levels of third party support. It is likely that party loyalty will better explain independent voting in the nineteenth century, when there was greater continuity in third party causes, than in the twentieth century, when these runs were sporadic and centered on candidates.

Constraints on Third Party Voting

As we have already argued, constraints favoring the two major parties make it extremely costly for citizens to vote for a third party candidate. Although the most important barriers against third parties—the single-member-district plurality system and the electoral college—have remained constant since 1840, there are periods when other constraints to exit have been particularly high, as well as times when they have been lower than usual. Moreover, for some citizens these hurdles are higher than for others. The lower the barriers to exit, the easier it is for people to abandon the major parties and to cast ballots for a third party alternative.

Allegiance

Loyalty to a major party or to the political system as a whole can serve as a barrier to third party voting. Loyalty raises the cost of exit and hence reduces the likelihood that citizens will pursue a minor party option. The stronger a citizen's allegiance to a major party, the more apt he is to interpret events in ways that are consistent with the outlook of his party, and the more difficult it will be for him to cast a third party ballot. By the same token, the more loyal a voter is to the political system, the more likely she will continue to look exclusively to the major parties for solutions. Conversely, third party voting should be easier for citizens who have weaker attachments, or who never developed system or party loyalties in the first place.

ALLEGIANCE TO THE MAJOR PARTIES

The stronger a person's attachment to the two major political parties, the less likely he is to vote for a third party candidate. Nearly all Americans identify with one of the two major parties. This identification serves as the lens through which people interpret politics and evaluate candidates (Campbell et al. 1960). Those without this bond are less likely to see the world as Democrats or Republicans and are thus less reluctant to vote for other candidates. As allegiance to the major political parties weakens, third party voting should rise.

Loyalty to a major party is likely to be strongest at the beginning of a party system and to weaken as the system ages.[4] The reason lies in the nature of a realigning election itself. As a consequence of a critical realignment, a dominant issue cleavage develops along which parties, candidates, and voters divide. This cleavage structures political debate: it defines party loyalties; it is what makes Democrats different from Republicans. But, with time, new issues arise and citizens who were not eligible to vote when the party system was founded comprise a larger and larger share of the elec-

[4] Scholars generally agree that there have been five party systems: 1789-1828; 1828-1860; 1860-1896; 1896-1932; and 1932 to the present. The 1828, 1860, 1896, and 1932 critical elections, it is argued, mark the beginning of new party systems because each brought about a reshuffling of the political cleavages between the parties and a redefinition of the issues that dominated political discourse. See Key 1955; Chambers and Burnham 1967; and Sundquist 1973.

torate. New voters come of age; the franchise is expanded (new states are admitted to the Union, blacks are enfranchised in 1865, women in 1920, 18- to 20-year-olds in 1972); immigrants arrive. These new entrants neither identify strongly with the issues that were the basis of the party system nor have partisan loyalties that are as strong as those held by the generation that experienced the realignment first-hand (Beck 1974; Clubb, Flanigan, and Zingale 1980, p. 121). These voters are apt to be more susceptible to third party appeals than people who were in the electorate at the time of the realignment.

If this argument about replacement holds, then age cohorts enfranchised after the critical election will be more likely to vote for third parties than will older cohorts. Furthermore, this likelihood should rise as the number of generations separating a cohort from the critical election increases. For similar reasons, we also expect that first-time voters will be especially likely to cast ballots for minor parties. Having no experience with electoral politics prior to their enfranchisement, and no habit of major party voting, this group should be less constrained to stick with the major parties. If this assumption holds, then the larger this pool of "non-immunized" citizens, the more minor party voting there will be.[5]

There is a scattering of evidence that points to new cohorts as being third party activists. The *New York Herald Tribune* estimated that a majority of the delegates to the 1924 Progressive convention were under the age of forty; students at Columbia, Harvard, Yale, and other universities sent delegates to the gathering (LaFollette and LaFollette 1953, vol. II, pp. 1111-12). The young were more apt to be supporters of Henry Wallace in 1948, George Wallace in 1968, Eugene McCarthy in 1976, and John Anderson in 1980.

[5] Confounding the cohort and new voter effects, of course, is age, which may also have an independent effect on third party voting. It may prove to be the case that it is mere youth that makes the new voters and younger cohorts more susceptible to a third party call. With age, attachment to the two major parties gets stronger (Converse 1976) and third party voting may decline.

The replacement argument helps explain why third party voting tends to be higher towards the end of a party system than in the years immediately following a realignment. As the system ages, the proportion of the electorate who were voters at the time of the critical election shrinks and the pool of citizens most susceptible to third party appeals grows. Except for 1860, the first four elections in a party system are relatively dormant periods for third parties (figure 5.3). Minor parties polled less than 6 percent of the presidential popular vote cast in the 1840, 1864-1872, 1896-1908, and 1932-1944 elections. Twenty years after a realignment, third party voting becomes more pronounced. Every instance of minor parties winning over 6 percent of the popular vote (save 1860) occurred at least five elections after the founding of the party system. This relationship is by no means a perfect one. There is a tremendous variance in third party strength at similar points in a party system. For example, compare 1844, 1876,

FIGURE 5.3

Third Party Presidential Vote by Age of Party System, 1840-1980

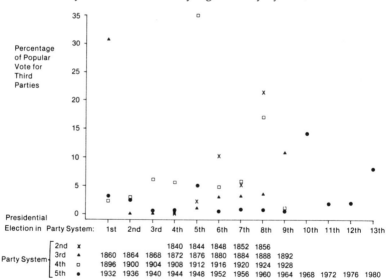

Party System		1st	2nd	3rd	4th	5th	6th	7th	8th	9th	10th	11th	12th	13th
2nd	x				1840	1844	1848	1852	1856					
3rd	▲	1860	1864	1868	1872	1876	1880	1884	1888	1892				
4th	□	1896	1900	1904	1908	1912	1916	1920	1924	1928				
5th	●	1932	1936	1940	1944	1948	1952	1956	1960	1964	1968	1972	1976	1980

1912, and 1948—all fifth elections. Likewise, although third party voting is on average higher in the second half of a party system, not all elections at the end of a system produce third party voting. For instance, in 1888, 1928, 1952-1964, 1972, and 1976, third parties gained less than 3 percent of the presidential vote.

ALLEGIANCE TO THE POLITICAL SYSTEM

Given the entrenchment of the two-party norm as part of American political ideology, loyalty to the political system itself may also make citizens reluctant to cast third party ballots. As this allegiance to the political order wanes, so may a citizen's propensity to stick with the major party candidates, and the third party route may come to seem a more attractive method for bringing about fundamental changes in the way the government is organized and run. Third parties have frequently advocated sweeping changes in the American political and economic order.

Alienation may produce disaffection from the political regime in a number of ways. First, citizens may feel that the government as a whole (as distinguished from the incumbent party) is incapable of effectively tending to the affairs of state. Voters may lose faith in the government's capacity to make wise decisions or may come to view the people who run the government as incompetent, wasteful, or ineffective. If citizens' faith in the capacity of government to manage the country diminishes, simply throwing the rascals out and voting for the other major party would be inadequate. The problem runs deeper. When loyalty to the political regime falters, so may allegiance to the two-party system. Third party voting could be one expression of this erosion of confidence (Citrin 1974, pp. 976-78).

A sense of powerlessness—the feeling that one's behavior cannot affect the actions of government—may also reduce the likelihood that people will support the major parties. The inefficacious may pursue the third party alternative out of frustration with their inability to influence what their government does (Carlson 1981, pp. 116-19). If people feel that they are incapable of having any effect on the affairs of state, one solution is to change, in a fundamental way, how the country is run.

Alienation from the political order may also grow out of a feeling of economic impotence or frustration over one's economic position in society. If economic powerlessness weakens a citizen's allegiance to the political order, then people at the low end of the economic ladder—the poor and those with low status occupations—will be alienated and less constrained from voting for a minor party. Historically, some third parties have garnered their support from the poor and the economically powerless. Manual workers and people with little or no property were more likely than the well-off to support the Know-Nothing Party in the 1850s (Unger 1964, p. 209; Lipset and Raab 1970, pp. 55-57). Poor white farmers in Georgia and Tennessee were likely to be Populists (Arnett 1922, p. 184; Martin 1933, p. 254). The least prosperous California counties were also Populist strongholds (Rogin 1969, p. 184). The poor were more apt to support George Wallace in 1968 (Lipset and Raab 1970, ch. 10; Ross et al. 1976, p. 85).

Social and economic changes that displace a group from a position of dominance in society may weaken their allegiance to the political order and the two major parties. The nativist political movements of the 1840s and 1850s, which found expression in the Know-Nothing Party, grew out of Protestant fear of growing immigrant political and economic power. In a sense, the farmer movements of the 1880s and 1890s can be characterized as a response to their perceived loss of power to commercial interests in the industrial East. Similarly, George Wallace's support has been attributed to white voters' feelings of status inconsistency from their displacement by blacks (Lipset and Raab 1970).

Structural Barriers to Third Party Voting

The lower the structural barriers to exit, the easier it is for citizens to abandon the major parties. Although the hurdles to third party voting have always been high, they have not remained constant. The introduction of the Australian ballot in the 1890s and the ballot access restrictions that soon followed made it difficult for candidates to place their names on the official ballot. Because it is relatively taxing for a person to cast a write-in vote (especially when voting machines or punch card ballots are used), and because voters can more easily recognize than recall a candidate's name (Mann and Wolfinger 1980), citizens are more prone to vote for a minor party when the candidate's name appears on the official ballot than when it does not. Since a citizen is more apt to cast a third party vote when the cost of doing so is low, it follows that the higher the proportion of voters with minor party candidates on their ballots, the greater the third party vote.

Disparities in campaign resources and media coverage have also always made it difficult for minor party challengers to compete with the major parties for votes. But this disparity is worse in some years than in others. The greater the minor party's disadvantage in campaign resources and media coverage, the lower is the third party vote. As the cost of gathering information about third party candidates goes up, so too does the probability that a voter will remain loyal to the major parties.[6]

Finally, anti-third party sentiment and respect for the two-party norm have always been present. Although the degree of disapproval has probably varied over time, this fluctuation is no doubt due chiefly to changes in some of the factors already discussed, such as age of the party system and the proportion of the electorate with weak allegiance to the major parties. Still, there have been some periods—the Red Scare, for instance—when third party activity was more perilous.

---

[6] Data on campaign spending, media expenditures, and press coverage are difficult to come by. Except in recent years, it is hard to say how disadvantaged each third party candidate was. Moreover, these data are often difficult to interpret. For instance, was John Anderson's media coverage in 1980 better or worse than James Birney's in 1840? At the time Birney ran, the media were quite limited, so he had little opportunity to make himself or his positions known to the public. In contrast, Anderson's media exposure reached a higher proportion of the electorate, but so did that of his major party opponents, whose coverage all but drowned him out.

When the cost of third party activity increases, the probability of defection from the two-party system declines.

SUMMARY

Citizens vote for third parties when certain motivations to abandon the major parties are high and the costs of doing so are low. When the two major parties deteriorate—when they fail to provide prosperity, responsive policies, and competent, trustworthy leadership—voters pursue the third party alternative. As the quality of minor party candidates and loyalty to third party causes increase, so does the probability that voters will abandon the major parties. Citizen loyalty to the American political system and to the two major parties makes it costly for people to choose the minor party route. Third party voting is also less likely to occur when these candidates are denied access to the ballot and when information about a third party cause is hard to come by. As these costs of third party voting increase, the probability that citizens will abandon the major parties goes down.

To be sure, there are many causes of third party support beyond the ones we have considered here. Indeed, any case study of a particular movement suggests additional reasons for that party's strength. The propositions we have identified are the ones that we think contribute to a general theory of third party voting. We are not asserting that there are no other causes, only that we have identified the important ones that will account for fluctuations in third party support in America.

CHAPTER 6

WHY CITIZENS VOTE
FOR THIRD PARTIES

WE HAVE identified a set of motivations and constraints that affect the likelihood of citizens abandoning the major parties. Yet thus far we have mustered only a limited number of historical examples in support of the theory. Our analysis in this chapter is more systematic. Here we test whether the theory is a general one: does it explain only a few instances of third party voting, or is it able to account consistently for changes in the level of minor party support over time? How much impact does each component of the theory have on third party voting once other factors have been taken into account?

Any effort to identify the conditions that prompt people to abandon the major parties, whether statistical or anecdotal, must examine not only instances of third party strength but periods of major party loyalty as well. Understanding why a party attracts no support at all is just as crucial to a general theory of third party voting as knowing why a party attracts a large number of voters. After all, when there is little or no third party voting, citizens are probably content with the major parties' performances. The total absence of third party activity is crucial information; it would be misleading to take as our universe for study only those instances when third parties emerged.[1]

One option would be to examine separately each of the forty-five parties that polled votes between 1840 and 1980. That is, one might estimate for each party an equation accounting for years of support as well as years of non-existence.

---

[1] Consistent estimates would result only if we took into account the "selection equations" that explain why each party appeared in the first place (Heckman 1976; Achen 1983).

But that would still not explain why some parties never emerged in the first place. Furthermore, it is impractical to estimate and analyze so many equations.

Instead, we focus on changes in the total level of third party support across elections. Our approach is to estimate how much a change in a particular motivation or constraint affects the probability of citizens casting third party ballots. We rely on both aggregate time-series data from the 1840 to 1980 presidential elections and survey data from the 1952 to 1980 contests to estimate the impact of each component of the theory. Some parts of the theory we test with aggregate data, others only with survey data. In a number of instances we are able to exploit both sources.

We treat each motivation for and constraint against third party support as a causal variable in the individual and aggregate equations we estimate.[2] Appendix B describes the sources of the data and the coding of each variable. Although we have relegated to footnotes most of the intricacies of the statistical procedure, the following general overview of the analysis will help the reader interpret the findings.

PRELUDE

Aggregate Analysis: 1840-1980

At the aggregate level the dependent variable is the proportion of the presidential popular vote cast in each presidential election for all third party candidates. The analysis begins with the 1840 election and ends in 1980, yielding thirty-six observations. Since the proportion of the presidential popular vote cast for third parties has a highly skewed distribution,

---

[2] In every year there are determinants of third party voting beyond those we consider here. Some may generate more minor party support, others less. We assume that they average out to zero, and that they are unassociated with the causes we are examining. We do think it is likely, however, that the other causes of third party voting in one year are associated with those in adjacent years. We take this into account in our analysis.

the variable is logged.[3] This means that an estimated regression coefficient represents the effect that a unit change in the causal variable has on a *percent* change in third party voting. For instance, a coefficient of .4 would imply that an increase of 1.0 units in the causal variable yields a 40 percent (or 1.4-fold) increase in the third party vote.[4] (By a 40 percent increase we mean, for example, a change from 5 percent of the vote to 7 percent, *not* a change from 5 to 45 percent.)

Two causes of the vote—the proportions of voters with prestigious and nationally prestigious third party candidates on their ballots—are themselves variables to be explained. Since they are endogenous, and since it is likely that the causes of third party support omitted from the vote equation are associated with the omitted causes of these candidates appearing on the ballot, we estimate the aggregate vote equation by two-stage least squares.[5] We defer to the next chapter our discussion of why prestigious and nationally prestigious third party candidates run and focus in this chapter on the causes of the vote itself.

We report the two-stage least squares estimates in table 6.1. As seen from figure 6.1, the aggregate model yields an ex-

---

[3] Logging the vote removes any association between the predicted values and the residuals. This transformation fits the data better than either the reciprocal or square root.

[4] For further discussion on interpreting logged variables, see Tufte 1974, pp. 108-31.

[5] The exogenous variables that appear in the equations for the two endogenous variables (the proportion of voters with prestigious and nationally prestigious third party candidates on their ballot) are discussed in chapter 7. The residuals are, surprisingly, not autocorrelated. When Fair's (1970) two-stages, maximum-likelihood estimator is employed, rho is estimated to be .19—small enough to ignore. The coefficients reported in table 6.1 are essentially the same (to the second decimal place) as those produced by correcting for autocorrelation. The error term is also homoskedastic. By the Gleiser test, there are only 39 chances in 100 that the residuals are heteroskedastic with respect to the log of the total votes cast. However, the standard deviation of the residuals in the nineteenth century is slightly smaller than in the twentieth century (.16 versus .21), which may slightly bias the standard error of the coefficients. We also tested whether variables had the same effect across time. With the exception of the lagged vote and the proportion of voters with prestigious third party candidates on their ballot, the coefficients are stable over the thirty-six elections.

TABLE 6.1
Determinants of Third Party Voting, 1840-1980:
Two-Stage Least Squares Estimates[a]

Variable	Coefficient	Standard Error
Proportion of voters with a nationally prestigious third party candidate on the ballot (squared)[b]	1.70	.17
Proportion of voters with a prestigious third party candidate on their ballot (squared), 1892-1980[b]	.14	.07
Proportion of the electorate eligible to vote for the first time (logged)	.49	.11
Proportion of the electorate eligible to vote for the first time who immigrated from countries with viable socialist parties (logged)	.54	.15
Long-term change in agricultural prices	− 1.21	.23
Change in the incumbent party's congressional vote	− 3.15	1.27
Third party presidential vote$_{t-4}$, 1840-1892 (logged)	.46	.07
Third party presidential vote$_{t-4}$ for non-prestigious candidates, 1896-1980 (logged)	.43	.06
Constant	1.17	.51

Standard error of estimate = .22
N = 36

[a] The variable being explained is the logarithm of the proportion of presidential popular vote cast for non-major party presidential candidates.
[b] Endogenous variable.

tremely good fit to the data. It closely accounts both for fluctuations in aggregate third party voting over time and for peak periods of strength. Bursts of third party voting prior to the Civil War, in the decades surrounding the turn of the century, and in the years since 1968 are all anticipated, as are the intermittent lulls in support. Half the years are predicted within .4 percentage points; three out of four are missed by less than 1.0 percentage point.

FIGURE 6.1
Actual and Predicted Third Party Vote for President, 1840-1980

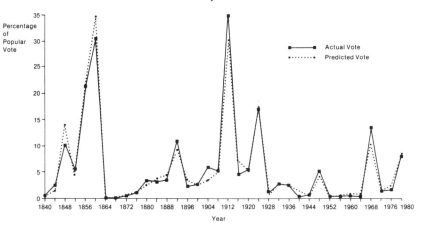

Individual-Level Analysis: 1952-1980

The individual-level analysis focuses on the 1952-1980 presidential elections. Here we rely on data gathered by the Center for Political Studies in its presidential election-year random sample surveys of the U.S. voting age population. In order to identify the conditions that prompt people to abandon the major parties in general, we pool respondents from these eight surveys. This procedure allows us to explain both what kinds of people vote for minor party candidates and how shifts in the political environment and in the composition of the electorate affect third party voting. This analysis focuses on why the person, in the year interviewed, did or did not vote for a minor party candidate. There are 5,780 cases in the analysis once we delete respondents who were polled in more than one election or who did not complete a relevant part of the questionnaire.[6]

Because some causes of third party voting are indirect (they

[6] The CPS interviewed some people in both 1956 and 1960 and others in both 1972 and 1976. To avoid autocorrelation problems, we dropped respondents when they appeared for the second time.

have an impact on one or more of the determinants of the vote, but not directly on the vote itself), we also estimate equations for the mediating variables. Figure 6.2 illustrates the structure of the individual-level model. Endogenous variables appear in ellipses; exogenous variables are listed in brackets.[7] We estimate six equations: one for how respondents

FIGURE 6.2
Determinants of Third Party Voting, 1952-1980: Structural Model

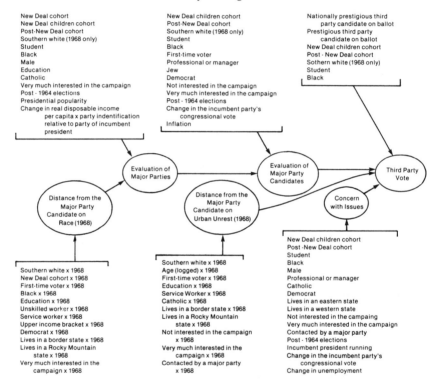

[7] We considered more complicated models—ones with additional variables, reciprocal relationships among the endogenous variables, and more direct effects of variables on the vote. Preliminary analysis allowed us to rule out other specifications. Variables deleted from an equation can be safely regarded as having coefficients equivalent to zero.

vote and one each for the voters' concern with issues, their evaluation of the major party candidates, their evaluation of the major parties, and their proximity to the major party candidates' positions on both racial and civil unrest issues in 1968.[8] Because the variables that appear as causes of voters' attention to issues and their distance from the major party candidates on racial and civil unrest issues are exogenous, we estimate these three equations by ordinary least squares. The equations for the voters' evaluation of the major parties and the major party nominees are estimated by two-stage least squares. None of these five variables was transformed, so there are no special problems in interpreting their coefficients. Whether people vote for a third party candidate is dichotomous; hence we use two-stage probit to estimate the coefficients in this equation.[9] We report the estimated coefficients for the six individual-level equations in table 6.2.

A probit coefficient is not as easy to interpret as the familiar least squares estimate: it represents the amount of change on the standard normal distribution that results from a unit change in the causal variable. To simplify the interpretation of these estimates, we convert the coefficients to probabilities and discuss the percentage-point impact of each variable on the likelihood that people will vote for an independent. (Here a 5

[8] Since each of these variables is measured with error, treating them as endogenous prevents attenuation of their coefficients.

[9] Ordinary least squares is inappropriate when an endogenous (or "dependent") variable is dichotomous. Two things go wrong: the OLS error term is heteroskedastic, and the predicted values on the endogenous variable are not constrained to the 0-1 interval. Moreover, it is unlikely that a variable has the same effect on everyone—people uncertain about whether to defect are going to be moved more than citizens who are staunch supporters of either a major or a minor party—so a linear model is inappropriate. Probit resolves these problems: its errors are homoskedastic and its predicted scores fall within the 0-1 interval. In probit a variable has very little impact on people who are either very unlikely or nearly certain to vote for a third party candidate. It has its greatest impact on voters who are between 40 and 60 percent likely to cast a third party ballot and are most susceptible to the forces affecting third party voting. For further information on probit, see Cox (1970, pp. 1-29); Pindyck and Rubinfled (1976, pp. 227-47); and Hanushek and Jackson (1977, ch. 7). The two-stage probit estimator we employed is described in Maddala and Lee (1976) and Achen (1983).

TABLE 6.2
Determinants of Third Party Voting, 1952-1980: Estimated Equations

			Equation[a]			
	(1)	(2)	(3)	(4)	(5)	(6)
Variable	Third Party Vote	Evaluation of Major Party Candidates	Evaluation of Major Parties	Concern with Issues	Distance from the Major Party Candidates on Urban Unrest (1968)	Distance from the Major Party Candidates on Race (1968)
Evaluation of major party candidates[b]	−4.562 (.940)					
Evaluation of major parties[b]		.642 (.173)				
Concern with issues[b]	1.896 (.682)					
Distance from the major party candidates on racial issues in 1968[b]			−.033 (.015)			
Distance from the major party candidates on urban unrest issue in 1968[b]	1.442 (.214)					
Nationally prestigious third party candidate on ballot	.528 (.122)					
Prestigious third party candidate on ballot	.103 (.074)					

	(1)	(2)	(3)	(4)	(5)
New Deal cohort				−.012 (.007)	
New Deal children cohort	.104 (.061)	−.018 (.007)	.012 (.007)	−.010 (.004)	
Post-New Deal cohort	.191 (.137)	−.029 (.010)	.044 (.010)	−.016 (.006)	
Southern white (1968 only)					.086 (.009)
Student	.247 (.173)	−.046 (.022)	.072 (.034)	−.037 (.015)	.258 (.015)
Black	.268 (.216)	−.057 (.032)	.024 (.012)	.040 (.019)	
Male	−.627 (.249)	.015 (.012)	.057 (.006)	.028 (.007)	
First-time voter		.031 (.014)		−.014 (.003)	
Education				−.006 (.001)	
Professional or manager			.011 (.006)		
Catholic		−.014 (.006)	−.017 (.007)	.017 (.004)	
Jew		.034 (.016)			
Democrat		−.039 (.006)	−.043 (.006)		
Lives in an Eastern state			−.022 (.007)		
Lives in a Western state			.029 (.010)		
Not interested in the campaign		−.048 (.008)	−.022 (.007)		
Very much interested in the campaign		.045 (.008)	.016 (.007)	−.009 (.004)	
Contacted by a major party			.015 (.007)		
Post-1964 elections		−.003 (.001)	.006 (.001)	−.001 (.000)	
Incumbent president running			−.070 (.009)		

TABLE 6.2 (cont.)

Variable	Equation[a]					
	(1) Third Party Vote	(2) Evaluation of Major Party Candidates	(3) Evaluation of Major Parties	(4) Concern with Issues	(5) Distance from the Major Party Candidates on Urban Unrest (1968)	(6) Distance from the Major Party Candidates on Race (1968)
Presidential popularity			.027 (.012)			
Change in the incumbent party's congressional vote		−1.492 (.247)		3.363 (.333)		
Change in real disposable income per capita × party identification relative to party of incumbent president			.189 (.063)			
Change in unemployment				.820 (.645)		
Inflation		−.758 (.185)				
New Deal cohort × 1968						.268 (.026)
Age (logged) × 1968					.138 (.003)	−.143 (.026)
First-time voter × 1968					.100 (.016)	−.387 (.024)
Black × 1968						

Variable	(1)	(2)	(3)	(4)	(5)	(6)
Education × 1968					−.036 (.002)	.085 (.003)
Unskilled worker × 1968						.159 (.015)
Service worker × 1968					−.077 (.018)	.081 (.031)
Upper-income bracket × 1968						−.012 (.013)
Catholic × 1968					.044 (.009)	.100 (.012)
Democrat × 1968						.206 (.019)
Lives in a Border state × 1968					−.076 (.012)	
Lives in a Rocky Mountain state × 1968					−.121 (.021)	−.073 (.035)
Not interested in the campaign × 1968					.068 (.012)	
Very much interested in the campaign × 1968					.044 (.008)	.026 (.012)
Contacted by a major party × 1968					.046 (.008)	
Constant	.305 (.750)	.419 (.087)	.528 (.008)	.512 (.021)	.001 (.001)	.008 (.002)
Standard error of estimate	.148	.129	.205	.231	.089	.148
R^2					.725	.523

N = 5,780

[a] Equation (1) is estimated by two-stage probit; equations (2) and (3) are estimated by two-stage least squares; equations (4), (5), and (6) are estimated by ordinary least squares. A blank cell in the table indicates that the variable (read off the row) had an estimated coefficient indistinguishable from zero in that equation (read off the column). The coding of the variables is described in appendix B.

[b] Endogenous variable.

percent effect represents a change from, say, 10 to 15 percent in a voter's probability of casting a third party ballot.) Because some variables have direct effects, some have indirect effects, and others have both, we report the variable's *total* impact (indirect plus direct) on the voters' probability of abandoning the major parties.[10]

The remainder of this chapter is taken up with the analysis and interpretation of the findings reported in tables 6.1 and 6.2. While each of the causes of minor party support is examined in detail, one general and important finding emerges that merits attention at the outset. The story of why people vote for third parties is a story of major party deterioration. To be sure, third parties can help their own causes by selecting high caliber candidates or by building a loyal following over the years. But, overwhelmingly, it is the failure of the major parties to do what the electorate expects of them—reflect the issue preferences of voters, manage the economy, select attractive and acceptable candidates, and build voter loyalty to the parties and the political system—that most increases the likelihood of voters backing a minor party. Citizens by and large cast third party ballots because they are dissatisfied with the major parties, not because they are attracted to the alternatives.

Issue Unresponsiveness

To assess the impact on third party voting of citizen discontent with the major party candidates' positions requires measures of both the voters' and the major party candidates' preferences on the issues of the day. Because survey data are nec-

---

[10] This is estimated by computing, separately for each respondent, the total impact of the variable on his probability of abandoning the major parties. The mean of these individual effects is the population estimate of the variable's impact on third party voting. To ensure that each election is counted equally in this calculation, we weight the cases so that each year has the same number of respondents. Some of the effects we discuss may appear to be small, but if everyone in the electorate were just 5 percent more likely to cast a minor party ballot, aggregate third party voting would go up 5 percentage points—a big change in the American context.

essary to measure the electorate's political proclivities, we can estimate the electoral impact of issues solely for the 1952-1980 period.

We find that voters' estrangement from the positions of the major party candidates leads to third party voting only when there is substantial distance between the voters and the candidates. On most of the prominent issues of this period—Korea in 1952, Vietnam in 1964, 1968, and 1972, civil rights in 1964, and the role of government in providing social services in 1980—the major party nominees positioned themselves in ways that did not leave much distance between their stands and those of the majority of the electorate. (Most voters in 1964, for example, were close to either Johnson's or Goldwater's civil rights positions.) Hence we do not find these issues prompting third party voting.

However, in 1968, Hubert Humphrey's and Richard Nixon's views on the questions of civil rights and urban unrest left some voters standing a considerable distance away from the two nominees. As a result, on these issues, we find that the larger the voters' distance from the position of the closest major party candidate, the more likely they are to cast their ballots for a third party challenger. Although urban unrest seems (surprisingly) to have been the more important issue, both had independent effects. Compared to a citizen whose position or urban unrest was equivalent to either Nixon's or Humphrey's, voters very distant from the major party nominees were 24 percent more likely to follow the third party route. The effect of such distance from the civil rights positions of the major party nominees is much smaller—only 2 percent. Furthermore, the impact of civil rights is indirect: distance from the major party nominees undermined a person's evaluation of the major parties in 1968, which in turn led to increased third party voting. (The urban unrest issue, of course, had obvious racial overtones.)

Thus disaffection with the stands of the major party candidates can produce third party support, but only when a substantial distance separates voters from the nominees. Citizens can apparently tolerate low levels of disaffection on issues without being pushed into a minor party camp.

A second set of results supports the contention that concerns about issues motivate third party voting. Throughout the 1952-1980 period we find that citizens who evaluated the major parties and their candidates predominantly by their stands (as opposed to their personalities or group appeal) were consistently more likely to appear in a third party camp. The effect varies with the type of third party candidate running. Voters who assessed the major parties and their nominees exclusively on issues were 28 percent more likely than their neighbors to support third parties when a nationally prestigious third party candidate ran, and about 20 percent more likely to do so when a prestigious or non-prestigious candidate appeared on their ballots. People intensely concerned with issues are apt to be disappointed with what the major parties have to offer. Major party candidates strive for ambiguity and resist taking controversial positions that concern only a small share of the electorate (Downs 1957; Page 1978). In any election there are dozens of issues about which the major party candidates have nothing to say. Voters concerned with these issues are not likely to find that the major party contenders have taken up their causes.[11]

Finally, we find that even once issues have been taken into account, Southern whites in 1968 were still 12 percent more likely to cast a third party ballot than were other citizens. "Friends-and-neighbors" politics, similar to the variety V. O. Key, Jr., found at work at mid-century in the South (particularly in Alabama), probably explains their support for George Wallace. Key argued that a Southern candidate wins support "not primarily for what he stands for or because of his capacities, but because of where he lives" (1949, p. 41). This phenomenon still seems to be at work in the South. Regional

---

[11] We are unable to devise a direct test of whether third party voting is prompted by the major parties ignoring specific issues that large segments of the electorate consider important. The anecdotal evidence reported in chapters 3 and 4, however, suggests that neglect of issues by the major parties does indeed lead to increased levels of third party support.

pride, Southern bonds to a candidate who was "one of us," and the belief that Wallace would promote Southern interests boosted his vote in his native South.[12]

ECONOMIC PERFORMANCE

Agricultural Adversity

Voters abandon the major parties during periods of agricultural adversity. Between 1840 and 1980 we find that the agricultural sector responded to long-term[13] changes in farm prices; short-term fluctuations had no effect on support for third party causes. Only after extended periods of decline, when both major parties have been given a chance but failed, when methods for refinancing debt have been exhausted, and when organizations have been built, do farmers pursue the third party route. In addition, farmers seem to be more sensitive to changes in prices than in personal income.[14]

The precise impact of long-term changes in farm prices depends on what proportion of the electorate is engaged in agriculture: the larger the agricultural sector, the greater the effect of agricultural adversity on third party voting. From our aggregate vote equation we have calculated the impact of long-term price changes when various proportions of the electorate are in this sector. These estimates appear in figure 6.3. For example, the top curve shows that when half the electorate made their living in agriculture (through about 1880), a 50 percent drop in long-term farm prices caused third party

[12] Rosenstone's aggregate analysis of the 1948-1980 elections finds a similar, though smaller, regional friends-and-neighbor's effect for Strom Thurmond, George Wallace, and Jimmy Carter (1983, p. 88).

[13] We define "long-term" changes in farm prices as those occurring over a period of sixteen years. Twelve- to eighteen-year lags in prices all work; the sixteen-year lag is the best fit to the data.

[14] Boulding (1953, p. 111) and Mayhew (1972) make a similar argument. Over the 1840-1980 period, long-term changes in agricultural prices better fit the data than changes in agricultural prices relative to changes in non-agricultural prices either in the short or long run. Between 1900 and 1980 changes in real per capita agricultural income did not affect the vote (slope = -1.06; standard error = 4.14).

FIGURE 6.3
Partial Effect of Long-Term Change in
Agricultural Prices on Third Party Voting,
1840-1980

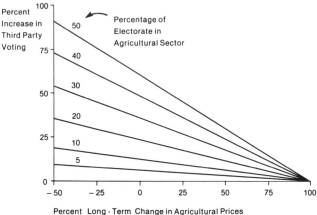

support to nearly double compared to the best years, when prices were up 100 percent in the long run. As the number of people engaged in farming dropped, so did the effect of agricultural adversity on third party voting, as shown by the dampened slopes of the lower curves. When about one in three citizens made their living off the land, a 50 percent drop in prices caused a 36 percent increase in third party voting. Now that less than 4 percent of the electorate is engaged in farming, the impact of agricultural adversity on third party voting is minimal.

In the past, long-term declines in farm prices while large portions of the population were in farming have indeed produced third party fervor. In 1880 farm prices were down 51 percent from their 1864 level. With nearly half the electorate dependent on agriculture for their economic survival, a huge pool of voters mobilized behind the Greenbacks. The depressed prices that persisted into the mid-1890s provided a basis of support for the Populist Party as well. When farm prices recovered at the end of the century, third party backing waned. When prices again bottomed out in the early 1930s, some farmers turned to William Lemke. However, in 1936 only one in five citizens were engaged in agriculture, substantially reducing farmers' impact on total levels of third party voting.

General Economic Adversity

Although economic conditions clearly motivated third party voting by farmers from 1840 to 1980, the evidence is mixed regarding whether other citizens are similarly moved. On the one hand, changes neither in prices, in unemployment, nor in income affected the level of third party support over these years.[15] General economic adversity (other than agricultural) turned citizens neither to nor away from third parties.

However, when we focus just on the 1968-1980 elections (the only years for which there are survey data on respondents' economic well being and evaluations of the incumbent's management of the economy), we find that economic considerations did affect the level of third party support.[16] (The model and estimated coefficients are reported in figure 6.10 and table 6.4, which appear as an appendix to this chapter.) In these four elections the unemployed were about 13 percent more prone than other citizens to vote for an independent; those who felt personally worse off financially were about 3 percent more likely to abandon the major parties. Not only did voters' personal economic well being affect their probability of casting a third party ballot, but they were even more willing to defect if they thought that the country as a whole was worse off as well. Citizens who saw a deteriorating na-

---

[15] The coefficient for election-year change in prices is .42 (standard error = .87). The effect of the absolute value of the election-year change in prices is also insignificant: .78 (standard error = 1.34). The impact of unemployment and the change in real GNP per capita were estimated beginning in 1892, the first year for which data are available. Change in unemployment is collinear with the change in real GNP per capita, which has a coefficient of −.52 (standard error = 1.33).

[16] We of course recognize the extremely limited generalizability of these results.

tional economy were about 10 percent more likely to vote for an independent challenger than their counterparts who thought the country was in good shape. This fact suggests that to some extent the gradual increase in third party voting since the boom years of the mid-1960s is a response to the major parties' mismanagement of the economy.[17]

There are a number of possible explanations for why general economic conditions only seem to have affected third party voting in the last few elections. First, it is possible that economic considerations became important in presidential voting only recently. Until the modern presidency, few voters held the chief executive accountable for the state of the economy. However, we do not find that aggregate economic conditions affected third party voting even when we examine just the twelve elections since 1936. A second possible explanation is that the important variables are *perceptions* of economic well being, which can only be measured with survey data and are not necessarily reflected in aggregate statistics. Usually, however, the two are associated.

Finally, it is conceivable that economic mismanagement was an important electoral consideration only during these years, and that in general it is not. We think this explanation is most plausible. The survey findings, we suspect, reflect the uniqueness of the 1968-1980 period. Historically, bad economic years like 1932 and 1960 have produced little third party voting. Recent third party candidates, though, have stressed economic concerns at a time when the economy was a salient issue. The finding that in the last four elections both personal economic well being and voters' assessment of the national economy have affected the general electorate's likelihood of supporting a third party is not generalizable to other periods of American history—except, of course, for farmers.

[17] The impact that voters' assessments of their personal economic well being have on the vote is mediated by their assessment of the nation's well being. People who feel personally worse off are about 33 percent more likely to think the country is worse off; this assessment in turn increases their probability of defecting to a third party. Nearly all of the impact of unemployment on the vote is direct, although some is indirect (the unemployed are naturally more likely to feel worse off financially).

UNACCEPTABLE MAJOR PARTY CANDIDATES

The less attractive the major party candidates are perceived to be, the more likely citizens are to vote for a third party alternative. Between 1952 and 1980 voter assessment of the major party nominees (measured by the number of positive and negative comments voters make about them) had a bigger impact on the level of third party support than any other variable. Not surprisingly, the more positive the electorate's evaluation of the major parties' nominees, the more likely voters will stick with them in November. As disaffection with the major party candidates grows, desertion becomes nearly certain, as seen in figure 6.4. Compared to citizens who evaluate the major party nominees favorably, those with the most critical assessments are 91 percent more likely to vote for an independent when a nationally prestigious candidate runs.

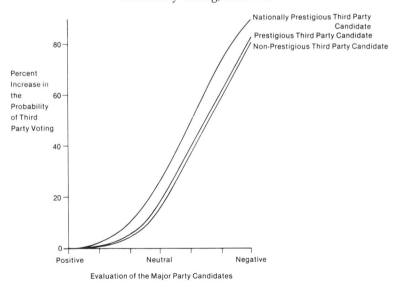

FIGURE 6.4
Effect of Evaluation of the Major Party Candidates on
Third Party Voting, 1952-1980

They are about 83 percent more prone to abandon the major parties if a prestigious or non-prestigious candidate appears on the ballot.

In short, when the major parties deteriorate—when they fail to represent people's issue preferences, when they seem to mismanage the economy, or when they run unacceptable candidates—citizens are likely to turn to a third party alternative.[18] Although for the most part, third party voting occurs when *neither* major party presents an attractive alternative, voters' disaffection with the incumbent party's performance in office can by itself prompt defection to a third party. We saw this effect with regard to economic performance between 1968 and 1980, but it also holds more generally for the entire 1840-1980 period. When voters were unhappy with the incumbent party, as measured by the size of the in-party's loss of votes in the midterm election, they were more likely to abandon *both* major parties. Over the 1840-1980 period, when the incumbent party's midterm congressional vote dropped 5 percentage points below its vote in the last presidential election, the vote for third parties in the subsequent election increased 16 percent. Although most voters disaffected with the incumbent party find a home in the opposing major party, some are moved to try the third party route.

ATTRACTIVE THIRD PARTY ALTERNATIVES

Floundering major parties push voters into third party camps, but attractive independent candidates make the decision to defect easier. The quality of the available third party alternative has a substantial effect on whether citizens will abandon the major parties. When nationally prestigious third party candidates appear on all November ballots, third party voting is 2.7 times higher than it otherwise would be. The peak periods of third party support (1856, 1860, 1912, 1924, 1968) were all due in large part to the presence of nationally prom-

[18] Lemieux finds that issues and evaluations of government performance are the primary causes of voter defection to Liberal candidates in Britain (1977, ch. 3).

inent third party candidates. Prestigious third party candidates appearing on the general election ballot also caused increased defection from the major parties, but as expected, their effect was only a fraction of that of the nationally prestigious candidates. Moreover, this effect does not appear until 1892. Beginning in that year, when a prestigious third party candidate qualified for every state's general election ballot, third party voting was 1.14 times higher than it otherwise would have been.

Similar findings emerge from the 1952-1980 individual-level analysis: nationally prestigious third party candidates poll more votes than prestigious candidates, and both do better than non-prestigious contenders. Voters are 4.8 percent more likely to abandon the major parties when a nationally prestigious third party candidate appears on the ballot and .8 percent more likely to do so when a prestigious candidate runs.[19]

A candidate who fails to attain ballot positions not surprisingly loses votes. Some of this loss comes from the increased cost that citizens must bear when they are forced to write in a candidate's name, but the situation is complicated: the marginal boost of additional ballot spots increases as the proportion of the electorate with the opportunity to vote for prestigious and nationally prestigious third party candidates grows (figures 6.5 and 6.6). When a nationally prestigious challenger appears on 50 percent of the ballots instead of 25 percent, there is a 1.32-fold increase in his vote. If he were to appear on 75 percent of the ballots instead of 50 percent, his support would be another 1.53 times higher.

A similar, though weaker, relationship holds since 1892 for prestigious candidates. If a prestigious challenger were listed on 50 percent of the ballots instead of 25 percent, third party voting would be 1.02 times greater; the marginal effect of the

[19] The appearance of this effect in the twentieth century probably reflects an increased importance of candidate-related factors in voting. Who the candidates are has become more consequential than party organizations. Alternatively, it may be that the political offices we label "prestigious" were not thought of as such in the 1800s (Kernell 1977). In any case, even in the current century, the effect of prestigious candidates is rather small.

FIGURE 6.5
Partial Effect of Nationally Prestigious Third
Party Candidate on Third Party Voting, 1840-1980

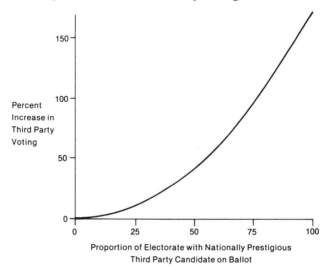

Proportion of Electorate with Nationally Prestigious
Third Party Candidate on Ballot

FIGURE 6.6
Partial Effect of Prestigious Third Party Candidate
on Third Party Voting, 1840-1980

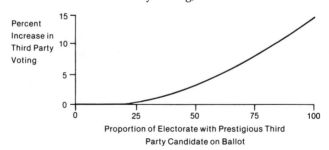

Proportion of Electorate with Prestigious Third
Party Candidate on Ballot

next quarter of the electorate having the candidate on their ballot is another 1.04-fold boost in support.

It is important to note that, in most instances, increasing the percentage of ballots a candidate is on does not provide him with a proportionate change in support. For example, if a prestigious candidate raises from 75 to 100 the percentage of citizens who find his name on their November ballots (a one-third increase), his vote total will go up merely 6 percent. Only nationally prestigious candidates, when they begin to approach universal ballot access, are rewarded with at least commensurate increases in support. For instance, when a nationally prestigious politician goes from being on three-quarters of the ballots to appearing on all of them, he enjoys a 75 percent boost in his vote.

These findings highlight an important difference between prestigious and nationally prestigious candidates. Prestigious challengers by and large court the support of a particular geographic region of the country with issues of interest only to that area. Once they have secured ballot positions in their locales, they gain little from winning additional ballot access. Strom Thurmond, for example, would have benefited negligibly from being on the Massachusetts ballot.

In contrast, nationally prestigious candidates, pursuing more universal issues, must demonstrate that they are indeed addressing the nation as a whole. They *are* well served by making it onto each state ballot, not only because they have supporters in every region of the country, but because the media, voters, and political elites view candidates who qualify for all fifty-one November ballots as more "serious" contenders than those who run in only a few states. Thus, when a nationally prestigious candidate qualifies nationwide, he benefits not only in the additional states he appears in but in his original pool of states as well.

A second reason for the increase in the marginal impact of additional spots on the ballot is that restrictive laws and major party tactics often deny candidates access to ballots in states where they are likely to do well. Eugene McCarthy's experience in 1976 is a good example. He failed to qualify in New

York and California, not because he had few supporters in those states, but because of onerous laws and the Democratic Party's vigorous campaign to keep him off those ballots.

Finally, it is more cost-effective, particularly in recent years, to run a campaign in every state than, say, in twenty or thirty. National network advertising, for instance, is cheaper than local media buys. And the exposure a candidate receives in one state often spills over to adjacent states in the same market (New York, New Jersey, and Connecticut, for example), but goes to waste if the candidate does not appear on all the ballots.

One way to illustrate the impact of ballot access restrictions on third party voting is to simulate what would have happened had McCarthy been on 100 percent of the ballots in 1976, instead of just the 63 percent he qualified for. Had he appeared on every state's ballot, McCarthy would have polled 4.3 percent of the vote, a dramatic improvement over his actual total of .9 percent. By the same token, if Anderson in 1980 had qualified for only as many ballots as McCarthy did in 1976, Anderson's vote would have dropped from 6.6 percent to only 1.7 percent, leaving him well below the critical 5 percent he needed to qualify for retroactive federal funding.

THIRD PARTY LOYALTY

Although voter loyalty to third parties can be quite strong, we find different patterns of minor party allegiance in the nineteenth and twentieth centuries. This difference directly reflects the metamorphosis of independent campaigns from party- to candidate-centered organizations.

Between 1840 and 1892 about 46 percent of those who voted for a third party in one election continued to do so in the subsequent one. However, the nature of this loyalty changed in the twentieth century, for few third parties persisted long enough to build voter allegiance. Prominent candidates no longer ran on the tickets of established minor parties, preferring instead to start their own parties. Moreover, when these candidates—Roosevelt, LaFollette, Lemke, Henry Wallace, Thurmond, and McCarthy—chose not to make a second run, their "parties" disappeared as well.[20] Hence only a few twentieth-century "parties" (most notably the socialists of various stripes and the Prohibitionists) could develop much loyalty among voters. These parties very seldom nominated prominent candidates to head their tickets.

Thus, in the twentieth century, the only continuity in third party voting occurred among citizens who supported non-prestigious candidates. People who voted for prestigious or nationally prestigious third party contenders in the twentieth century were no more likely than others to cast third party ballots in the next election because those prominent independents generally did not reappear. On the other hand, citizens who supported third parties led by non-prestigious candidates displayed about the same amount of loyalty as nineteenth-century voters; about 43 percent cast third party ballots in the subsequent election.

The findings suggest that although voters are initially driven to third parties by the short-term failures of the major parties, many, when given the opportunity, develop an allegiance to the minor party to which they defect. In the nineteenth century, a sizable share of third party support came from loyal voters. In the current era, however, third party support is due almost entirely to conditions unique to particular elections.

There is a second source of loyalty to third parties. We find that when immigrants from countries with viable socialist parties first enter the electorate, they are more prone than other voters to cast minor party ballots. As their proportion of the electorate rises 1 percent, third party support goes up .5 percent.[21] Because this group has never comprised more than 3 percent of the electorate, their contribution to aggregate

[20] At the time of this writing, Anderson had not yet decided whether to run in 1984.

[21] This effect does not hold for immigrants in general (coefficient = -2.3; standard error = -5.7), nor does it hold for immigrants from countries with multi-party systems (coefficient = -21.6; standard error = 27.8).

shifts in third party voting has been small. Yet their presence helps explain why support for American socialist parties crested when it did. The peak years for parties of the left—1904 to 1920—were also years when immigrants from countries with socialist parties comprised the largest share of the electorate. The Socialist Party vote reached its zenith in 1912, the year that first-time voters from countries with a socialist party tradition topped off at 2.9 percent of the electorate. As immigrants with socialist ties shrank to a smaller and smaller proportion of the electorate, Socialist support also declined. The big drop-off between 1920 and 1924 in the Socialist vote was due to a 50 percent reduction in the number of new voters with these preexisting loyalties.[22]

ALLEGIANCE TO THE MAJOR PARTIES

Allegiance to one of the two major parties substantially reduces the probability of citizens defecting to a third party cause (figure 6.7). Between 1952 and 1980, when a nationally prestigious third party candidate ran, voters with weak ties to the major parties were 37 percent more likely than the most attached to cast their lot with a third party candidate. The increase was about 27 percent when either a prestigious or non-prestigious third party contender appeared on the ballot. The impact is indirect: attachment to the major parties boosts voters' evaluations of the Democratic and Republican nominees, which in turn reduce their probability of third party voting.

Replacement of the realignment cohort with new voters who are less loyal to the major parties also produces third party voting. Citizens who entered the electorate between 1936 and 1956 (who were socialized during the New Deal but

[22] Because voters who cast a third party ballot can have strong loyalties to their third party causes, about four out of ten immigrants who vote for a third party will remain faithful third party voters in the election subsequent to their initial entry. Descriptively, then, foreign-born immigrants from countries with a viable socialist party, as a group, are more likely to be third party voters in any future elections. But they are no more loyal than other third party voters. (The coefficient for foreign-born from countries with a socialist party tradition is − .06 [standard error = .12].)

FIGURE 6.7
Effect of Evaluation of the Major Parties on
Third Party Voting, 1952-1980

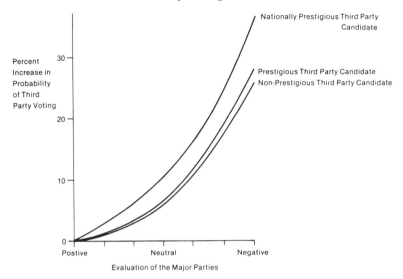

were not in the electorate at the time of the realignment) were about 2 percent more apt to vote for third parties than people who were eligible to vote in 1932 (figure 6.8). Voters who entered the electorate since 1960 have been about twice as likely as the 1936-1952 cohort to be third party supporters.[23]

This cohort effect is both direct and indirect. The post-1960 generation is twice as likely as the New Deal cohort to have both negative evaluations of the major party candidates and neutral or negative feelings towards the two major parties. The younger cohorts are also more attentive to issues than their New Deal counterparts. Thus a large part of the cohort effect is mediated by voter attentiveness to issues and by evaluation of the major parties and their nominees.[24]

[23] These findings also hold when AIPO data from the 1940-1948 elections are included in the analysis.

[24] Although the generation voters belong to has a clear effect on the likelihood they will abandon the major parties, youth itself does not increase the probability of defection. (The coefficient for age is .002 [standard error

FIGURE 6.8
Effect of Age Cohort on Third Party Voting, 1952-1980

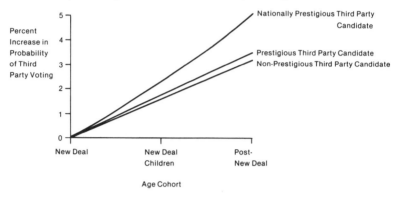

New voters, with weaker allegiance to a major party, were more likely to cast a third party ballot over the 1840-1980 period than were other members of the electorate. An increase in the proportion of first-time eligible voters in the electorate boosts the level of third party support. A 10 percent rise in the proportion of voters new to the electorate produces a 5 percent increase in third party backing. This, in part, explains the extent of third party voting that occurred between 1840 and 1924. During these years the electorate expanded much faster than in subsequent decades, providing a bigger pool of voters susceptible to third party appeals. For example, in the 1916 election, 23 percent of the electorate was voting for the first time, as compared with 10 percent in each context between 1952 and 1964. The rise in third party voting since 1964 stems in part from a slight increase in the rate at which the electorate has grown. (Most of this is due to the enfranchisement of 18- to 20-year olds and the baby boom generation coming of age.)

= .008]. Non-linear transformations of age do not improve matters.) Furthermore, there are no age-cohort interactions: age effects do not appear for a particular cohort, and the cohort effect does not vary with one's age.

ALLEGIANCE TO THE POLITICAL SYSTEM

Voters' social and economic class has no bearing on the likelihood that they will abandon the major parties. Those at the bottom rungs of the socio-economic ladder are no more disloyal to the major parties than are other citizens. The very poor are no more likely to defect to third parties than the very rich; those with the least prestigious occupations are no more prone to defect than people with the most enviable jobs; the less well-educated are no more apt to abandon the major parties than the well-educated.[25] None of these variables, at least over the 1952-1980 elections, has a significant direct effect on third party voting. Their indirect effects are also negligible (less than .2 percent). In sum, social class has absolutely nothing to do with the likelihood that people will remain loyal to the two parties.[26]

Blacks constitute the one social group that has remained persistently loyal to the two major parties. Between 1952 and 1980 blacks were 4 to 7 percent more loyal than whites to the major parties (chiefly the Democrats). (This finding is not solely an artifact of George Wallace's 1968 candidacy; black loyalty was high in other years as well.) It seems this result is a general one: Hanes Walton, Jr. found that despite Prohibitionist, Greenback, Populist, and Progressive appeals, few blacks defected to these parties (1969). Several factors explain their hesitency to defect. Some third party candidate's racist appeals naturally have made them anathema to blacks. Many candidates who did advocate increased civil rights usually found those stands would cost them more votes than they would gain, leading them to weaken their commitment to racial progress. Finally, the major parties have responded to

[25] The coefficient for education was .001 (standard error − .03); the effect of income was − .01 (standard error = .12) for the richest third of the population and .09 (standard error = .16) for the poorest third. We estimated the effect of occupation with separate dummy variables for each occupational category and none had either a substantive or statistically significant effect. Union families were no more prone than other citizens to support third party causes.

[26] Lemieux reaches a similar conclusion in his analysis of the Liberal Party's vote in Britain (1977, ch. 2).

minor party attempts to attract black support. Truman's reaction to Henry Wallace's 1948 freedom pledge is one example. Blacks have generally seen the major parties as offering their best hope for achieving their goals.

Feelings of powerlessness, though widely believed to have
been an important cause of defection to George Wallace in
1968, do not in general produce third party voting. Once other
variables have been taken into account, people who feel unable to affect the decisions of government do not turn to third
parties as a recourse any more often than does anyone else.[27]
Similarly, those who experience status inconsistency—whether
measured by gaps between their level of education and income, occupation and income, education and occupation, or
income and subjective social class—are not more likely to
abandon the major parties.[28]

Although citizens with less stake in the political and economic system by virtue of their position in society are not apt
to see third parties as an avenue of recourse, voters who are
unhappy with the performance of the government are more
willing to try a third party alternative. Between 1968 and 1980
citizens least trustful of government—those who felt that the
people running the government were crooked, wasted money,
could not be trusted to do the right thing, and were controlled
by a few big interests—were about 10 percent more prone to
abandon the two major parties at election time. The effect is
indirect: those who distrust the government are more likely
to evaluate the parties and candidates in terms of issues; this
kind of evaluation in turn leads to increased third party voting. The decline in citizen trust in government since the mid-

[27] The effect of efficacy between 1952 and 1980 was $-.10$ (standard error
$= .15$). The effect when a prestigious or nationally prestigious third party
candidate ran between 1968 and 1980 was $.27$ (standard error $= .17$). This
conclusion is intuitively sound. Given that a third party candidate will certainly lose, it seems hard to believe that the inefficacious would be more
likely to cast a third party ballot than citizens who feel their actions have
political consequence.

[28] Regardless of the measure used, the effect is insignificant. When all four
measures are combined into a single scale, the effect remains insignificant
(coefficient $= -.19$; standard error $= .21$).

FIGURE 6.9
Effect of Political Disaffection on
Third Party Voting, 1968-1980

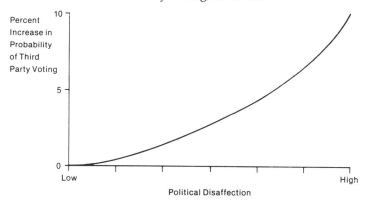

1960s partly explains the aggregate rise in third party voting since that time.

In summary, although distrust in government increases third party voting, allegiance to the political and economic system as a whole does not anchor voters to the Democrats and Republicans. Loyalty to the major parties is the prime deterrent to third party voting. Loyalty to the political system plays a very small role.

CONCLUSIONS

Major party failure is the primary force motivating third party voting in America. When the two major parties deteriorate—when they neglect the concerns of significant blocs of voters, mismanage the economy, or nominate unqualified candidates—voters turn to a third party alternative. Prominent third party challengers, and to a lesser extent minor party loyalties, also prompt citizens to abandon the major parties.

In addition to the factors that drive the electorate to support third parties, unavoidable demographic shifts weaken aggregate allegiance to the major parties and thus increase the level of third party voting. The arrival of immigrants from countries

with viable socialist parties, the enfranchisement of new generations of native-born voters, and the gradual replacement
of the loyal realignment cohort, all cut into major party dominance. These factors, of course, are beyond the control of
either the major parties or third party challengers. Hence,
regardless of how well the major parties perform, periodic
bursts of third party voting are unavoidable.

The theory presented here is a general one: it accounts for
fluctuations in minor party strength over time and explains
seemingly disparate kinds of third party movements. One
way to illustrate this generalizability is to show that the conclusions apply equally well to two ostensibly very different
candidates—George Wallace and John Anderson. Wallace's
support was strongest in the South, Anderson's in the Northeast; Wallace drew from the poor, Anderson from the well-
off; Wallace from the least educated, Anderson from the best
educated; Wallace from conservatives, Anderson from liberals. Despite these descriptive differences in their constituencies, our aggregate model explains fairly accurately the vote
in both years. It predicts that 10.4 percent of the electorate
would abandon the major parties in 1968 and that 8.7 percent
would do so in 1980—off by 3.5 and .5 points respectively.
Similar factors motivated people to vote for each candidate
(table 6.3). Disaffection with the major parties and their nominees increased the likelihood of citizens casting ballots for
both independent candidates. The more concerned voters were
with the issues, the more prone they were to end up in a
third party camp. In both instances, the latest cohorts to enter
the electorate—those with the weakest allegiance to the major
parties—were most likely to support the independent candidates. And black loyalty to the major parties was evident
not only in 1968 but in 1980 as well.

Our findings identify fundamental changes in third parties
at the turn of the century. Who the candidates were became
more significant than the parties they headed. Experienced
politicians became more willing to form new organizations,
so important parties were not on the scene long enough to
build allegiance in voters. Loyalty to minor parties *can* be

TABLE 6.3
Sources of Support for George Wallace and John Anderson

	Percentage Voting for George Wallace	Percentage Voting for John Anderson
Evaluation of the major parties		
Positive	5.2	4.2
Neutral	7.5	10.5
Negative	16.0	11.5
Evaluation of the major party candidates		
Positive	6.1	4.2
Neutral	21.9	10.4
Negative	38.7	29.8
Age cohort		
New Deal	8.7	1.9
New Deal children	11.8	5.4
Post–New Deal	15.9	9.7
Race		
White	12.5	7.8
Black	0	1.0
Concern with issues		
Low	10.9	6.1
Medium	10.9	9.1
High	15.5	10.3

cultivated, but obviously only when parties endure. The continuous parties of the twentieth century have enjoyed the same level of voter allegiance as their nineteenth-century counterparts, but few prominent candidates have taken advantage of this potential for enduring loyalty.

APPENDIX

FIGURE 6.10
Determinants of Third Party Voting, 1968-1980: Structural Model

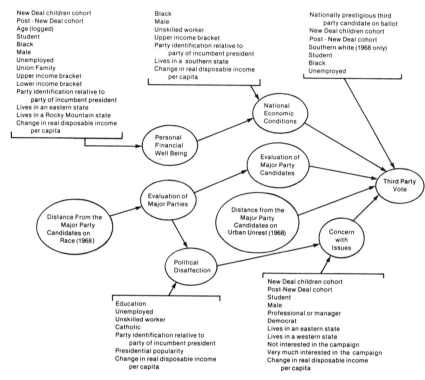

TABLE 6.4
Determinants of Third Party Voting, 1968-1980: Estimated Equations

	Equation[a]				
	(1)	(2)	(3)	(4)	(5)
		Concern		*National*	*Personal*
	Third Party	*with*	*Political*	*Economic*	*Financial*
Variable	*Vote*	*Issues*	*Disaffection*	*Conditions*	*Well Being*
Evaluation of the major party candidates[b]	−4.199 (1.085)				
Evaluation of the major parties[b]			−.668 (.311)		
Concern with issues[b]	1.197 (.669)	.583 (.101)			
Political disaffection[b]	−.737 (.329)				
National economic conditions[b]					
Personal financial well being[b]				.330 (.079)	
Distance from the major party candidates on urban unrest issue in 1968[b]	2.031 (.424)				
Nationally prestigious third party candidate on ballot	.165 (.137)				
New Deal children cohort	.312 (.183)	.039 (.020)			−.088 (.034)
Post–New Deal cohort	.404 (.205)	.051 (.020)			−.098 (.056)

TABLE 6.4 (cont.)

	Equation[a]				
Variable	(1) Third Party Vote	(2) Concern with Issues	(3) Political Disaffection	(4) National Economic Conditions	(5) Personal Financial Well Being
Age (logged)					−.278 (.053)
Southern white (1968 only)	.227 (.181)				−.217 (.072)
Student	.283 (.207)	.094 (.051)			−.040 (.032)
Black	−.861 (.339)			−.064 (.031)	.033 (.018)
Male		.051 (.013)	−.014 (.004)	.040 (.004)	
Education					
Unemployed	.674 (.236)		.073 (.030)		−.206 (.051)
Professional or manager		.034 (.013)			
Unskilled worker			.034 (.014)	−.053 (.023)	
Union family				.046 (.019)	−.033 (.021)
Upper-income bracket					.074 (.021)
Lower-income bracket					−.055 (.026)
Catholic			−.035 (.013)		
Democrat		−.050 (.013)			
Party identification relative to party of incumbent president			−.040 (.005)	.044 (.009)	.028 (.009)
Lives in an Eastern state		−.011 (.015)			
Lives in a Western state		.052 (.019)			−.064 (.021)
Lives in a Rocky Mountain state					−.096 (.043)

	(1)	(2)	(3)	(4)	(5)
Lives in a Southern state					.033 (.020)
Not interested in the campaign		−.066 (.020)			
Very much interested in the campaign		.088 (.014)			
Presidential popularity			1.822 (.220)		
Change in real disposable income per capita	.719 (.825)	1.427 (.388)	−8.670 (.847)	8.754 (.443)	2.062 (.457)
Constant		−.095 (.074)	.376 (.137)	.167 (.040)	1.606 (.231)
Standard error of estimate	.228	.276	.220	.364	.383
R^2					.109
N = 1,910					

[a] Equation (1) is estimated by two-stage probit; equations (2), (3), and (4) are estimated by two-stage least squares; equation (5) is estimated by ordinary least squares. A blank cell in the table indicates that the variable (read off the row) had an estimated coefficient indistinguishable from zero in that equation (read off the column). The coding of the variables is described in appendix B. Equations for the voter's evaluation of the major party candidates, evaluation of the major parties, distance from the major party candidates on urban unrest in 1968, and distance from major party candidates on racial issues in 1968 were also estimated, although their coefficients are not reported in this table.
[b] Endogenous variable.

CHAPTER 7

CANDIDATE MOBILIZATION

THE RELATIVE success of a third party depends in part on who heads its ticket: support is highest when a prestigious or nationally prestigious politician runs. Because the quality of the challengers has such a large impact on the level of minor party strength, our theory of third party voting must account for why these candidates bolt the major parties when they do.

Few if any third party challengers seriously think they will win. Experienced politicians certainly recognize that as third party candidates they will suffer from all the biases and disadvantages that have plagued their predecessors. Even Theodore Roosevelt, the most advantaged third party candidate of the century, understood that he was unlikely to be victorious. In a letter to a friend the former president confessed: "Do not get the idea into your head that I am going to win this fight, it was a fight that had to be made and there was no alternative to my making it" (Bishop 1920, p. 319).

And yet prominent politicians do run. Despite the biases and the inevitable risk of political excommunication, prestigious third party candidates have emerged in two out of five elections since 1840, and nationally prestigious candidates have run in one out of every four contests.

Some candidates run more willingly than others. Nineteenth-century third parties frequently had to persuade prominent politicians to head their tickets. Free Soilers, for instance, had to convince former President Martin Van Buren to overcome his stated "unchangeable determination never again to be a candidate," before he would lead their cause in 1848 (Lynch 1929, p. 514). In contrast, most prestigious and nationally prestigious third party candidates of the twentieth century have been self-starters. The candidate recruited the movement, not the other way around. As Carlson observed, "the AIP [American Independent Party] was not an integrated, functioning party; it existed only as a vehicle for Wallace's candidacy" (1981, p. 74). Similarly, John Anderson created the National Unity Campaign. It did not exist before him and probably will not survive without him.

Although some politicians must be persuaded to become independents, ultimately, of course, the decision to run rests with the candidates themselves. A politician will not mount a third party challenge unless he believes it is in his best interest to do so. There is no shortage of examples of people who resisted the pressure because they felt a campaign would be futile or too costly. As we all remember, Arkansas Governor Orval Faubus chose to run for reelection rather than head the National States' Rights Party ticket in 1960. George Wallace sat out the 1964 campaign, as did Eugene McCarthy in 1968.

Given that the chances of victory are so remote, other considerations must motivate these candidates to embark on third party crusades. Some run to promote important issues, others to establish themselves as incontrovertible political forces, and still others to seek revenge or vindication in their fight for a political cause. A few may even believe, if only for a fleeting moment, that they can win. But, regardless of a candidate's specific goal, the only way he can hope to achieve it is by winning votes. To advance a cause, a challenger cannot merely publicize it, he must demonstrate public support for it as well. Only then will one or both of the major parties adopt the issue as their own. Votes are also needed to exact revenge. Without them the most a candidate can hope to be is a nuisance. It is reasonable, then, to expect that prestigious and nationally prestigious politicians will run when they think their candidacies will attract votes. Moreover, since a third party bid may cost a prominent politician his career, it is also reasonable to think that he will be selective about when he runs.

We assume that, like all politicians, potential third party candidates think strategically.[1] Prominent politicians, who have

---

[1] For other treatments of politicians as strategic actors, see Schlesinger (1966), Black (1972), and Jacobson and Kernell (1981).

had years of electioneering experience and have demonstrated their political savvy with their previous electoral successes, presumably have the skills necessary to identify those occasions when a third party run might prove profitable.

The decision to mount a minor party challenge is not made in a vacuum. Politicians monitor the political and economic environments to gauge the vote-getting potential of a third party candidacy and embark on campaigns only when they perceive that they will be able to garner votes to advance their causes. As conditions change, so do the odds that prominent challengers will emerge. Our purpose in this chapter is to determine how prestigious and nationally prestigious politicians decide whether to run.

In an effort to assess the likelihood of successfully reaching their goals, potential candidates may take into account four general sets of considerations. Politicians, like the voters, may bolt when the major parties have deteriorated—when the major party nominees fail to represent a large issue constituency, when one or both of the major parties have had a particularly divisive nominating convention that left a faction discontented, or when there is widespread economic suffering. Potential candidates also notice whether these conditions have dislodged other political elites—campaign contributors and organizers—and ultimately voters.

Intra-party feuds usually leave an important figure on the losing side. When they do, the slighted politician may give up on his old party as a means of achieving his goals and instead try to capture the White House as an independent. With the possible exception of Breckinridge, all nine nationally prestigious third party candidates who emerged over the past 140 years were snubbed by their own parties before they ran. Van Buren, Fillmore, Roosevelt, LaFollette, George Wallace, McCarthy, and Anderson all lost bids for their own party's nomination. Henry Wallace was ousted from his post as Commerce Secretary by President Truman.

Like the voters, political leaders regard a minor party as a path of last resort. National politicians first pursue their goals within the major parties. Only when this route has been closed off do they make a third party run.

Prominent politicians may also be more willing to abandon the major parties when a minor party looks particularly strong. Periods of third party vitality, as reflected by the standing of third parties in previous presidential or congressional elections, may signal would-be candidates that a third party challenge would prove profitable. When third parties have been doing well, politicians may reason that popular and elite support will continue and that they will benefit from prior groundwork and organizational efforts.

Prestigious and nationally prestigious politicians may also be sensitive to changes in the composition of the electorate, making them more likely to mount a third party challenge when those voters who are most susceptible to third party appeals are abundant. If this is a valid assumption, then when voter allegiance to the party system is weak—when the critical election is long past, when a large proportion of the electorate is newly enfranchised, or when many are first-time voters from countries with viable socialist parties—prominent politicians will be more likely to run.

Finally, candidates may be sensitive to procedural changes in the electoral system and may be most willing to challenge the major parties when the barriers to running as an independent are lowest. If so, then changes in the rules governing third party access to the general election ballot should significantly affect the likelihood that prominent challengers will emerge.

Given the differences between prestigious and nationally prestigious candidates' political experience, the personal risk they assume from a third party run, and the goals they hope to achieve, we do not expect that these two groups of politicians will necessarily respond to the same political cues. It should take more to move a nationally prestigious figure to candidacy than it takes to get a prestigious politician to run. National prestige should indicate a candidate has more political acumen than a challenger without a national base. Furthermore, prestigious politicians with national reputations have obviously gone further up the political ladder and therefore have more to lose by antagonizing their major party.

In addition, their goals often differ. Nationally prestigious candidates have historically struck out in behalf of national concerns, whereas prestigious contenders have advanced the needs of particular regions of the country. Preserving the union, taming corporate barons, and toning down the Cold War—these are the causes of nationally prestigious candidates. In contrast, regionally prominent figures have carried the farmers' banner. For all these reasons, we expect to find differences between the decision rules that nationally prestigious and prestigious candidates use when contemplating third party runs.

We estimate two equations to assess the causes of candidate mobilization: one for the probability that a nationally prestigious third party challenger will emerge in a given year, and the other for the probability that a prestigious third party contender will run. The unit of analysis is a presidential election; 1840 is the first observation, 1980 the last. The dependent variable in each equation is whether that type of candidate ran for president outside the major parties in that year. The independent variables are the factors that prompt prestigious and nationally prestigious politicians to run. (The coding of the variables and the sources of the data are described in appendix B.) Because the dependent variables are dichotomous (1 if a nationally prestigious third party challenger ran, O otherwise; 1 if a prestigious third party challenger ran, O otherwise), we use probit analysis to estimate the marginal effect of each variable on candidate mobilization. As noted in the last chapter, a probit coefficient is not as easy to interpret as the more familiar least squares estimate: it represents the amount of change on the cumulative normal distribution that results from a unit change in the causal variable. To simplify the interpretation of these estimates, we again convert the probit coefficients to probabilities and discuss how much each variable affects candidate mobilization.[2]

---

[2] This is estimated by computing, separately for each year, the marginal effect of each variable on candidate mobilization. The mean of these thirty-

Why Nationally Prestigious Third Party Candidates Run

Table 7.1 reports the estimated coefficients for the variables that affect the likelihood of nationally prestigious politicians running on a third party ticket. Variables deleted from this equation had substantively and statistically insignificant effects on the emergence of these candidates. Each variable that remains in the equation has at least a .93 probability of being different from zero.[3] The equation provides an extremely good fit to the data: 94 percent of the cases are correctly predicted; only two of the thirty-six years are missed. We fail to account for Van Buren's run in 1848, and we incorrectly predict that a nationally prestigious third party candidate would appear in 1852. (Of course, the error may have been Van Buren's.)

When the major parties deteriorate, prominent politicians, like the voters, turn to third parties. Leaders abandon the

TABLE 7.1

When Nationally Prestigious Third Party Candidates Run, 1840-1980: Probit Estimates

Variable	Coefficient	Standard Error
Age of the party system (logged)	3.52	1.85
Major party factionalism (national level)	26.08	15.52
Incumbent president running	3.45	2.02
Closeness of previous presidential election	1.16	.65
President denied his party's renomination	3.98	2.21
Constant	−12.01	6.50

$R^2 = .77$
X^2 (5 degrees of freedom) = 27.79 (pr < .001)
Standard error of estimate = .26
94 percent of cases correctly predicted (null model = 75 percent)
N = 36

six probabilities is the aggregate estimate of the variable's impact on candidate emergence.

[3] The coefficients are stable over the thirty-six elections, as is the variance of the residuals. There is also no autocorrelation (rho = −.19).

major parties because they are encouraged to do so by other disgruntled elites, because they are discontented with the political choices the party's majority faction has made, and because the major parties appear to be vulnerable. Weak major parties lead prominent politicians to believe that a third party candidacy would attract voters' support. In general, the more vulnerable the major parties, the more likely it is that prominent politicians will run.

Dissension within the Major Parties

A politician will not even contemplate a third party run until the major parties force him to. Realizing that the constraints against third parties are formidable, if not insurmountable, prominent politicians first try to reach their goals through the major parties. Some seek the adoption of a particular policy position, others the presidential nomination itself. When a politician and his followers are rebuffed by their party, discord results. This conflict within the ranks of the major parties usually surfaces in the selection of their presidential candidates. If the losing factions are large, widespread elite and mass disaffection with the nominees probably exists. To a would-be candidate, a large bloc of disgruntled delegates indicates that the major parties are vulnerable and that there is a pool of potential supporters that could be wooed by a third party effort.

We find that between 1840 and 1980 the larger the size of the losing faction at the major party conventions, the more likely it is that a nationally prestigious politician will mount a third party campaign[4] (figure 7.1). Years with the least major party factionalism (1872, 1900, 1916, and 1936) do not produce nationally prestigious third party candidates. As party divisiveness rises, so does the likelihood of a nationally prestigious politician bolting. When 10 percent of the delegates to the major party conventions are on the losing side (as in 1864,

[4] Nationally prestigious third party candidates look at the size of the losing faction in both parties, not only their own.

FIGURE 7.1
Partial Effect of Major Party Factionalism
(National Level) on Nationally Prestigious
Third Party Candidate Mobilization, 1840-1980

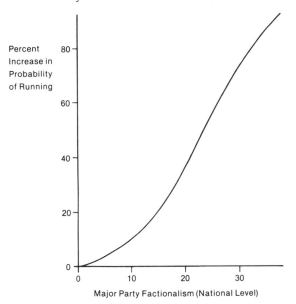

1896, and 1904), a nationally prestigious politician is 10 percent more likely to run than during the most harmonious
years. When the losing factions comprise 20 percent of the
delegates (as in 1852, 1884, 1920, 1940, and 1980), a nationally
prestigious politician is 36 percent more likely to run. When
25 percent of the delegates support a runner-up (as in 1868,
1912, and 1948), the probability of a nationally prestigious
third party candidate running jumps by 55 percent. In the
most factionalized years—1856 and 1860—nationally prestigious politicians are 93 percent more likely to emerge than
during the most harmonious times.[5]

[5] We must consider whether it is factionalism that produces third party
candidacies or third party candidates that generate divisive conventions. The
former seems to be the case: historically, factionalism has preceded prominent

Theodore Roosevelt's Progressive candidacy is a clear example of a nationally prestigious politician running because his faction lost its bid to control one of the major parties. Roosevelt came to the 1912 Republican convention with strong backing from the progressive wing of the party, but his sweeping primary victories were not enough to overcome incumbent Taft's control of the convention and eventual nomination. Although Roosevelt sensed the depth of his support before the Republican convention began, he did not make himself available as a third party candidate until after he failed to capture the nomination.

Of course, factionalism at a convention is not a cause of a candidate's emergence in and of itself. Rather, it indicates two conditions that are likely to produce major party vulnerability: intra-party disagreement over prominent issues, and large-scale disaffection with the party nominees (for reasons other than their stands on issues).

Disputes over issues are an important cause of major party divisiveness. When two factions hold conflicting positions, they usually end up doing battle over the party's platform and the nominee. Discontented delegates are the result. The presence of large losing factions means there are politicians, and probably voters, who are unhappy with the policy positions of at least one of the major party candidates. A nationally prestigious politician examines the fit between the policy stands of the major party nominees and the preferences of the electorate on the salient issues of the day. As the proportion of the voters estranged from the positions of the major party candidates grows, the emergence of a nationally prestigious third party candidate becomes more likely.

Several third party candidacies fit this pattern. Clearly Teddy Roosevelt's faction at the convention disagreed sharply with

---

politicians' decisions to mount third party campaigns rather than the other way around. In some instances where there were high levels of factionalism and a nationally prestigious third party candidate—Theodore Roosevelt, Martin Van Buren, and John Breckinridge—the candidates emerged only after the major party conventions had taken place. In none of the divisive years when nationally prestigious politicians ran can the third party be said to have caused the factionalism.

Taft's. The Bull Moose campaign was precipitated by this feud. George Wallace ran in 1968 because the major party nominees' stands left conservatives on racial and urban unrest issues unrepresented. Wallace seized the opportunity to capture the conservative vote. This is to be contrasted with 1964, when Wallace aborted a third party campaign after Goldwater, a civil rights conservative, secured the G.O.P. nomination.

Prominent politicians are also prompted to run as third party candidates when the major party nominees fail altogether to address an issue that is important to a large number of voters. Former President Martin Van Buren's decision to run on the Free Soil ticket in 1848 was heavily influenced by his inability to get the Democratic Party leadership to grapple with several issues he considered crucial, slavery chief among them. Van Buren forces arrived at the 1848 convention ready to fight for adoption of the anti-slavery platform. However, when the Cass–Polk faction that dominated the proceedings was able to stifle discussion of the issue, Van Buren's supporters protested by marching out of the convention hall. Since the Whigs were equally unwilling to address the slavery question, Van Buren subsequently accepted the nomination of the newly formed Free Soil Party "owing to the combination of principle and a thirst for revenge" (Hamilton 1971, p. 870).

The presence of party factionalism also suggests that many politicians and voters find the major party nominees unacceptable for reasons other than their stands on issues. When the candidates barely win nomination, it sometimes indicates that elites and voters do not perceive them as trustworthy, capable, competent, honest, or up to the job of being president. Voters in 1980, for instance, were twice as likely to have negative rather than positive evaluations of the major party nominees. (In contrast, positive evaluations outnumbered negative ones by as much as four to one in 1952, 1956, and 1960 [CPS National Election Studies]). This widespread disaffection with Reagan and Carter clearly was an impetus to Anderson's decision to run.

Incumbent Presidents as Targets

Third party campaigns are frequently campaigns *against* an incumbent president. Between 1840 and 1980 nationally prestigious politicians were 28 percent more likely to mount a third party challenge when an incumbent president was seeking another term than when one was not. Five nationally prestigious third party candidates have challenged sitting presidents: Roosevelt, LaFollette, Henry Wallace, McCarthy, and Anderson. With the possible exception of McCarthy, each of these independents zeroed in on the incumbent president. It is easy to understand why the man in the White House serves as a lightning rod. A sitting president makes a good target: his positions and his accomplishments (or lack of them) are clear.[6] When no incumbent president is in the race, this source of irritation is absent and the target of a third party effort is more ambiguous.

Theodore Roosevelt's decision to run in 1912 was clearly spurred by animosity towards President Taft. Roosevelt felt personally betrayed by his hand-picked successor's failure to implement progressive reforms, Taft's dismissal of Roosevelt appointees, and the U.S. Steel suit. Until this suit, Roosevelt adamantly distanced himself from the 1912 Republican race.[7] His resulting animosity towards Taft was at least partially responsible for Roosevelt's Bull Moose candidacy. Had Taft not sought renomination, Roosevelt probably would have sat out the 1912 race. But faced with the prospect of four more years of policies that he vehemently opposed, and armed with the belief that large numbers of voters shared his distaste for Taft's actions, Roosevelt launched his independent challenge.

[6] All five campaigns against incumbents occurred in the twentieth century. Nineteenth-century presidents, considerably less powerful than their twentieth-century counterparts, were less relevant targets. Third party campaigns of the era were just as negative as more recent ones, but the objects of scorn were parties, not presidents. This parallels our other observations that individuals have replaced parties as the political actors of importance.

[7] Mowry claims that "the only logical explanation" for Roosevelt's sudden entry into the campaign "is that his irritation with Taft, which had been almost continual since 1909, had broken all bounds with the institution of the steel suit" (1946, p. 197).

Our finding that nationally prestigious politicians are more likely to run when incumbent presidents are in the race implies that these candidates are not guided strictly by their calculated probability of victory. Incumbents, after all,

> have advantages over their challengers—advantages that can be directly translated into votes on election day. They control political resources, enjoy the prestige and symbols of office, profit from their tremendous amount of press coverage, both before and during the campaign, and are likely to be more widely known than their opponents, to encounter weak challengers, and to structure events in their favor. (Rosenstone 1983, p. 86)

If third party challengers were trying to win, they would not run against incumbent presidents.

Rebuffed Presidents

When a current or former president is rebuffed in an attempt to capture his party's renomination, as were Martin Van Buren in 1884, Millard Filmore in 1852, Chester Arthur in 1848, and Theodore Roosevelt in 1912, some party leaders and supporters are sure to be disaffected. In these circumstances, the probability that a nationally prestigious third party candidate (the jilted ex-president) will emerge within the next two elections increases by 40 percent. Three of these four deposed presidents mounted minor party challenges following their rejection. The pattern is familiar: politicians abandon their major party only when pushed.[8]

Electoral Signs of Major Party Vulnerability

Recent election returns that signal major party vulnerability affect the likelihood of a nationally prestigious politician head-

---

[8] Although one vice-president (Henry Wallace) who later ran as a third party candidate was also rejected by his party, deposed vice-presidents, as a rule, are not more likely to become independents (coefficient = .80; standard error = 1.61).

ing a third party. The greater the winner's margin of victory in a presidential election, the higher is the probability that a nationally prestigious third party candidate will emerge in the subsequent contest (figure 7.2). Compared to the closest elections (1880, 1884, 1888, 1960, and 1976), a 15 percent margin of victory (as in 1892, 1928, and 1932) boosts the probability of a nationally prestigious third party candidate running by 23 percent. Electoral landslides (as in 1920, 1924, 1936, 1964, and 1972) where the winner trounces his opponent by over 20 points raise by about 30 percent the likelihood of a nationally prestigious politician embarking on a third party crusade in the subsequent election.

There are several reasons why nationally prestigious politicians are more apt to run when the president's margin of victory in the previous election is high. If it appears that support for one of the major parties is weak, then an astute

FIGURE 7.2
Partial Effect of Closeness of Previous
Presidential Election on Nationally
Prestigious Third Party Candidate
Mobilization, 1840-1980

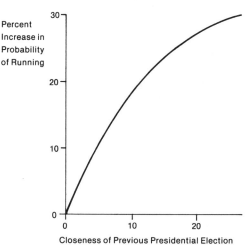

Closeness of Previous Presidential Election

politician may believe that many voters are disgruntled with the party and can be persuaded to join a new one. Alternatively, he may reason that a party coalition has grown too large and too diverse to be stable (Broder 1971; Cameron 1981). Several factions will inevitably be disappointed by the president's actions. Some supporters will likely desert in the next election, and an independent may run in an attempt to scoop up the defectors.

This finding further supports our claim that third party candidates run to gain votes, not to affect election outcomes. If nationally prestigious candidates were mounting campaigns in an effort to change outcomes, then close presidential elections—when a shift of a few votes to a third party candidate could make a big difference in who wins—would prompt them to run.[9] But just the opposite holds: nationally prestigious politicians appear after landslides, not cliffhangers. Nationally prestigious politicians are not more likely to run in tight contests or in years when a small change in popular vote in a few states might alter the outcome or cause a deadlock in the Electoral College.[10]

Age of the Party System

Finally, we find that nationally prestigious candidates are more likely to emerge when party systems are old and decaying than when they are relatively new. Immediately after a critical

[9] The margin of victory in a given election is an indicator of the margin in the subsequent contest. The following equation represents the strength of the relationship between the closeness of the outcome of adjacent elections:

$$\text{Closeness}_t = -.66 + .74\,(\text{Closeness}_{t-4})$$
$$(.11)$$

$\text{Rho} = -.68$
$R^2 = .60$

where $\text{Closeness}_t = \text{Log}_e |\text{Democratic percent of presidential popular vote}_t - \text{Republican percent of presidential popular vote}_t|$.

[10] Citizens do not engage in strategic considerations either. Their likelihood of supporting a third party candidate does not increase as the candidate's probability of affecting the outcome rises. This conclusion is inconsistent with those reached by Lemieux (1977, p. 177) and Cain (1978, p. 645) for Britain.

realignment, the major parties enjoy the loyalty of both voters and elites. With time, the probability of a nationally prestigious third party candidate running increases (figure 7.3). By the fifth election in the party system (for example, 1844, 1876, 1912, and 1948), nationally prestigious third party candidates are 8 percent more prone to run than at the beginning of the system. By the tenth election (for example, 1968), they are 34 percent more apt to run, and by the thirteenth (for example, 1980), 47 percent more likely to emerge.

With the exception of 1860, when the Republicans were running in only their second presidential election (perhaps a reason to believe that they could be displaced), no nationally prestigious candidate has emerged before the fifth election of a party system. Early in the system, parties align around

FIGURE 7.3
Partial Effect of Age of Party
System on Nationally Prestigious
Third Party Candidate Mobilization,
1840-1980

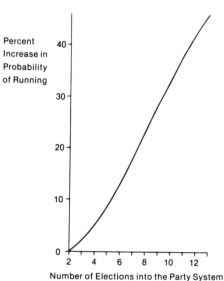

Number of Elections into the Party System

salient issues, major parties address those concerns, and voters divide along those lines. With time, the issues that form the basis for the political alignment fade in importance and the predominant cleavage between the major parties becomes less relevant. The proportion of voters who were not in the electorate at the time of the critical election increases. Towards the end of a party system, some prominent politicians are more willing to embark on a third party venture because they, like the voters, have concerns different from the major parties, and because there is a large reservoir of citizens who are weakly tied to the existing political alignment. In short, nationally prestigious third party candidates emerge when the party system is so old that new issues have become salient, a new cohort less committed to the prevailing alignment has been enfranchised, and the cleavages between the major parties have become cloudy.

This observation implies that the longer the interval *between* realignments, the more likely nationally prestigious politicians are to bolt the major parties. Thus the proliferation of nationally prestigious candidates in recent years (Wallace in 1968, McCarthy in 1976, and Anderson in 1980) is due in part to political elites' restlessness with the failure of the major parties to realign around a new, more salient set of concerns.

Summary

Nationally prestigious third party challengers do not just pop up at random; rather, they employ a clear decision rule. These candidates emerge when they perceive weaknesses in the two major parties. They run either when the major parties have disappointed a large minority faction, when the major parties do not pay sufficient attention to the issues of concern to the voters, when there is an incumbent president on which to focus discontent, or when the previous election suggests that one major party may be too weak or too large to hold its supporters together. Finally, jilted ex-presidents are especially likely to become independents.

Why Prestigious Third Party Candidates Run

We performed a similar analysis to identify the forces that prompt prestigious third party candidates to run. The resulting probit estimates are reported in table 7.2. As before, we deleted variables from this equation that had an insignificant effect on the emergence of candidates. Each remaining variable has at least a .97 probability of being different from zero. The equation correctly predicts 72 percent of the cases.[11]

Several important differences between the motivations of the two kinds of candidates are immediately apparent. First, we are better able to explain why nationally prestigious politicians make third party runs than why prestigious candidates do (94 percent of the cases in the first group are correctly predicted; 72 percent of the latter).[12] This difference is to be expected: an occasional former congressman may run for idio-

TABLE 7.2
When Prestigious Third Party Candidates Run, 1840-1980:
Probit Estimates

Variable	Coefficient	Standard Error
Major party factionalism (regional level) (squared)	2.58	1.28
Long term change in agricultural prices	− 3.78	1.62
Third party presidential vote $_{(t-4)}$ (logged)	.88	.34
Constant	2.08	.98

R^2 = .59
X^2 (3 degrees of freedom) = 12.55 (pr < .001)
Standard error of estimate = .44
72 percent of cases correctly predicted (null model = 58 percent)
N = 36

[11] These coefficients are also stable over the thirty-six elections, as is the variance of the residuals. No autocorrelation appears here either (rho = − .09). The residuals from this equation are also uncorrelated with the residuals from the equation for nationally prestigious third party candidate emergence (r = − .03).

[12] The standard error of the estimate for the nationally prestigious third party candidate equation is .26; it is .44 for the prestigious third party candidate equation.

syncratic reasons, but ex-presidents, vice-presidents, and other national figures, having more to lose and being more adept at reading political tea leaves, are more careful to respond to cues that signal the availability of votes. The second difference is that the factors motivating prestigious politicians to mount a third party challenge are different from the forces moving nationally prestigious politicians to do so. No variable affects both groups of candidates; prestigious and nationally prestigious candidates run for different reasons. This too is to be expected: prestigious candidates have different goals and respond to different constituencies than their nationally prestigious counterparts. Whereas nationally prestigious candidates react to signs that the major parties have ignored national concerns, prestigious candidates respond more to the specific concerns of their own region.

Regional Dissension within the Major Parties

Prestigious third party candidates, like their national counterparts, react to party factionalism. When the parties are factionalized nationwide, a nationally prestigious third party candidate surfaces. But prestigious third party candidates run when discontent is concentrated in a particular region of the country. The larger the proportion of the major party delegates from any region supporting the first runner-up at either major party's convention, the higher is the probability a prestigious candidate will emerge (figure 7.4). Compared to a year when every region supports the parties' nominees (as in 1900, 1916, and 1936), a prestigious challenger is 8 percent more likely to mount a third party effort when about one in three delegates in a single region backs the first runner-up (as in 1840, 1896, 1920, and 1956). The marginal effect of regional factionalism increases with the amount of divisiveness. When half a region's delegates oppose the nominee, the probability of a prestigious politician bolting jumps 17 percent. When approximately 90 percent of a region supports the losing candidate (as in 1852, 1868, 1948, and 1976), the probability of a prestigious politician running increases by 54 percent.

FIGURE 7.4
Partial Effect of Major Party Factionalism
(Regional Level) on Prestigious Third
Party Candidate Mobilization, 1840-1980

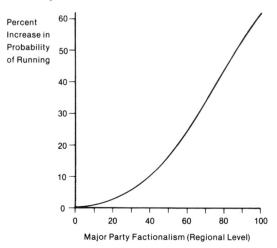

Major Party Factionalism (Regional Level)

It stands to reason that prestigious politicians respond to regional cues whereas national politicians react only to more universal signs. National candidates, after all, have more to lose and can only consider running if their potential base of support extends beyond a single section of the country. Prestigious candidates, on the other hand, who by definition have never run a national campaign, can and do respond to regional forces. They share their constituencies' concerns, and they are accustomed to representing them. Historically, popular local figures have suffered little from third party ventures, no matter how unsuccessful they turn out to be. The constituencies whose causes they sought to advance were simply grateful to the candidates for efforts on their behalf.

Strom Thurmond exemplifies a prestigious politician whose candidacy grew out of regional dissatisfaction with a major party and who suffered no setbacks to his career as a result of his bolt. At the 1948 Democratic convention, Southerners, unable to block adoption of a strong civil rights plank, responded by opposing Truman's nomination. Of the South's 298 convention votes, 262 were cast for Georgia Senator Richard B. Russell. Only 13 of Truman's 926 votes came from the former Confederacy. (The rest of the Southern delegates did not vote, as some of them had walked out by the time the balloting began.) Shortly after the convention, the States' Rights Party formed with Strom Thurmond as its nominee. Although he attracted but 2.4 percent of the national vote, Thurmond easily won a Senate seat as a write-in candidate in 1954. He was reelected as a Democrat in 1956 and 1960, but was unopposed until 1966, the first time he ran as a Republican.

Agricultural Adversity

Prestigious candidates respond to a second regional cue: agricultural adversity. The larger the long-term decline in farm prices, the greater is the likelihood that a prestigious third party candidate will emerge. Our estimate takes into account the proportion of the population engaged in agriculture (see appendix B), so the precise effect of this variable varies with the size of this sector. In figure 7.5 we have drawn separate curves for the effect of long-term price changes when different proportions of the electorate are in agriculture. For example, the top curve displays the effect of long-term changes in farm prices when 50 percent of the work force were farmers (about 1840-1860), the second when 40 percent were in agriculture (about 1880-1892), and so on. When half the electorate earned their living off the land, a 50 percent drop in farm prices increased by 65 percent the probability that a prestigious candidate would run. When only 40 percent of the electorate were in farming, the same drop increased the probability of a prestigious candidate running by 56 percent. As the proportion of the workforce engaged in agriculture has dwindled, so has the effect of economic adversity on candidate mobilization. Now that less than 4 percent of the electorate is in the agricultural sector, changes in farm prices have a negligible

FIGURE 7.5
Partial Effect of Long-Term Change in
Agricultural Prices on Prestigious Third
Party Candidate Mobilization, 1840-1980

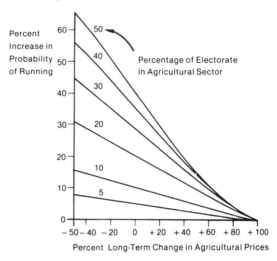

impact on the likelihood of a prestigious politician mounting a third party campaign.

Agricultural adversity prompted Congressman James Weaver to run on the Greenback ticket in 1880 and as a Populist in 1892. It moved Massachusetts Governor and former member of the House Benjamin Butler to run in 1884. Poor economic conditions among farmers also weighed heavily in Congressman Lemke's decision to run in 1936. Although the entire nation had been suffering from seven years of depression, farmers had been toiling under the burden of low farm prices for a decade and a half. As Schlesinger noted, Lemke's district "was a study in economic desperation; two thirds of the farms had been foreclosed since 1929" (1960, pp. 559-60).

Beyond the effect of agricultural adversity, economic conditions have little impact on politicians' decisions to embark on third party campaigns. Wild price fluctuations, steep inflation or deflation, high unemployment, or drops in income are not factors that prompt either prestigious or nationally prestigious politicians to bolt.[13]

Recent Third Party Performance

The recent performance of third party candidates is the final factor that prestigious candidates take into account when they contemplate a third party run. The more votes cast for third parties in the previous presidential contest, the higher the probability a prestigious politician will run in the current election (figure 7.6). Prestigious candidates are 28 percent more likely to run in the subsequent presidential election when

FIGURE 7.6
Partial Effect of the Third Party Vote
in the Previous Presidential Election
on Prestigious Third Party Candidate
Mobilization, 1840-1980

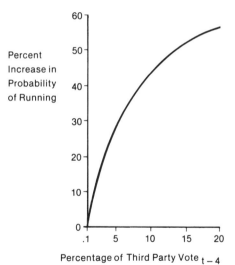

Percentage of Third Party Vote $_{t-4}$

[13] None of these coefficients has more than six chances in ten of being significantly different from zero.

third parties poll 5 percent of the popular vote than when the major parties monopolized all but .1 percent of the ballots cast. If minor parties get 15 percent of the vote, the probability of a prestigious politician bolting in the next election increases by 52 percent.

From the candidate's point of view, taking recent third party success into account may make sense. The challenger presumes he is better off running when third parties have been doing well than when they have not. However, this is a sensible calculation only if there is a high degree of continuity in voter support for third parties from one election to the next. As we saw in chapter 6, such continuity existed only in the nineteenth century. After 1892, few minor parties persisted over time. Thenceforth, the level of third party voting in one contest became a poor indicator of future levels of support. So, though relying on past third party performance when deciding to run may seem reasonable, it is an inaccurate guidepost in the current century.

Although prestigious politicians look at the third party vote in the last election when considering whether to run, candidates in general do not pay much attention to other indicators of third party strength. Moreover, nationally prestigious politicians are not moved at all by such concerns. The proportion of seats third parties hold in Congress, and the vote they received in the previous midterm election, do not affect the likelihood that a prestigious or nationally prestigious third party candidate will run.

Nor do recent prominent third party candidacies discourage new attempts. Memories of a third party failure do not have to fade before another prominent politician will run. There is no relationship between the number of years since the last prestigious or nationally prestigious candidate ran and the likelihood that a new one will emerge.

Furthermore, although resources and votes are scarce, a prestigious politician's decision to mount a third party campaign is not affected by whether a nationally prestigious third party candidate has already emerged, nor is a nationally prestigious politician's decision influenced by whether a prestigious politician is in the race.

CONCLUSIONS

Strategic considerations motivate prominent politicians to abandon the major parties. Yet, unlike other politicians, third party candidates run, not because they believe they can win, but because they see signs that they can garner votes to advance their cause. A potential third party candidate evaluates and reacts to the cues he is accustomed to studying. A politician "responds to the immediate forces in his political environment"—those that he can readily see and experience (Black 1972, p. 145). As these forces change, so does the likelihood that a politician will bolt the major parties.

Prestigious and nationally prestigious politicians employ similar decision rules, though the specific cues they respond to are different. Both try to pursue their goals within the major parties before they run as third party candidates. Both act on behalf of concerns relevant to their own political arenas. Both respond to signs that large segments of their followings are unhappy with the way the major parties have treated their concerns.

The differences between the decision rules that prestigious and nationally prestigious politicians employ reflect differences in the constituencies they represent. Nationally prestigious politicians look for signs of potential support among a national following. They are more likely to emerge when the major parties' nominating conventions are divisive, when an incumbent president runs for reelection, or when an incumbent president has been denied renomination by his party. Prestigious politicians, who by definition do not have a national constituency, are more attuned to state and regional concerns. Although they also look for signs of major party weakness, they respond to disputes that primarily affect their section of the country. Disaffection with the major parties within a particular region is sufficient for these candidates to run. Prestigious politicians also respond to another regional cue: agricultural adversity. In essence, minor party candidates emerge when there are real-world signs that they will enjoy substantial support.

We do not claim that potential third party candidates actually tally up values for any of the variables described here. Rather, they behave in the way that politicians generally behave—they react to their constituencies. They detect dissatisfaction, not with elaborate computations, but with political sensitivity. Astute politicians have a sense of when they are likely to run well and when they are not. The factors we identify are simply indicators of conditions to which they are likely to respond.

The candidates' decision rules have mixed success. We saw that voters do support third party candidates when the major parties have failed to address their concerns or have mismanaged the government. In general, prominent candidates are there to lead them under these circumstances. But there are signs of potential support that would-be challengers miss. Voters are willing to show loyalty to third parties; however, few candidates, especially in the twentieth century, have sought to take advantage of this potential by building a lasting party. Furthermore, although the wholesale enfranchisement of new voters boosts the level of third party voting, there is no evidence that potential candidates recognize or respond to this cue.

A candidate's decision on whether or not to run is not always an optimal one. It is quite possible that even though he has carefully considered the move, his appeals for support will fall on deaf ears. Conversely, there are periods when the electorate is susceptible to third party appeals, but neither a prestigious nor a nationally prestigious candidate emerges.[14]

---

[14] As Black has noted: "Politicians, like everyone else, make errors; errors that can derive from an incorrect estimate of the probabilities attached to various alternatives or from an incorrect evaluation of the cost and benefits attached to a given alternative. These errors arise because information is almost always limited and expensive, and the decision maker must generally arrive at his decisions through the process of an educated 'guess.' Thus, politicians can err in their choices even though they are trying to behave rationally" (1972, p. 146).

We should note that other political elites, not just potential candidates, also probably engage in the strategic considerations described in this chapter. Campaign organizers, contributors and workers, as well as interest groups, surely attend to these same signs and respond as prominent politicians do. Thus the effect on candidate mobilization of the cues we have identified may be indirect: other political elites react to indicators that the major parties are vulnerable; their response in turn may convince potential candidates that it is an opportune time to run.

Potential third party candidates do not seem to be deterred by legal barriers to candidacy. The institution of laws restricting candidate access to the general election ballot made it harder for minor party candidates to get their names before the voters, but it has not inhibited would-be third party candidates from running. Although a progressively larger portion of the electorate has confronted ballots governed by candidate access restrictions, the probability of a prominent politician mounting a third party campaign has not declined.[15] Similarly, neither the institution of primaries nor their expanded use since 1968 has encouraged (or discouraged) the emergence of prestigious or nationally prestigious politicians.[16] Although presidential primaries provide many more politicians with the opportunity to gain exposure outside of their home states, expand their name recognition, pick up popular support, and build national organizations even if they lose the nomination,[17] primaries have not prompted more candidates to run outside the major parties.

Other institutional changes may or may not contribute to a candidate's decision to run. Federal funding of presidential

---

[15] The coefficient for the proportion of voters with ballot access restrictions is .81 (standard error = .91) in the nationally prestigious third party candidate equation and .76 (standard error = .66) in the prestigious third party equation.

[16] This holds regardless of whether one considers the proportion of the states with presidential primary elections or the proportion of the delegates selected through primaries.

[17] LaFollette, George Wallace, McCarthy, and Anderson all attained national recognition in part through presidential primaries.

campaigns has been instituted so recently that it is difficult, at this point in time, to assess its impact on candidate mobilization. Although advances in media technology and mass marketing techniques have obviously had an impact on campaign strategy, it is unclear whether they affect would-be independents' willingness to run.

Politicians, like the electorate as a whole, react to the major parties. Both groups utilize the third party option when the major parties fail to meet their needs. Given that the behavior of third party candidates and voters is largely an indicator of major party performance, it is appropriate to consider what the fluctuations in minor party activity reveal about the vitality of the American two-party system. This is our task in the final chapter.

CHAPTER 8

MAJOR PARTIES, MINOR PARTIES, AND AMERICAN ELECTIONS

THIRD PARTIES are a response to major party failure. It is around this notion that we have developed a general theory of minor party voting and candidate mobilization. Since 1840 there have been over one hundred third parties driven by very disparate concerns. And yet one can still predict with a relatively high degree of precision when independent challengers are likely to emerge and when voters are apt to support them.

How Voters Choose

Third party voting occurs when citizens feel the major parties have failed to live up to their implicit contractual obligations. Voters expect the major parties to be responsive, to manage the government competently, and to provide trustworthy leadership. When both major parties deteriorate to unacceptable levels, third party voting results. However, because the costs of defecting are so high, small transgressions by the major parties do not cause people to bolt. Only the most egregious violations motivate voters to overcome the costs.

Citizens do not regard all parties as equally legitimate. The two major parties enjoy a privileged position in American politics; third parties are the path of last resort. Voters first look over the Democrats and Republicans; they consider other alternatives only if they are dissatisfied with these choices. It is a two-step process. The second search does not begin unless the voter rejects both major party candidates.

We have identified the actions that voters consider the most serious breaches of contract by the major parties. We now know precisely what the voters expect of the major parties—issue responsiveness, competent management, and attractive electoral choices. Voters are willing to let others worry about the details of politics; they just want their most basic needs tended to. As long as one of the major parties comes close to representing their views on specific issues, as long as the candidates nominated are not hopelessly incompetent, and as long as their economic survival is not threatened, voters will remain loyal to the major parties.

The situation is somewhat different for people just entering the electorate. They have the same basic expectations, but the costs of defecting are lower since they have not yet settled into major party habits. In their first election, they are some-what more vigilant and more demanding. Hence their tolerance for major party failure is lower.

Third parties are expressions of negative sentiment. An examination of individual parties finds that third party backers are usually united, not in *support*, but rather in *opposition* to some person or issue. Candidates emerge when there is an incumbent president to run against; voters join the cause when they oppose some policy or major party nominee. Third parties are coalitions of opposition to the major parties. Their members ordinarily have few common goals to bind them, and thus the parties break apart easily.

No single variable by itself explains why Americans abandon the major parties. Contrary to most spatial theories of elections, proximity to the candidates does not alone account for levels of third party support (Downs 1957, ch. 8). The performance of the major parties over a series of years, the quality of the available candidates, partisan attachment, the nature of the times, and the formal and informal rules that govern the contest all affect the likelihood of people casting minor party ballots.

Current retrospective theories of voting also cannot account for fluctuations in third party support. What do citizens do when both the Democrats and Republicans have deteriorated to the point that giving the out-party a chance to govern offers no more hope than staying the course with the ineffectual incumbent? Retrospective voting models assume that voters confront only two parties (for example, Fiorina 1981). When people are indifferent between them, the choice is neither difficult nor crucial. However, there are two sorts of indifference. If citizens are *satisfied* with both candidates, voting for one is just as good as voting for the other. There is little psychic pain. They could abstain, but certainly there would be little motivation to search out other alternatives. But when one party is just as bad as the other, then *dissatisfaction* with both options prompts voters either to abstain or to hunt for another choice.

Class theories of politics do not in general help explain third party support in America either. Although minor parties have at times spoken out for the disadvantaged and have won the allegiance of those at the bottom rungs of the economic ladder, other parties, like the National Democrats or John Anderson's National Unity Campaign, have represented the middle or upper classes. The absence of class-based third party voting in America should not be too surprising: it is consistent with the generally muted impact of class on most political preferences, cleavages, and political activities in the United States.[1]

Although citizens arrive at their decisions to support third parties by a fundamentally different path from the one they take when voting for major parties, some of the considerations they employ are the same. The quality of the candidate, the

---

[1] This lack of a class basis to minor party support in the United States may also help to explain the ephemeral nature of third parties. When a third party's issue evaporates or its leader disappears, so does the minor party. With no enduring focus (like a class-based issue) around which to organize support, third parties in America tend to wither and die. This tendency is in marked contrast to the experience of minor parties in most other countries, which have class bases and, probably not coincidentally, endure. When a party organizes around class interests, the party does not lose focus if the salient issues change. With a basic agenda that seems capable of lasting for as long as there are governments (or at least until Marx's revolution), these parties are more durable because they are able to adapt to changes in the details of political debate.

prominent issues of the day, the state of the economy, and the strength of their party allegiance all influence the probability of a person casting a third party ballot. Our findings suggest that fluctuations in third party support stem from changes in the political, social, and economic environment that citizens face. Voters are deliberative: they recognize when the major parties have failed and adjust their political behavior accordingly. People respond in sensible ways to changes in the real world and make connections between electoral outcomes and policy results.

But minor party voting also derives from changes in the types of people who comprise the electorate. Defection from the major parties stems not only from citizens reacting to shifting conditions but from the replacement of old voters by new ones. Times when there are large pools of citizens with weak allegiance to the major parties are opportune moments for independent candidates. When the composition of the electorate is relatively stable, and the party system comparatively young, third party voting is uncommon. Improved major party performance can potentially counter deliberate defection, but the major parties can do little to combat these secular dips in allegiance.

Our conclusions are probably unique to the United States. At best, the theories of third party voting and candidate mobilization presented here may be generalized to other two-party systems that have only periodic outbursts of minor party sentiment. But there are few political systems where the two parties have dominated for so long or have enjoyed such deep-seated respect. Even in Britain, Canada, and Australia, minor parties are more common and enduring than in the United States. Differences in the electoral rules of the game, the greater legitimacy that Americans bestow on the Democrats and Republicans, and the tendency of American third parties, particularly in the twentieth century, to rely solely on the individuals who head the ticket make the situation in the United States fairly special.

Strengths and Weaknesses of the Parties and the Two-Party System

There is much talk these days about the decline of political parties. Parties, it is said, no longer perform their traditional functions. They do not develop policies, they stand for no consistent ideology, they are of little use in elections, and they rarely command loyalty within the Congress or state legislatures. Yet these are not the sorts of conditions that promote minor party support. In fact, as we have seen, third parties have suffered a similar decline in their ability to affect the course of elections. Like the major parties, they have been replaced by individual candidates who supply their own portable machinery.

Third party voting is a response to major party *failure*, not *decline*. Minor parties do well when the major parties fall short of what the electorate expects of them. Voters do not turn away from major parties because they offer no consistent ideology or are unable to discipline their congressmen; these are not failures to the voters.

The parties may be in decline, and they may occasionally fail to fulfill their pact with the voters, but the American two-party system itself remains healthy. It has withstood massive shocks—the replacement of a major party, a civil war, the desertion of three ex-presidents, changes in the rules of the game, sweeping changes in the prominent issues, and continual replacement of the electorate. Only egregious major party failures have produced significant levels of third party support. And even the most fervent third party activity has not eroded the two-party norm. Nearly a century has elapsed since a single minor party has been able to mount a sustained challenge.

The resilience of the two-party system is evident not only in its ability to retain voter loyalty but in its success at discouraging politicians from leaving the major parties. After all, in nearly a century and a half, only seventeen prestigious and nine nationally prestigious politicians have embarked on third party challenges. The barriers against third parties are powerful deterrents to elite desertion. Moreover, because it is often difficult for defectors to return to the party they abandoned, the decision to exit rather than fight is a risky path that few choose.

The two-party system shows no signs of faltering. The multitude of legal, constitutional, and psychological constraints described in chapter 2 continue to protect the two-party arrangement. The single-member-district plurality system will doubtless keep on discouraging candidates and supporters. Major parties will continue to adjust their appeals to accommodate and thus absorb the minor parties that do emerge. There is no reason to expect that the major parties will take steps to equalize the resources available to them and third party challengers, nor will they relax any of the barriers to third party activity. Furthermore, citizens are not clamoring for them to do so. As long as these constraints are in place, the two-party system will endure. No permanent third party able to garner a sizable share of the popular vote threatens to emerge. There seems little reason to believe that the basic pattern of Democratic and Republican dominance, with intermittent periods of third party activity, will change.

The two-party arrangement persists, not because it is a "good" system, but because the constraints that discourage third party challenges also encourage the major parties eventually to accommodate many (though not all) political preferences.

We cannot go so far as to say, however, that if the major parties were responsive, there would never be third party voting. Intra-party feuds will always produce losers who occasionally respond by turning to third parties. There will also always be a pool of voters who have weak allegiances to the major parties and are thus susceptible to third party appeals. The inability of the major parties to induce all new voters to join their ranks from the moment they enter the electorate can hardly be regarded as a failure of the two-party system. If anything, the loyalty to the major parties that new entrants display testifies to the system's strength, not its weakness.

Our analysis of third party voting identifies an important deficiency in the American electoral system. Although the major parties are relatively good at managing conflict, building majority coalitions, and holding voter loyalty, this success has its costs. While consensus over a broad range of policies is likely to ensue, the major parties tend to ignore issues that concern only a minority of citizens and threaten the interest of the majority. Even when farmers comprised over a third of the electorate, the major parties ignored their cries until their defection seriously threatened a party's chances of victory. The current plight of farmers and their inability to gain a sympathetic ear in Washington suggests that not much has changed in this regard. So long as each party calculates that it can capture the Electoral College without the support of a minority faction (such as farmers, Southerners, or whomever), that group, if its preferences run counter to those of other larger groups in the coalition, will be ignored. Only by threatening a major party's electoral majority does a group have much hope of its needs being met.[2]

In sum, moments of third party strength indicate that the major parties have failed to harmonize the different political interests in society and have failed to adjust to the economic and social demands that citizens have placed on the political system. "A new party does not arise until the existing institutions have clearly proved their unreadiness to respond" (Herring 1965, p. 180).

THE ROLE OF THIRD PARTIES IN AMERICAN POLITICS

Third parties in America fulfill two critical functions: they popularize ideas that the major parties would otherwise ignore, and they serve as political vehicles for citizens discontent with the policies put forth by the major parties. The Democratic and Republican parties do not (and perhaps can-

---

[2] Because third parties are a crucial means of minority representation, barriers restricting minor party activity disproportionately hinder these groups. Majority interests have no need for third parties and are thus unaffected by constraints against independents.

not) always build coalitions that represent all voters. Third parties provide citizens with the opportunity to affect electoral outcomes in the hope of winning attention from a major party.

The major parties, rationally, react to signs of voter discontent. We have seen numerous instances of the major parties embarking on a policy course with the explicit intention of stealing away the independent's reason for being. The impact that George Wallace's candidacy had on the Nixon administration's civil rights policies demonstrates how profound an effect a third party can have. Minor parties help shape the issues and programs the two major parties pursue in office. Note, however, that the major parties adopt these new positions, not out of an altruistic concern to "represent the people," but rather so that they can put the third party out of business. It is ironic that when they do so, both the third party supporters and the major parties benefit.

Thus third parties, like the major parties and other political organizations, perform a constituent function: they are vehicles for aggregating and promoting citizen preferences. Minor party activity is just one of several political strategies citizens employ to make claims on government. Third party agitation is a natural, reasonable means of recourse when other political avenues have failed. Minor parties are not so much safety valves for voters who want to blow off steam as they are checks on the major parties. They are a weapon citizens can use to force the major parties to be more accountable. The threat of exit provides voters and their leaders with an important resource when bargaining with both major parties. Third parties are not aberrations in the American political system; they are in fact necessary voices for the preservation of democracy. They represent the needs and demands of Americans whom the major parties have ignored.

Minor parties are also policy innovators. Policy ideas at times arise outside the two-party system because the major parties remain preoccupied with issues that defined the party alignment in the last critical election. The major parties are often unable or unwilling to deal with new issues, even those concerning a sizable portion of the electorate. When the major party leadership continues to focus on an increasingly irrelevant agenda, third parties become an important voice of change.

In short, third parties should not be viewed as organizations that stand outside the mainstream of the American political system. They are very much a central part of it. The stands of the major political parties, the political strategies they pursue, and the motivations underlying their choice of nominees often anticipate the response of potential third parties. Minor parties provide voters with an important opportunity to express their discontent. This makes third party support one of the clearest barometers we have of the electorate's evaluation of the Democrats and Republicans.

How would politics in the United States be different if opportunities for third party activity were reduced? The constraints against third parties clearly encourage consensus building. Because exit is so difficult, disgruntled party elites tend to work for compromise within the major parties. With only Democrats and Republicans from which realistically to choose, politicians try to reconcile their differences and form broader coalitions than do their counterparts in multi-party systems. They view third parties as nothing more than a path of last resort.

But the steep costs of an independent challenge have negative consequences as well. The constraints on third parties limit their political impact. The obstacles facing third parties slow the consideration of some new policy proposals and force some minorities to go unrepresented. Disgruntled citizens who see no hope for their cause in the major parties frequently give up because the third party route is so discouraging. The difficulties of raising money, getting publicity, winning votes, and, most important, earning legitimacy as a third party movement deter even the most energetic reformers.

Some of the tactics the major parties employ to stymie third parties diminish the benefits we have been discussing. When the Democrats and Republicans harass third parties, restrict their access to ballots and resources, and delegitimize their candidates, they reduce the ability of independent challengers to hold the major parties accountable. The more difficult it is for citizens to support third parties, the greater is the major party deterioration required before voters are induced to back an independent. If the costs are too great, of course, the check on the major parties evaporates.

Proposals to raise the costs of third party voting would have severe negative consequences for American democracy. If the major parties closed off the third party route entirely, an important means of political representation would be lost. As long as minorities can threaten to damage both parties by a third party campaign, the major parties are encouraged to compromise with these groups. It is not clear what strategies disgruntled minority factions would pursue if the third party option were unavailable. It is unlikely that they could force the major parties to be more accommodating. Since they would have nowhere else to go, these groups might have to turn to less accepted forms of action.

Because third parties help to hold the major parties accountable to certain minority interests, one way to enhance minority representation in the political arena is to increase the opportunities for third party activity. The less the major parties are able to monopolize control of the government, and the more uncertainty there is over which party will enjoy an Electoral College majority, the greater the incentives for the major parties to tend to the minority concerns they would otherwise ignore. The less the rules of the game permit groups to be written off, the more accountable the major parties have to be. Because the current set of electoral rules reduces the likelihood of a third party significantly affecting election outcomes, the major parties can afford to be relatively unattentive to minority concerns.

THE FUTURE OF THIRD PARTIES IN AMERICA

The marked increase in third party voting since 1964 can be attributed to several factors. Increased intra-party factionalism and the inability of the major parties to realign around more salient concerns have been the two most important forces prompting prominent politicians to bolt the major parties. But the decline in major party support is not due solely to the greater propensity of prominent candidates to run. Changes have occurred in the electorate as well (figure 8.1). Between 1952 and 1980 the percentage of voters who negatively evaluated the major parties nearly doubled; the proportion of the electorate who had negative evaluations of the major party nominees increased threefold. Voters also became increas-

FIGURE 8.1
Trends Causing an Increase in Third Party Voting,
1952-1980

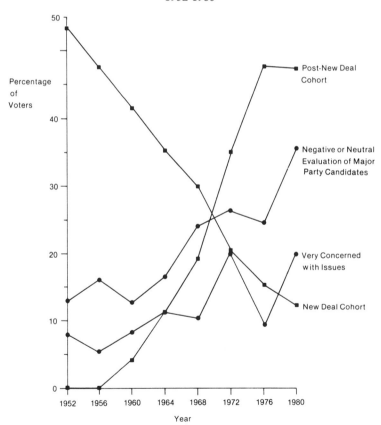

ingly concerned with issues, leading inevitably to disappointment with the major party nominees. Finally, through replacement, the electorate was increasingly comprised of voters enfranchised since the New Deal realignment. In 1952 over half the electorate had witnessed the formation of the New Deal coalition; by 1980 only about one voter in ten was a member of this cohort. Nearly half the 1980 electorate was enfranchised after 1956. These citizens, as we have seen, have weaker major party allegiance and provide a reservoir of support for third party causes.

Minor parties may also have benefitted from changes in campaign technology and the political environment. The major parties' control over campaign resources (money, expertise, volunteers, and the like) has never been as actively challenged as it is today. Hired consultants provide mailing lists, targeting information, and individual fundraising support once available only through a party organization. The proliferation of presidential primaries in recent years has made it easier for politicians to gain national exposure that can later be used to their advantage in a third party run. The media have a greater impact than ever before on public perceptions of the candidates and on views of who are legitimate contenders. This decentralization of control over campaigns has probably aided third parties.

A minor party challenger is unlikely to capture the presidency, but there will continue to be times when a substantial share of the electorate will abandon the major parties. The theories of third party voting and candidate mobilization developed here identify with a fair amount of certainty when prestigious and nationally prestigious third party candidates will emerge and what proportion of the electorate will cast minor party ballots.

To illustrate the theory's predictive validity, we forecast the 1968 to 1980 elections using only data available prior to each contest (table 8.1).[3] For 1968 our model forecasts that there

_____

[3] The 1968 forecasts, for instance, were generated by reestimating the aggregate equations reported in tables 6.1, 7.1, and 7.2 with data from the 1840-1964 elections and applying these new estimates to the 1968 values of the explanatory variables.

TABLE 8.1

Forecasts of Candidate Mobilization and Third Party Presidential Voting, 1968-1984

Year of Forecasts	Data Used for Forecasts	Forecasted Probability of a Prestigious Third Party Candidate Running	Did a Prestigious Third Party Candidate Actually Run?	Forecasted Probability of a Nationally Prestigious Third Party Candidate Running	Did a Nationally Prestigious Third Party Candidate Actually Run?	Forecasted Third Party Vote	Actual Third Party Vote	Error
1968	1840-1964	.23	no	.63	yes	11.5%	13.9%	+2.4%
1972	1840-1968	.63	yes	<.01	no	2.4%	1.8%	− .6%
1976	1840-1972	.49	yes	>.99	yes	3.9%	1.9%	−1.0%
1980	1840-1976	.25	yes	.71	yes	9.9%	8.2%	−1.7%
1984	1840-1980							
Scenario 1		.38	?	<.01	?	1.0%	?	?
Scenario 2		.99	?	>.99	?	10.8%	?	?
Scenario 3		.65	?	.99	?	4.4%	?	?

were 23 chances in 100 that a prestigious third party candidate would run and 63 chances in 100 that a nationally prestigious third party candidate would emerge. It predicts that 11.5 percent of the electorate would support third party candidates in that year's presidential contest. These predictions are fairly close to the actual result: no prestigious third party candidate ran, while George Wallace, a nationally prestigious candidate, did. The vote forecast is off by 2.3 percentage points.

The theory performs about as well in 1972, 1976, and 1980. As expected from our discussion in chapter 7, predictions of nationally prestigious candidates' emergence are more precise than those for prestigious candidates. The model fails to anticipate the Rarick candidacy in 1980, but does indicate a high probability that a nationally prestigious third party candidate (Anderson) would run. A total of 8.2 percent of the voters actually cast a third party ballot in 1980; the model forecasts 9.9 percent—an error of 1.7 percentage points. Between 1972 and 1980 the third party popular vote forecast was off by an average of about 1 percent.

Although the obvious next step would be to predict future levels of third party support, it would be foolhardy to make unconditional forecasts this far in advance of the 1984 or 1988 elections. At this point in time we can only guess how factionalized the major parties will be, whether Reagan will seek another term, or whether 1980 was a critical election. Instead, we will generate 1984 forecasts under three different sets of assumptions.[4]

The first forecasts assume that 1980 was a critical election, that both parties harmoniously select their 1984 nominees, that Reagan does not run, and that there is a significant rise in farm prices before the election. Given the relationships between these variables and third party candidate mobilization and voter support, this is the most pessimistic third party scenario that we can devise. If these conditions were to prevail in 1984, there is a .38 probability of a prestigious third party

[4] Additional equations might someday allow reasonable forecasts of future values of these variables.

candidate running and less than 1 chance in 100 that a nationally prestigious politician would mount a third party challenge. Only about 1 percent of the popular vote would be cast for the minor parties.

The second scenario embodies the set of assumptions that would maximize third party voting: Reagan runs again, 1980 did not mark the beginning of a new party system, the major parties are extremely factionalized, and farm prices fall precipitously. Under these conditions there is a .99 probability that both a prestigious and nationally prestigious third party candidate would run. About 10.8 percent of the popular vote cast in 1984 would go to third party candidates. Even under these ideal circumstances, third party voting in 1984 would not exceed the level in 1968.

Finally, we assume plausible conditions: Reagan seeks another term, 1980 was not a realigning election, the Republican convention is as consensual and the Democratic as divisive as they were in 1980, and farm prices remain constant in 1983 and 1984. If these conditions were to hold, there is a .65 probability that a prestigious candidate would run and 99 chances in 100 that a nationally prestigious challenger would emerge in 1984. About 4.4 percent of the electorate would abandon the major parties.

Thus, given even the best of conditions, it is quite unrealistic to expect that third party voting will in the near future approach levels seen in 1856, 1860, or 1912. This conclusion stems in part from demographic changes in the composition of the electorate. In the nineteenth and early twentieth centuries, new entrants, newly enfranchised immigrants from countries with viable socialist parties, and farmers made up a relatively large proportion of the electorate. These groups, who are prone to back minor parties, now comprise a much smaller share of those eligible to vote. In addition, third parties are less able to retain voter allegiance than they were in the nineteenth century.

Minor parties in America are condemned to their fate as third place finishers. We perceive the circumstances under which a third party could replace a major party to be so extraordinary as to be unrealistic. The parties that compete for control of the government will, in all likelihood, continue to be the Democrats and the Republicans. How much of their energy they can safely devote to combating one another, however, will ultimately depend on how well they develop issues, respond to the electorate's concerns, and manage the country's governmental and economic affairs.

H. ROSS PEROT

IN 1992, one out of five Americans abandoned the major parties to support a third party alternative. Nearly all of those who bolted—18.9 percent—cast a ballot for Texas billionaire H. Ross Perot. Not since 1912, when former President Theodore Roosevelt ran as the Bull Moose candidate, had so many Americans voted for an independent challenger.

Our purpose in this chapter is to explain Perot's phenomenal success and to see how well our account of the ebb and flow of third party support between 1840 and 1980 explains the surge in third party voting that took place in 1992. Was the Perot vote really an anomaly, or was his support what one would have expected given the circumstances? Did something happen in 1992 that made this election different? Was Perot a more effective or more popular candidate than his predecessors? Were voters more angry than ever before? The fundamental question we pose here is the same one that we posed at the outset of the book: What prompts citizens to seek a third party alternative?

What we find is that in many ways, the story behind H. Ross Perot's historic level of support is the story we have already told about the success of third party candidates in earlier periods of American history. Citizens were angry with government, anxious about the nation's future, and disaffected from the major parties and their candidates. Ross Perot, like his predecessors, tapped into this deep discontent. But as fashionable as this account is, disaffection is only part of the story behind Perot's success in 1992. As we will show, in 1992 Americans were no more disaffected from the parties, from the candidates, or from the political system than they were back in 1980 when only 6.6 percent of the electorate bolted to vote for the independent, John Anderson. Disaffection alone does not explain much more than about a third of Perot's support.

The reason Perot did so well in 1992, we will show, is that he was able to break through many of the constraints that had impeded his predecessors. What distinguishes Perot from his predecessors, foremost, and what explains much of his phenomenal showing in 1992, is money, and plenty of it. Throughout American history, every independent candidate for President has been strapped for resources, but not the Texas billionaire, Ross Perot. The nearly $73 million Perot pumped into his crusade was more money than any third party candidate had ever spent on an independent bid for the White House. With money, Perot was able to build a campaign organization, to fund ballot access drives in all fifty states, and to purchase unprecedented blocks of television time to air his political ads. With money came credibility.

Perot broke through two other barriers that had handicapped his predecessors. Thanks to his strong standing in the polls and his skillful working of the television and radio talk show circuit, Perot enjoyed more extensive and more positive media coverage than third party candidates usually do. This too boosted his vote on election day. Finally, Perot was the only independent challenger ever to appear shoulder-to-shoulder with both major party candidates in televised presidential debates. The debates gave Perot unprecedented national exposure, legitimacy, and momentum in the final weeks of the campaign.

We begin by describing the Perot phenomenon: the context in which he emerged; his candidacy, message, and campaign organization; and his sources of support. Next, we scrutinize the most popular accounts of Perot's success in 1992: declining allegiance to the major parties; surging disaffection with the major party candidates; increasing political alienation; rising economic insecurity; his personal appeal; the sense that he could win; and his ability to mobilize new voters to his cause. We then show how Perot's money, media coverage, and participation in the presidential debates boosted his vote total way beyond what it would have been had he been an ordinary third party challenger. We conclude by reflecting on Perot's impact on American politics.

THE 1992 ELECTION CONTEXT

A year before the primary season got rolling, few observers would have given much credence to the idea that in 1992 a third party candidate would capture nearly 20 percent of the presidential vote. In fact, it is only a slight exaggeration to say that at one point, few observers thought that *any* candidate other than President George Bush would garner 20 percent of the vote.

It was February 1991. Under the leadership of President George Bush, American-led, multinational ground forces took just 100 hours to roust Iraqi dictator Saddam Hussein from Kuwait and southern Iraq. The media dramatically portrayed the effectiveness of America's military forces, especially its high-tech weapons. There were only 148 American casualties. Public support for Bush topped 90 percent—the highest figure ever recorded for *any* American President.

The election seemed all but over. One by one, the best-known Democratic candidates—New York Governor Mario Cuomo, New Jersey Senator Bill Bradley, Tennessee Senator Al Gore, Missouri Congressman Richard Gephardt—announced they would not run for President.

But over the next few months, the triumph in the Persian Gulf faded from people's memories, helped in large part by a biting recession. Many Americans felt hopelessly trapped in a "middle-class squeeze," caught between rising prices and stagnating wages. When the economically distressed turned to Bush for help, they found a President denying there was even a problem. When they turned to Congress, they found paralysis over scandal and bickering over charges of sexual harassment by Supreme Court nominee Clarence Thomas. They also discovered that their representatives in Congress had regularly exempted themselves from the laws they had passed.

To many Americans, it seemed as though the country was going downhill and nobody who had the power to do anything about it cared. Citizens were frustrated. According to one survey, three out of four Americans agreed with the proposition that "the entire political system was broken— that it was run by insiders who didn't listen to working people and couldn't solve their problems" (Goldman and De-Frank 1992, p. 23).

The first tangible sign that something was amiss came when Pat Buchanan, an ultraconservative gadfly, drew 37 percent of the vote from George Bush in the New Hampshire Republican primary. Buchanan had no chance of being nominated, or even winning a single state primary. He was out of touch with all but the most conservative elements of the Republican Party. He couldn't raise enough money to compete. Buchanan's message was a snarl of resentful anger—anger at Washington, at foreigners, at blue bloods, at declining moral values. And yet nearly four in ten Republicans abandoned their President to vote for him. Only Eugene McCarthy, in 1968, had ever run better against an incumbent President in the New Hampshire primary, and his 42 percent was enough to convince President Lyndon Johnson that he should not seek another term.

At the time, some observers read New Hampshire as a referendum on George Bush. And in part it was. But in retrospect, New Hampshire was also the first concrete sign that many Americans were unhappy with politics as usual, and when presented with an opportunity to do so, they were perfectly willing to vote for a candidate who would tell the system to "go to hell."

Over the coming months, Buchanan's message continued to resonate. Though Bush had little trouble capturing the Republican nomination, Buchanan continued to draw well, winning 22 percent of the votes that Republicans cast nationwide in the 1992 presidential primaries.

Meanwhile, a strikingly similar story was unfolding in the Democratic Party. The campaign began as a wide-open race featuring six moderately prominent candidates—each claiming to be an agent of "change." Though beset by an endless number of seemingly fatal allegations and disclosures about his past, Arkansas Governor Bill Clinton emerged from the pack in the second week of March when he swept the six

Southern primaries held on Super Tuesday. Nine days later, only the most implausible challenger—former California Governor Jerry Brown—remained in the race. Like Buchanan, Brown was a voice of anger.

To dramatize his claim that he was the only candidate for President who could not be bought by the special interests, Brown turned away contributions larger than $100 and set up an "800" number to take in donations from ordinary citizens. Thousands responded. To bypass the skeptical and cynical establishment media, Brown took to radio talk and call-in shows, the favorite information source for many of America's angriest voters.

Like Buchanan, Brown aimed some of his fiercest fire at his own party. He was not just running against George Bush and the Republicans; his opponents were "the Incumbent Party," the political establishment that did the bidding of the special interests and ignored the needs of ordinary Americans.

With a flaky reputation, a liberal record out of touch with even most Democratic primary voters, and a relatively modest amount of money to spend, Brown should have met with little success. Instead, he captured 20 percent of the votes cast in the Democratic primaries.

By most measures, Jerry Brown and Pat Buchanan had little in common. Buchanan was a darling of the religious right and a loyal aide to Richard Nixon who knew how to play to Americans' worst fears. Brown was a Yale educated darling of the California liberal elite who had little firsthand experience with the day-to-day hopes and fears of ordinary Americans. Still, they shared an important common denominator: they both carried the "go to hell" message. The political system was corrupt, the federal government was bankrupt, and the American economy was being sold off to foreign investors; it was time to stand up and protest.

THE PEROT CANDIDACY

As Buchanan and Brown were out campaigning for votes within their respective parties, H. Ross Perot was pushing the same themes, tapping the same emotions, and exploiting the same avenues of communication as an independent candidate for President.

At first glance, a billionaire industrialist was hardly an ideal presidential candidate in the television age. Perot was not photogenic, not comforting, and knew little about most of the issues facing a President. But at a time when many Americans believed that their elected officials either didn't care about their problems or didn't know how to fix them, Perot offered himself as the ultimate no-nonsense, can-do leader.

The myth of Ross Perot was carefully cultivated by Perot himself. He was "the ultimate self-made man . . . who started his company with one thousand dollars." "He was a Rambo in a business suit, whether sending in his private commandoes to get two of his employees out of jail in Iran or fighting for twenty years to bring the last missing boys home from Southeast Asia." Perot was "a tough, determined and often lonely warrior willing to take on politicians, bureaucrats, industrialists, financiers, third-world dictators, or anybody else who got in his way" (Goldman et al. 1994, pp. 415, 416).

An eccentric billionaire who was a prominent volunteer in public issues ranging from Texas school reform to investigations into Vietnam MIAs, Perot had never run for public office. He portrayed himself as a reluctant candidate: a patriot who "the people—the owners of this country" could draft to do their bidding against lobbyists, special interests, and the elected officials who serve them. Perot did not need the job, of course, and said he would run only if "the people" summoned him to be their servant. This was the challenge Perot put forth when he launched his campaign during his February 20, 1992, appearance on CNN's television talk show, *Larry King Live*. On the show, Perot said he would run for President "if voters in all 50 states put me on the ballot—not 48 or 49 states, but all 50."

Two themes were at the heart of Perot's campaign: the federal budget deficit and the "mess in Washington." Perot blamed the $4 trillion national debt on the failure of the Democrats and Republicans to make the hard choices needed to balance the budget. "The United States government must pay its way," he argued (Perot 1992, p. 35). His fix was to cut discretionary spending; enact the line item veto and a tougher deficit reduction law; eliminate special tax breaks that subsidized the rich; control entitlements; increase tobacco and gasoline taxes; and get Japan and Germany to pay their fair share of the costs of defending Asia and Europe. For America to be economically competitive, "governmental policies should be redirected to stimulate growth, to encourage the private sector, to create jobs, and to open opportunities for all Americans" (Perot 1992, p. 113).

Before the deficit could be reduced, however, Americans first needed to "overhaul the political system that created it" (Perot 1992, p. 23). Here too, Perot maintained that the major parties had failed. They failed to restrict campaign contributions; they failed to curb political action committees; they failed to insulate themselves from the money of special interests. Perot blasted the influence of foreign governments and businesses, advocating that it should be a "criminal offense for any foreign government or individual or company to attempt to influence American laws or policies" (1992, p. 26). And to clean up the mess in Washington, he called for cutting special perks (airplanes, gymnasiums, barber shops, free mail); pruning congressional and executive staffs; reorganizing the legislative system; and getting federal employees to treat citizens as the owners of the country.

Like Buchanan and Brown before him, Perot railed against the North America Free Trade Agreement with Mexico and Canada, and he blamed many of the country's ills on high-priced lobbyists who "owned" elected officials lock, stock, and barrel.

Perot's message, folksy style, simple, direct language, and quick fixes to all the nation's problems initially appealed to many Americans. Ordinary citizens thought that "since Perot had built [a] $2 billion fortune he could handle the country's financial troubles." Others thought that "he's no nonsense," that he can "make decisions," and that "he cares about America and keeping money in the country" (Market Strategies

Inc. 1994, p. 673). Within a month of his appearance on *Larry King Live*, fully one-quarter of the electorate said they intended to vote for Ross Perot (figure 9.1), and by the middle of May, Perot was running neck-and-neck with President George Bush and Governor Bill Clinton in the Gallup trial heats. By early June Ross Perot was the presidential front-runner with fully 39 percent of the electorate saying they were going to vote for him on election day. But, like his predecessors' (figure 2.2), Perot's support faded over time. As we argued in chapter 2, citizens may flirt with minor party candidates early in the season, but harsh treatment by the press, the battle of the campaign, the pull of partisanship, and the inevitable "he can't win—it's a wasted vote" argument bring many voters home to the major parties on election day.

As we will see in much more detail later in this chapter, Perot's campaign was anything but a typical third party run for the presidency. In July he suspended his campaign midstream, rejoining the fray with only four weeks to go. He fired professional campaign managers and media consultants, replacing them with close friends and business associates. He refused help from professional speech writers, which led to political faux pas such as the one before the National Association for the Advancement of Colored People where he repeatedly talked about his concern for "your people." He broke with campaign orthodoxy by supplementing the usual thirty-second television spots with millions of dollars worth of thirty- and sixty-*minute* "infomercials" that featured Perot, by himself, before the camera with charts and pointer in hand discussing the budget deficit. He captured hours of free media exposure by appearing on scores of radio and television talk shows.

The Perot Campaign Organization

Perot unremittingly portrayed his campaign as a grass-roots effort by "the people"—no consultants, no handlers, no image makers. In fact, it was nothing the sort. To be sure, many Americans volunteered to work for Perot, and many others signed his petitions or phoned his toll-free number to voice support for his candidacy. But it was Perot himself who paid

FIGURE 9.1
Voter Support for H. Ross Perot, 1992

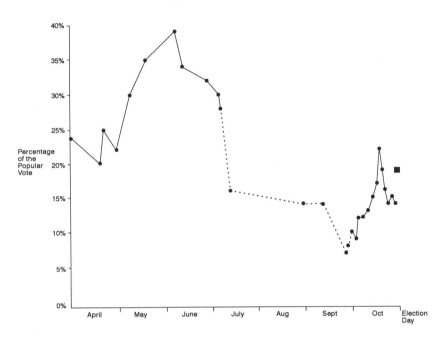

SOURCE: *Gallup Poll*

for and controlled the "grass-roots" movement. Perot Systems provided office space, employees, phone lines, and technical support. Perot employees set up the national headquarters in a Perot building on Merit Drive.

From the beginning, Perot maintained top-down control of the emerging campaign. As ballot petition drives got under way, Perot dispatched key employees to oversee and nurture their development. When a Perot for President office spontaneously popped up in Washington, D.C., Perot shut it down. When more than one competing group sprung up in a state, Perot dispatched his "whiteshirts" to resolve the conflict (Germond and Witcover 1993, pp. 224-29).

At the peak of his support in June, Perot hired two of the

most prominent political consultants in the country—former Ronald Reagan campaign manager Ed Rollins and former Jimmy Carter manager Hamilton Jordan—to help plan the world-class campaign that Perot had promised supporters. Soon after, stories emerged of bitter battles between the staff and a candidate "too headstrong to take advice from his managers," as CBS's Bill Lagatutta put it. Perot rejected the $147 million campaign blueprint that Rollins and Jordan drew up, vetoed the idea of staging a midsummer media campaign, objected to the scores of campaign professionals added to the staff, and despised the pilot ads that former Reagan ad-man Hal Riney had prepared. Within six weeks, Rollins resigned and Perot "withdrew" from the race. Jordan did not return when the campaign resumed in October.

All sorts of reasons surfaced for Perot dropping out. Some reports had him "wilting under the fire of negative campaign" (Barrett 1992, p. 32). Others said he "lost heart" after realizing what it would take to eliminate the budget deficit (Ceaser and Busch 1993, p. 95). Still others reported that Perot was unwilling to spend the money needed to wage a serious presidential effort. In his withdrawal statement, Perot made the dubious claim that it was the revitalized Democratic Party and his concern that the House of Representatives would have to decide a three-way contest—a prospect that would disrupt the country. (Seven weeks later when he formally reentered the race, Perot claimed that the real reason he dropped out was that the GOP had planned dirty tricks aimed at disrupting his daughter's wedding.)

In retrospect, however, Perot's withdrawal looks more like a shrewd and deliberate plan to stop the barrage of negative publicity, to preserve what was left of his good name, and to save money for a stretch run in the fall.

Though he denied it all summer, the facts clearly show that "Perot began plotting his comeback within hours of his withdrawal" (Turque 1992, p. 31). Two days after dropping out, Perot told a select group of volunteers in Dallas that "If anybody thinks I've quit, they're going to be in for an October surprise" (Turque 1992, p. 30). Two weeks later, Perot formed

"United We Stand"—portraying it as a group that would pressure candidates to embrace his economic program. In letters sent to state election officials in thirty states, Perot affirmed his desire to remain on the presidential ballot. Between July 17 and September 30—the time during which he was presumably out of the race—Perot pumped over $11 million into his presidential campaign, as documents filed with the Federal Election Commission later revealed. This money was used to staff the Dallas headquarters, sustain sixty-four state and regional campaign offices around the country, and underwrite the petition drives that were still under way in nineteen states. To keep his issues in the public's mind during his seventy-six-day hiatus, Perot published *United We Stand: How We Can Take Back Our Country*, which outlined his prescriptions for balancing the budget and cleaning up the mess in Washington. With Perot's money, "the volunteers" bought 100,000 copies of the paperback, which helped make it a national bestseller.

Perot used the campaign hiatus to consolidate his control over the local organizations that had arisen the past spring. He took over state organizations, replacing volunteers with paid professionals with whom he had personal or business connections. He opened new campaign offices that were funded directly out of Dallas, bypassing local volunteers entirely. He ran credit checks and conducted private investigations of state coordinators, weeding out those he deemed untrustworthy. He formed a new brain trust, replacing Ed Rollins, Hamilton Jordan, and Tom Luce with United We Stand executive director Orson Swindle, crony Martin Murphy, longtime aide Sharon Holman, and son-in-law Clay Mulford (Turque 1992). Perot centralized decision making in Dallas.

In the closing pages of his political manifesto, Perot wrote: "The Perot phenomenon that swept the country through the spring and summer of 1992 had little to do with me. It was a spontaneous grassroots outpouring" (1992, p. 111). Nothing could have been farther from the truth. As Perot's Kentucky coordinator, Charles M. Hellebusch, put it, Perot's devotion to grass-roots democracy was a charade. "There's no information coming from the ground up. It's all a sham" (Balz 1993, p. A8). Perot's former chair of the New York metropolitan area, Matthew Lifflander, concluded: "this whole thing with the volunteers is a cruel hoax" (Noah 1992, p. A16). The volunteers did not own this organization. United We Stand was organized, financed, and controlled by Perot. Although Perot insisted that his decision to "reenter" the race would come "from the bottom up," it wasn't "the volunteers in all 50 states," but Perot himself who decided to "reenter" the race on October 1.

Few, if any, candidates could get away with dropping out of a race and reentering a month before election day. Campaign workers would defect; money would dry up; the campaign organization would crumble; news coverage would turn to ridicule. But Perot did not need to convince any campaign contributors; he could keep his organization going out of petty cash; the volunteers were nothing but props; and the news media remained in awe of his willingness to spend.

Like other prominent independent candidates in the twentieth century, Perot was able to "construct . . . a pseudo-party and present himself as the people's voice" (Wilentz 1993, p. 35). Like his twentieth-century counterparts, Perot was more an independent campaign than a political party. There was no real organization distinct from the candidate's own following. The "party" would not have existed without the candidate.

Sources of Support

Ross Perot's vote total on election day surprised most everyone. Polls published the weekend before the election showed Perot would win about 16 percent of the popular vote. Political pundits predicted he would end up with less than 13 percent.[1] Instead, Perot captured 18.9 percent of the popular vote—more votes than any third party or independent candidate had won in eight decades.

[1] The final preelection polls were reported in *The Public Perspective*, November/December 1992, p. 11. The forecasts made by twenty-nine political pundits were reported in American Political Network, Inc. (1992).

Perot drew support from nearly every segment of the American electorate: from men and women, from rich and poor, from well-educated and those with few years of formal schooling, from liberals and conservatives. He ran best among those who said the budget deficit was the nation's most pressing problem. No region stood out as a Perot stronghold, though he ran slightly better in Maine, Kansas, Alaska, Idaho, Montana, Nevada, Utah, and Wyoming, where he won over a quarter of the vote.

Perot did not win a single electoral vote, however. The Electoral College system worked as we described in chapter 2, discriminating against this nationally based independent candidate who in every state fell short of a popular vote plurality.

Perot did not play the role of a spoiler. Bill Clinton would still have been elected President even if Perot had not run. Data gathered by Voter Research and Surveys (the consortium of news organizations that interviewed voters as they left the polling place on election day) show that Perot's vote would have divided evenly between Bush and Clinton had Perot's name not been on the ballot.[2] Nor did Perot appear to have had a significant impact on the Electoral College results. Though Bush was the second choice of Perot voters in southern and mountain states, Clinton was the second choice in New England. Everywhere else, Perot voters would have divided themselves evenly between Bush and Clinton. Allocating the Perot vote to Bush and Clinton based on each voter's second choice suggests that Perot may have cost Bush 20 electoral votes (from Georgia, Nevada, and Montana)—nothing close to the 140 electoral votes that George Bush needed to catch up with Clinton.[3]

Having said all that, Perot *did* prevent Clinton from winning a majority of the vote—the new President received only 43 percent of the popular vote. Entering the White House as a minority President certainly contributed to the trouble Clin-

[2] Market Strategies Inc.'s post-election survey for the Republican National Committee reaches the same conclusion. See Shaw (1993, p. 13).
[3] Market Strategies Inc. for the Republican National Committee, as reported in Shaw (1993, p. 14).

ton had pushing his legislative agenda through Congress. Perot did not affect the outcome of the Presidential election, but he almost certainly affected the outcome of the Clinton presidency.

Voters abandoned the major parties in 1992 for many of the same reasons that citizens cast third party ballots in earlier eras. The same factors that caused people to bolt to George Wallace in 1968 and John Anderson in 1980 also explain why people cast a ballot for Ross Perot in 1992 (table 9.1). Citizens with the weakest allegiance to the major parties were about five times more likely to vote for Perot than were those who strongly identified with the Democratic or Republican Party. Citizens were four times more likely to cast a vote for Perot if they thought the major parties' nominees were unacceptable than if they had a positive impression of at least one of the major party candidates. The youngest cohorts, who entered the electorate long after the New Deal realignment and thus had the weakest allegiance to the major parties, were most likely to support Ross Perot in 1992, just like they were most likely to vote for Wallace and Anderson in early eras. Black loyalty to the major parties was about as evident in 1992 as it was in 1968 and 1980.[4] Although there were ostensibly very different candidates—running in different decades, campaigning on different issues, and appealing to different regions of the country—on each occasion, the same underlying factors motivated people to vote for the third party challenger.

However, weak voter allegiance to the major parties, dissatisfaction with the major parties' candidates, and deep concern about issues are only a part of the story behind Ross Perot's success. These considerations, as well as the others we deployed in chapters 6 and 7, cannot alone account for the level of third party voting that occurred in 1992. Our aggregate time-series equation reported in table 7.1 predicts that there were 97 chances out of 100 that a nationally prestigious

[4] Others who have analyzed data from the 1992 National Election Study have reached conclusions similar to those reported here. See Alvarez and Nagler (1994); Abramson et al. (1994); Gilbert, Johnson, and Peterson (1994); Gold (1994); and Miller and Shanks (1995, ch. 16).

TABLE 9.1
Sources of Support for George Wallace,
John Anderson, and H. Ross Perot

	Percentage Voting for George Wallace	Percentage Voting for John Anderson	Percentage Voting for H. Ross Perot
Strength of partisanship			
Strong partisan	5.6	3.6	6.4
Weak partisan or independent who leans to a major party	13.5	8.0	22.2
Pure independent	20.7	14.1	35.9
Evaluation of the major parties			
Positive	5.2	4.2	2.9
Neutral	7.5	10.5	12.8
Negative	16.0	11.5	22.0
Evaluation of the major party candidates			
Positive	6.1	4.2	6.2
Neutral	21.9	10.4	13.9
Negative	38.7	29.8	27.3
Age cohort			
New Deal	8.7	1.9	6.2
New Deal children	11.8	5.4	13.8
Post–New Deal	15.9	9.7	21.2
Race			
White	12.5	7.8	20.7
Black	0.0	1.0	3.7
Concern with issues			
Low	10.9	6.1	15.9
Medium	10.9	9.1	18.2
High	15.5	10.3	19.9

SOURCE: National Election Studies, 1968, 1980, and 1992.

third party candidate would emerge in 1992. Our aggregate vote equation (reported in table 6.1), however, grossly underestimates the number of Americans that cast a third party ballot in 1992. When we plug in the values observed in 1992 (treating Perot as a nationally prestigious third party candidate),[5] the model predicts that 6.0 percent of the electorate would bolt the major parties. Instead, 19.6 percent of the electorate cast a third party ballot—a whopping 13.6 point error.

Why was support for third parties in 1992—and for Ross Perot in particular—so much higher than we would have expected based on the analysis of third party voting over the last century and a half? And why did Ross Perot manage to garner nearly three times as many votes as John Anderson did back in 1980?

The most widely accepted interpretation of Perot's performance in 1992, as we suggested at the outset of this chapter, is that Americans had grown increasingly dissatisfied with the major parties, with the candidates, with politics, and with the mess in Washington. In the section that follows, we show that this line of argument, as seductive as it may be, does not explain the surge in third party voting between 1980 and 1992. The real explanation for Perot's exceptional performance, which we lay out in the subsequent section, is that he was able to break through the constraints that third party and independent candidates before him had faced.

SEVEN MYTHS ABOUT WHY SO MANY AMERICANS
VOTED FOR H. ROSS PEROT

Myth #1: Declining Allegiance to the Major Parties

Some observers say that waning allegiance to the major parties is the reason Ross Perot did so well (Black and Black 1992;

---

[5] By the strict definition we offered in chapter 5, Ross Perot does not cut mustard as a nationally prestigious third party candidate. In reality, however, by the fall campaign Perot was just as much a national political figure as, say, Eugene McCarthy was in 1976 or John Anderson was in 1980. When we created these categories more than a decade ago, we did not anticipate billionaires buying national standing that in the past had been reserved for Presidents, vice presidents, governors, U.S. senators, and representatives.

1994). To be sure, there was a vast pool of independent voters that Perot could tap. Americans were much less likely to profess attachment to the Democratic or Republican Party in 1992 than they were in the 1960s. And as we saw in table 9.1, citizens with the weakest party attachments and most uncharitable evaluations of the major parties were most likely to bolt to Perot.

Waning allegiance to the major parties, however, cannot explain why Ross Perot did so much better than John Anderson. *Allegiance to the major parties did not decline between 1980 and 1992.* In 1980, 26 percent of the American people identified themselves as either strong Democrats or strong Republicans (table 9.2). In 1992, the proportion of the electorate that professed strong partisan leanings was actually three percentage points *higher* than in 1980. Similarly, the proportion of the electorate that called themselves apolitical or denied leaning toward a political party *declined* two points between 1980 and 1992. Other indicators also fail to show a drop in party allegiance since John Anderson ran. Citizens were just as likely in 1992 as they were in 1980 to say they saw important differences between what the Democrats and Republicans stand for. And although Americans were two points less likely in 1992 than in 1980 to say that one of the major parties can deal with the nation's most important problems, they were also nineteen points *more* likely to say they did care which *party* wins the presidential election. Our measure of citizen evaluation of the major parties (based upon the number of positive and negative comments voters make about them) declined a measly two points between 1980 and 1992.

In short, waning allegiance to the major parties can help explain why Perot did as well as John Anderson, but not why he did any better.

Myth #2: Surging Disaffection with the Major Party Candidates

A second, widely accepted interpretation of 1992 is that Perot did so well because citizens were unhappy with Bush and Clinton. As we have already seen, voters most disaffected from the major party nominees are much more likely to aban-

TABLE 9.2
Disaffection in 1980 and 1992

Characteristic of the Electorate	1980	1992	Change
Allegiance to the major parties			
Strength of partisanship			
Strong partisans	26%	29%	+ 3%
Pure independents and apoliticals	15%	13%	− 2%
Important differences between what the	63%	63%	0%
Democrats and Republicans stand for			
One of the major parties is likely to get the	54%	52%	− 2%
government to do a better job in dealing with			
the nation's most important problem			
Care which party wins the presidential election	56%	75%	+19%
Evaluation of the major parties (100-point scale)	51	49	− 2
Assessment of major party nominees			
Evaluation of the major party candidates	27	33	+ 6
(100-point scale)			
"Feeling thermometer" rating of major party	73	71	− 2
candidates (100-point scale)			
Distance from a major party candidate on	1.0	.9	− .1
(7-point) liberal/conservative scale			
Political alienation			
Political disaffection			
Trust the government to do what is right none	74%	71%	− 3%
or some of the time			
Government is run by a few big interests	77%	79%	+ 2%
People in government waste a lot of money	80%	68%	−12%
Quite a few government officials are crooked	48%	47%	− 1%
Political disaffection (100-point) scale	74	72	− 2
Government unresponsiveness			
Government does not pay much attention to	42%	26%	−16%
what the people think			
Elections do not make the government pay	13%	12%	− 1%
much attention to what the people think			
Political efficacy			
Public officials don't care much what people	55%	58%	+ 3%
like me think			
People like me don't have any say about what	40%	39%	− 1%
the government does			

Source: National Election Studies, 1980 and 1992.

don the major parties than voters who positively evaluate one of the major party candidates. This relationship held in 1968 when George Wallace ran; it held in 1980 when John Anderson ran; and it held in 1992 for H. Ross Perot.

Though disaffection with the major party candidates was relatively high, it cannot explain why Ross Perot captured nearly three times as many votes as John Anderson. The simple fact is that *the American people were no more disenchanted with the major parties' nominees in 1992 than they were in 1980* (table 9.2). The electorate's evaluation of the major party candidates (based upon the positive and negative comments citizens make about them) was actually six points *higher* in 1992 than it was in 1980. "Feeling thermometer" ratings of the most preferred major party candidate were only two points lower in 1992 than they were in 1980. Nor is there any evidence that citizens in 1992 regarded the major party candidates as more ideologically aloof. For example, when asked to place themselves and the candidates on a seven-point liberal/conservative scale, the average citizen stood 1.0 points away from the closest major party candidate in 1980; in 1992 the closest major party candidate was only .9 points away.[6]

In sum, rising disaffection with the major party candidates cannot explain this rise in third party voting because citizens were no more disaffected with the major party nominees in 1992 than they were in 1980.

Myth #3: Increasing Political Alienation

A third, popularly held interpretation of 1992 is that Perot's support grew out of a rising tide of political alienation—from politics, from politicians, and from government as a whole. Soundings from 1992 *were* bad: 71 percent of the electorate said that they rarely trusted the government to do what is right; 79 percent said that government was run by a few big

---

[6] Gold (1994) finds that measured across a broad range of issues, 25 percent of the 1980 electorate stood far away from both major party candidates; only 23 percent of the electorate stood far from both major party candidates in 1992.

interests; 68 percent said that people in government wasted a lot of money; 47 percent thought that quite a few government officials were crooked (table 9.2). To borrow the title of Germond and Witcover's account of the 1992 election, Americans were *Mad as Hell* (1993).

But again, 1992 was not much different from 1980. If anything, political disaffection actually *declined* a bit between 1980 and 1992, judging from the disaffection scale built from responses to the four disaffection questions referred to above. Other indicators of political alienation produce about the same results: the electorate's perception of government unresponsiveness *declined* between 1980 and 1992. Feelings of political efficacy in 1992 were about what they were in 1980.

As appealing as the "mad as hell" interpretation of the 1992 election might be, there is little hard evidence that political disaffection played much role in vote choice in 1992. Perot's appeal was not limited to the angry. For example, although 20 percent of those citizens most disaffected from the political system cast a ballot for Perot, so did 13 percent of those *least* disaffected. And careful, multivariate analysis of vote choice in 1992 confirms what we reported in chapter 6 about 1968-1980 elections: those most disaffected from government, most likely to portray the government as unresponsive, or most likely to feel they are unable to affect the decisions of government do not turn to third parties as a recourse any more often than do the unalienated.[7]

Political alienation does not explain why H. Ross Perot did so much better than John Anderson. Americans were disaffected from politics, politicians, and government in 1992, but no more so than when John Anderson ran in 1980. Aliena-

---

[7] Neither Alvarez and Nagler (1994), Gilbert, Johnson, and Peterson (1994), Abramson et al. (1994), nor Zaller and Hunt (1996) find any relationship between disaffection from government and the propensity to vote for Perot. Although Gilbert, Johnson, and Peterson (1994) and Abramson et al. (1994) find that people who rate the federal government low on the 100-point feeling thermometer were more likely to vote for Perot, the effect is substantively very small. Abramson et al. (1994) find, as we did in our analysis of the 1952 to 1980 elections, that political efficacy (the belief that one can influence the decisions of government) has no impact on the propensity to vote for Perot.

tion did not make people more likely to cast a third party ballot.

Myth #4: Fear of a Declining Economic Future

Fear about the economy was critical to George Bush's demise. And although many observers have assumed that it was also key to Perot's appeal, it turns out that the economy cannot explain the historic proportions of Perot's vote.

The economy was bad in 1992, but by most indicators, the country was actually in much *better* shape than it was in 1980 (table 9.3). Although real disposable income per capita had grown a measly 1.8 percent in 1992, it had *dropped* 0.3 percent in 1980. Although over a third of the electorate felt worse off financially in 1992, 42 percent felt this way in 1980. And although nearly three out of four citizens thought that the nation's economy had gotten worse in 1992, a whopping 83 percent of the electorate felt that way in 1980.[8]

Second, despite all the talk in 1992 about America's insecure economic future, citizens were much *more* optimistic in 1992 than they were when John Anderson ran. In 1992, 10 percent of the electorate said they would be worse off financially a year from now; fully 22 percent of the electorate were that pessimistic in 1980. Less than one in five Americans in 1992 said that the national economy would decline over the next year; nearly one out of three Americans foresaw a declining national economy in 1980.

Finally, in 1992 citizens were *more* positive about the ability of the major parties to handle the economy than they were in 1980. Ten percent of the 1992 electorate said there was no difference between the ability of the Democratic and Republican parties to keep the country prosperous. Back in 1980, nearly twice as many Americans saw no difference between the two parties.

[8] Alvarez and Nagler (1994) find that citizens who felt worse off financially or who felt that the national economy had declined were no more likely than other Americans to vote for Perot. These findings are consistent with the very modest effects we reported in chapter 6.

TABLE 9.3
Economic Conditions and Outlooks in 1980 and 1992

Economic Indicator	1980	1992	Change
Election year change in real disposable income per capita	− .3%	+1.8%	+2.1%
Retrospective economic evaluations			
Personally worse off financially compared to a year ago	42%	35%	− 7%
Nation's economy has gotten worse over the past year	83%	72%	−11%
Prospective economic evaluations			
Will be personally worse off financially a year from now	22%	10%	−12%
National economy will get worse over the next year	31%	19%	−12%
No difference between the ability of the Democratic and Republican parties to keep the country prosperous	19%	10%	− 9%

SOURCE: *Statistical Abstract of the United States, 1994*; National Election Studies, 1980 and 1992; *The Gallup Poll Monthly*, September 1980 and October 1992.

So while many Americans did indeed fear that their birth-right of an ever-expanding economy was going by the way-side, this does not account for Perot's historic vote.

Myth #5: Ross Perot's Personal Appeal

A fifth interpretation of the 1992 results focuses on Ross Perot's charisma. Anderson staged a notoriously dull campaign in 1980, something that could never be said of Ross Perot. But when all is said and done, Americans did not warm up to Ross Perot as a person any more than they did to John Anderson. In interviews conducted over the two months before the 1980 election, NES respondents rated John Anderson a tepid 52 on the 100-point "feeling thermometer." During the last five weeks of the 1992 campaign (when Perot was officially in the race), NES respondents rated him a measly 47—

that is, five points *lower* than Anderson.[9] The surge in third party voting in 1992 cannot be attributed to Ross Perot's personal charm.

Myth #6: Ross Perot Can Win

Still another assertion about why Ross Perot did so well is that his standing in the polls, his participation in the presidential debates, and his media blitz in the final weeks of the campaign convinced voters that he was viable—that he could actually win. Unlike his predecessors, so the story goes, Perot short-circuited the argument that a third party vote is a "wasted vote." As appealing as this line of reasoning may be, it too does not jibe with the facts. First, citizens did not think that Perot stood much of a chance of winning—and the numbers here are not appreciably better than they were for Anderson. Back in 1980, only 0.5 percent of the electorate interviewed in the two months before the November election thought that Anderson would be elected President; only 1.2 percent thought that he would carry their state. In 1992, 2.6 percent of the electorate interviewed in the period that Perot was back in the campaign thought he would be elected President; 3.7 percent thought he would carry their state.[10]

Despite Perot's message that "this is not time to waste our vote on politics as usual," Perot, just like his predecessors, lost support to the wasted vote argument. Those citizens who

[9] There were no more impassioned supporters of Perot (as measured by scores of seventy points or more on the feeling thermometer) than there were impassioned supporters of Anderson. These findings also hold if one examines responses that citizens gave to the questions asking what it was they liked and disliked about the candidates: citizens did not like Perot any more than they liked Anderson. As John Zaller puts it, Perot had no "inherent degree of likability that was independent of the media coverage he was getting at the moment." He finds that the public's evaluations of Perot waxed and waned with the news about him (personal communication, September 20, 1995).

[10] NES data also show that only 3.4 percent of the respondents interviewed in the final two weeks of the campaign thought that Perot would be elected; 5.4 percent thought he would carry their state. Even before Perot suspended his campaign, only 7 percent of the respondents interviewed in the July 14-15 CBS News Poll thought Perot would win.

rated Perot higher than Bush or Clinton were two to three times more likely to abandon Perot on election day than were citizens who gave Clinton or Bush their highest rating (Brams and Merrill 1994). Although Perot's supporters were less likely than John Anderson's to defect, they were more likely to defect than were those most supportive of George Wallace in 1968 (Abramson et al. 1994). In sum, Perot did not neutralize the electorate's perception that he could not win.[11] Clearly, most of the people who voted for Perot thought they were voting for a loser.

Myth #7: Perot Mobilized New Voters

Another myth is that Perot did so well because he managed to bring to the ballot box for the first time millions of Americans who in the past had been sitting on the political sidelines.[12] Although voter turnout rose 5.1 points in 1992 to 55.2 percent—its highest level in over two decades—careful analysis of the evidence shows that Ross Perot's personal appeal, his straight talk, and his legion of "volunteers" did little, if anything, to bring new voters to the polls in 1992. The politically disaffected were not more likely to vote in 1992 than were other citizens. Perot's staunchest supporters were no more likely to turn out than those who supported Bush or Clinton (Rosenstone et al. 1993).[13] For all the talk of the Perot campaign mustering its supporters from the ranks of the disenfranchised, citizens who stayed home in 1988 but turned out to vote in 1992 were no more likely to cast a ballot for Perot than were citizens who had voted in both elections (Alvarez and Nagler 1994). Moreover, Perot's "grass-roots, citizen campaign" managed to contact personally a mere 2.8 percent of the electorate—and those who were contacted were only 5.5

[11] On this point, also see Shaw (1994) and Black and Black (1994).

[12] For a sampling, see Swanson (1992); Pear (1992); Pomper (1993); and Nichols and Beck (1995).

[13] Neither citizens who placed Perot high on the 100-point "feeling thermometer," nor citizens who rated Perot higher than both Bush and Clinton on the thermometer, nor citizens whose positive views of Perot outbalanced their negative views were more likely to cast a ballot in 1992 (Rosenstone et al. 1993).

percent more likely to vote—producing an aggregate increase in turnout of a measly 0.15 percentage point (Rosenstone et al. 1993).[14]

Perot's mobilization efforts were no less effective than his predecessors'. Historically, voter turnout has not fluctuated with the ebb and flow of support for third party or independent candidates (figure 9.2).[15] Even the most successful independent contenders have had no apparent impact on voter participation. Take, for example, Theodore Roosevelt's 1912 "Bull Moose" campaign—the most successful independent presidential campaign in American history. Like Perot, Roosevelt championed the sovereignty of the people, declaring, "we recognize in neither court, nor Congress, nor President any divine right to override the will of the people." Like Perot, Roosevelt attacked the Democratic and Republican Party as "husks" lacking "real souls . . . divided on artificial lines, boss ridden, and privilege controlled."[16] Like Perot, Roosevelt had charisma and flare, which made the 1912 contest an unusually spirited campaign. In the end, Roosevelt captured 27 percent of the popular vote and eighty-eight electoral votes from six states, but voter turnout plunged nearly seven points between 1908 and 1912. Turnout also fell five points when Henry Wallace and Strom Thurmond ran in 1948; it dropped a point in 1968 when George Wallace ran and dropped another point in 1980 with Anderson's candidacy. Turnout rose less than half a percentage point when Robert LaFollette ran in 1924.

In sum, Perot, like his predecessors, did not rally new vo-

---

[14] In contrast, the major parties personally contacted 20 percent of the electorate, boosting the turnout of those they contacted by 9.2 points.

[15] The details of this time-series analysis are reported in Rosenstone et al. (1993). When the voter turnout time series is modeled as a simple first-order, autoregressive process with interventions for the advent of women's suffrage in 1920, the extension of the franchise to 18-to-21-year-olds in 1972, and support for third party candidates, the coefficient for the vote for third party candidates is overwhelmed by its standard error ($b = .01$; $SE(b) = .09$). Restricting the analysis to the twentieth century does not alter the results. Neither does differencing the data nor taking the logarithm of third party vote. The results do not change either when the effect of prestigious and nationally prestigious third party candidates are taken into account.

[16] Mowry (1946, pp. 262-78; 1971, pp. 2135-66) and Pinchot (1958).

FIGURE 9.2
Third Party Vote and Turnout, 1844-1992

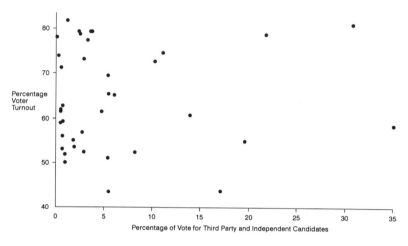

SOURCE: *Rosenstone el al. (1993).*

ters by offering hope to the disenchanted. Perot's campaign organization was ineffective in bringing new voters to the polls. Mobilization of new voters does not explain why Perot did so well in 1992.

Summary

The facts are fairly straightforward. Between 1980 and 1992 party allegiance did not decline, disaffection with the major party candidates did not surge, alienation did not rise, and economic uncertainty did not grow. Americans did not think Ross Perot stood a much better chance of winning than John Anderson did in 1980, nor were they more enthusiastic about Perot, the person, than they were about Anderson when he ran for President. Perot did not mobilize new voters to his cause. The reasons for the rise in third party voting lie elsewhere.

Breaking the Constraints on Third Parties in America

The key to Ross Perot's success was his ability to break through many constraints that had impeded third party challengers in the past. Unlike his predecessors, Perot had ample resources to deploy a national campaign organization, to stage ballot access drives in all fifty states, and to mount an unprecedented media blitz in the final weeks of the campaign. Unlike his predecessors, Perot participated in three presidential debates that put him on equal footing with the major party candidates. Unlike his predecessors, Perot gained considerable access to the media.

Abundant Resources

Money, and plenty of it, is what distinguishes H. Ross Perot from every other third party presidential candidate. Reports filed with the Federal Election Commission show that the Texas billionaire spent a whopping *$72.9 million* on his bid for the White House—nearly all of it his own. No other third party candidate in American history mustered this kind of cash for an independent campaign. To put things in perspective, after correcting for inflation, Perot spent 7.6 times more than former President Theodore Roosevelt did in his 1912 Bull Moose campaign, 2.5 times more than George Wallace mustered for his 1968 effort, and 2.8 times more than John Anderson laid out in 1980.

Unlike his predecessors, Perot had the resources to build and maintain a national campaign organization. Perot had the resources to mount the petition drives needed to get his name on the November ballot in each state. Perot had the resources to campaign—especially through the media.

Whereas in the past even the most successful minor party challengers had amassed only a fraction of the resources available to their Democratic and Republican opponents, Perot's expenditures outpaced those of his major party rivals. As we reported in table 2.2, Theodore Roosevelt spent only 60 percent of the average major party total in 1912, George Wallace spent 39 percent, and John Anderson only 49 percent. However, in 1992 Ross Perot spent *119 percent* of what Bill Clinton and George Bush expended on their campaigns. During his first two weeks back, for example, Perot shelled out an astounding $25.7 million—twice what Bush or Clinton each spent in the first half of October. Americans did not seem to mind that Perot was trying to buy his way into the White House. Instead, his money became part of his appeal. Many voters believed that Perot was too rich to be bought—he would not be beholden to special interests (Matalin and Carville 1994, p. 148).

Although Perot could not buy his way into the White House, his deep pockets surely bought a lot of votes on election day.[17] As evident from the data displayed in figure 9.3, a third party candidate's share of the popular vote tends to increase as the level of spending rises (relative to that of the major party candidates). After taking into account the diminishing marginal return of campaign money and the easier time that prestigious and nationally prestigious candidates have raising campaign funds, we estimate that when third party candidates double their spending, on average, they raise their vote total by about half.[18] Put differently, had Perot spent in 1992 what Anderson spent in 1980 (that is, had Perot spent only 49 per-

---

[17] For evidence on the impact of money on congressional elections, see Jacobson (1978; 1980) and Sorauf (1992).

[18] To make these estimates, we regress the log of the percentage of the vote received by the third party candidate onto the log of the percentage of spending by the third party candidate, controlling for whether the candidate was a prestigious or nationally prestigious candidate. There are 66 cases: the 46 third party candidates listed in table 2.2 and the 20 candidates who ran in 1984, 1988, and 1992. The ordinary least squares estimates (with standard errors in parentheses) are:

$\log(\text{vote} + 1) =$

.456 * log(spending + 1) + .774 * nationally prestigious third party candidate
(.060)   (.223)

+ .249 * prestigious third party candidate − .069. R^2 = .84.
(.153)

These data tell only part of the story. They do not take into account "soft money"—that is, money spent on party-building activities such as voter registration drives and efforts to get out the vote. This should not, however, distract from the central point: Perot was in a lot better shape than any of his predecessors.

FIGURE 9.3
Campaign Expenditures and Third Party Vote, 1908-1992
(Logarithmic Scales)

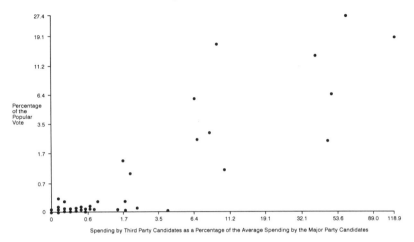

Spending by Third Party Candidates as a Percentage of the Average Spending by the Major Party Candidates

cent rather than 119 percent of what the major parties spent), Perot's level of support would have been 5.9 percentage points lower. This means that nearly one-half the 12.3 percentage points that separate Perot's vote from Anderson's can be attributed to the greater amount of money that Perot was able to plow into his campaign.

If anything, these calculations may underestimate by a few points the impact of Perot's money. These estimates do not take into account Perot's ten-week hiatus, which permitted him to concentrate his resources in the final month of the campaign. They do not factor in Perot's "electronic front-porch campaign," which spared him the expenses associated with going on the road in search of votes (Goldman et al. 1994, p. 429). They do not take into account that Perot was self-financing, which spared him millions of dollars in fund-raising costs. In short, not only did Perot have more money overall, but a much greater share of it went to helping him win votes.

Ballot Access

Although Perot was fond of portraying his ballot drive as a grass-roots effort run by "the volunteers," the petition drives were in large part financed by Perot himself. With deep pockets, Perot simply spent what was needed to get his name on all fifty-one ballots—in the final analysis, about $18 million (Black and Black 1992, p. 5).[19] During his campaign hiatus, Perot financed petition drives in the nineteen states that had not yet reached their filing deadlines. In New York, for example, Perot took out full-page newspaper ads and purchased radio spots urging people to sign his ballot petition; he hired six hundred temporary workers to gather the required signatures; he purchased voter registration lists from each of New York's sixty-two counties so that campaign workers in his Manhattan headquarters could electronically verify the information provided on the petitions (Isikoff and Goodstein 1992, p. A6). As Black and Black put it, "for Perot, getting on the ballot was nothing more than a matter of resources" (1992, p. 5).

In addition, the barriers to ballot access in 1992 were lower than in recent years thanks to the legal battles that George Wallace, Eugene McCarthy, and John Anderson had waged. Anderson needed 1.2 million signatures to qualify for every ballot in 1980; Perot needed only 716,000 signatures in 1992 (Winger 1992). Whereas Anderson's effort required expensive litigation in a dozen states, Perot filed not one lawsuit, profiting from the legal victories that those before him had won.

An Advertising Blitz

Unlike his predecessors who were strapped for funds in the final weeks of their campaigns, Perot's personal wealth enabled him to mount an unprecedented, massive media blitz. During the 1980 campaign, for example, John Anderson was able to allocate only $1.6 million to television and radio adver-

[19] This represented a quarter of Perot's $72.9 million total campaign effort. In contrast, Anderson's ballot access drive consumed $7.3 million of his $15.0 million campaign chest—nearly half.

tisement—about one-tenth the $16.5 million that Reagan and Carter each spent on media buys (Alexander 1983). In 1992 Perot allocated an astonishing $45 million to television advertisements—about 1.3 times more than Clinton and Bush each spent and 16 times more than Anderson spent in 1980 after correcting for inflation (Germond and Witcover 1993, p. 440).

This again illustrates how Perot's financial advantage lay not just in the raw number of dollars he spent, but also in the extent to which he was able to spend it persuading voters. While Perot's *overall* budget was 2.8 times the size of Anderson's, his *media* budget was 16 times as large; while Anderson was able to devote just over 10 percent of his total budget to media, Perot could spend nearly 62 percent of his treasury on ads.

In total, Perot aired ten infomercials, each reaching an average of 10.7 million homes—about 16.1 million viewers (Nielsen 1993, p. 10). More Americans saw Perot's first infomercial than tuned into the first few innings of the National League baseball playoffs that aired immediately after Perot. This media blitz made a big impression on the American people. Two-thirds of the electorate reported seeing one or more of Perot's commercials (Buchanan 1993, p. 11). Citizens interviewed in the final days of the campaign were just as likely to recall something about a Perot ad as they were to recall something that Bush or Clinton put on the air (Zaller and Hunt 1996, ch. 5). Voters reacted positively to Perot's ads—much more positively than to the commercials that Clinton or Bush ran (Visgaitis 1992). According to one estimate, the money that Perot devoted to his media blitz may have contributed as much as 8.5 percentage points to his vote total (Zaller and Hunt 1996, ch. 5). This estimated vote advantage is in the same ballpark as our estimate based upon Perot's overall level of campaign spending.

Participation in the Presidential Debates

Perot was the first independent candidate to appear shoulder-to-shoulder with both major party candidates in televised presidential debates. John Anderson debated Ronald Reagan in September 1980, but when Anderson's standing in the polls dipped below 15 percent, he was excluded from the more crucial Carter-Reagan clash the week before the election. When the bipartisan Commission on Presidential Debates invited Perot to join, he clearly did not meet the commission's criterion of having a reasonable chance to win anymore than John Anderson did in 1980. Perot was included because Bush, in a desperate effort to save his floundering campaign, wanted him to take part.

Perot's participation in the nationally televised debates on October 11, 15, and 19 had three powerful consequences. First, by placing Perot on equal footing with the two major party nominees, the debates granted visibility, legitimacy, credibility, and status—exactly what Perot desperately needed in the final month of the campaign, and exactly what third party challengers before him could never achieve. For four and one-half hours, over sixty million Americans saw Perot on the same podium with Bush and Clinton (Nielsen 1993). The visual images that appeared on the front pages of newspapers around the country, on the covers of the weekly news magazines, and on television news broadcasts showed three candidates for President. Reporters referred to them as the "major candidates." Although the media's debate postmortems said more about Bush and Clinton than about Perot, the coverage of Perot was about as positive as the coverage of Clinton and much more positive than the coverage of Bush (Downing 1994).

Second, the debates gave Perot an opportunity to frame his message. During the debates, he effectively portrayed Bush and Clinton as having been cut from the same political cloth. He blasted his opponents for giving in to special interests. Over and over, he hammered the Democrats and the Republicans for their failures, especially on the federal deficit. And he turned his political inexperience into an advantage, quipping at one point in the first debate: "Well, they've got a point. I don't have any experience running up a $4 trillion dollar debt. I don't have any experience in gridlock government. I have experience in not taking ten years in solving a ten-minute problem." Perot was not just one of three candidates for President; he was the *one* contender who was different.

Finally, public opinion polls showed that viewers thought that Perot had outperformed his competitors in two of the three encounters (Newport and Gallup 1992). Those who tuned in saw a successful businessman, deeply concerned about the budget deficit. As Goldman and his colleagues conclude, Perot's "strong performance had washed out some of the taint left over from the eccentric course and the abrupt end of his first campaign. He had made himself plausible again" (1994, p. 578).

Over the course of the three presidential debates, Perot's standing in the trial heats rose 5 percentage points; his favorable ratings doubled; his negatives were cut in half; confidence in his ability to deal with the economy rose.[20] Had he not taken part in the debates, it is unlikely that Perot's campaign would have regained its momentum.

Media Coverage of Perot

As we argued in chapter 2, the media generally ignore third party candidates. Yet, this did not happen in 1992, in part because Perot developed a strategy for successfully sidestepping the national press corps; in part because Perot appeared for a time to be a viable presidential contender and the media covered him as such; and in part because Perot participated in the presidential debates.

Like Jerry Brown, Perot exploited a new channel of political communication—television and radio talk shows and interview programs—that allowed him to get his message across, in his own words, to a huge national audience, with little mediation by the national press corps. During the initial months of his campaign Perot worked the radio and television news

[20] These numbers parallel Zaller and Hunt's more detailed analysis, which estimates that Perot's participation in the debates boosted his vote total by 4.2 percentage points (1996, ch. 5).

and talk show circuit, making some forty-seven appearances between February when he announced his availability and July when he suspended his candidacy (Zaller and Hunt 1996). Perot appeared on *CBS This Morning*, on NBC's *Today*, on ABC's *Good Morning America*, on *Nightline*, and on interview programs hosted by Phil Donahue, Tom Snyder, Barbara Walters, David Frost, and, of course, Larry King, to name a few. Zaller and Hunt estimate that during the initial month of his campaign, Perot's appearances on talk shows and viewer call-in programs allowed Perot to reach about 31.9 million people (1996, ch. 2). Perot's predecessors—including John Anderson—were never this efficient in getting their message out to the American electorate.

The media covered Perot much more extensively than they covered John Anderson in 1980. Between May 1 and June 15—Perot's period of peak support in the polls—media coverage of Perot kept pace with that of Bill Clinton.[21] Anderson never enjoyed this level of attention even when he stood at 25 percent in the polls. The same pattern held during the fall campaign: Perot received much more coverage than Anderson did (Magoon 1994; Zaller 1995).

Even more crucial than the amount of coverage is the tone. Here too, the media portrayed Ross Perot more positively than they portrayed John Anderson. Both Anderson and Perot enjoyed a honeymoon of sorts—an initial period during which reports on their candidacy were overwhelmingly favorable, even upbeat. Initial stories focused on the myth of Ross Perot and on the public's enthusiasm for his candidacy: the thousands of phone calls that poured into his headquarters each day and how "across the country ordinary people on their own are trying to get Perot on the ballot" (Jamie Gangel on NBC's *Today*, March 16, 1992). Perot graced the cover of all the weekly news magazines. *Time*'s May 25 cover, for example, read: "President Perot?" The media widely reported on

---

[21] During this six-week period, network television news devoted 108 minutes to Perot and 67 minutes to Clinton. The nation's thirty leading newspapers ran 2,305 stories mentioning Perot against 2,690 mentioning Clinton (Zaller and Hunt 1996).

Perot's standing as frontrunner in the polls. Never during the 1980 campaign was media coverage of Anderson as positive as was the coverage of Perot during the initial months of his 1992 presidential bid (Zaller and Hunt, ch. 3).

Then the coverage turned sour. Talk show hosts pushed for specifics. Journalists focused on Perot's shallow understanding of the issues, his inexperience, and his authoritarian style. The *Dallas Morning News*, for example, reported that Perot had fired an employee for refusing to shave off his beard. *The Wall Street Journal* revealed that Ross Perot had regularly engaged private detectives to gather information about his employees and competitors. A couple days later the *Los Angeles Times* recounted how during a power struggle with GM chair Roger Smith, Perot had told aides that they might have to "nuke" GM by shutting down its computer system. The *Washington Post* and *The Wall Street Journal* described Perot's various investigations of George Bush and his sons. The *Chicago Tribune* wrote about "The World of Inspector Perot," comparing Perot's investigative practices to former President Nixon's penchant for "enemy lists." Stories surfaced that Government Accounting Office auditors had "found pervasive, widespread problems" in work that Perot companies had done for the government. A *Los Angeles Times* article revealed that senior officers with whom Perot served in the navy judged him to be "emotionally maladjusted" and too immature to be a career naval officer.

By the end of June, the media relayed the "Doubts about Ross Perot" as *Time's* June 29 cover put it. The *New York Times'* Michael Kelly summed up the transformation this way: "Only a short while ago, Ross Perot had the sort of public image that would make any politician salivate: self-made billionaire, just folks tycoon, scourge of the Ayatollah, straight-talking guy. But lately, a more ominous portrait has emerged: J. Edgar Perot, a man obsessed by conspiracies and beset by enemies in his mind, willing to use tactics of espionage and intimidation to destroy those who stand in his way" (Kelly 1992). "The idea that Perot is a conspiratorialist and a paranoid," Morton Kondracke reported on the political talk show the *McLaughlin*

Group, "is now in the public conscience." The electorate's opinion of Ross Perot grew increasingly negative.

"Suspending" the campaign spared Perot ten weeks of bad press. And by the time he resumed his campaign on October 1, the media were preoccupied with the horse race, Perot's performance in the debates, and whether Perot's campaign could be revived. This is not to say that the media's concerns about Perot had disappeared. *Newsweek* greeted Perot's reentry with a cover story entitled "Ego Trip." New revelations (such as contradictory reports about Perot's reasons for dropping out in July, wild charges that Bush had planned to disrupt Perot's daughter's wedding, and Perot's claim that two decades ago terrorist death squads had targeted him) surfaced, but these stories no longer dominated coverage of Perot.

In the closing month of the campaign Perot not only received more press coverage than Anderson did in 1980, but much more positive coverage as well. For every positive Anderson horse race story that appeared in newspapers around the country in 1980, there were five negative ones. Perot's ratio in 1992 was only three to one. For every positive story written about Anderson on the issues, there were over four negative ones; for Perot, the ratio was only two to one—a figure not much worse than the 1.4:1 ratio for Clinton and Bush (Magoon 1994). Perot's coverage on network television news was slightly more negative than Clinton's but not noticeably more negative than Bush's (Zaller and Hunt 1996, ch. 5). In sum, Perot enjoyed better and more sustained media coverage than his recent predecessors—particularly in the closing weeks of the presidential campaign.

Summary

Ross Perot's historic level of support was not the result of unprecedented anger or disaffection. If that was all he had going for him, he would have garnered only about 6 percent of the vote.

Ross Perot's success was due largely to his ability to use his wallet to crush almost all of the constraints that had hindered his predecessors. His money bought ballot access, it bought news coverage normally accorded to major party candidates, it bought advertising, it bought appearances in the debates, and it bought credibility.

That is not to say that any candidate with deep pockets and a willingness to spend can expect to win close to 20 percent of the vote as a minor party candidate for President. Nor would Perot have done just as well had he run in another year. What made 1992 unique was the *combination* of dissatisfaction with the major parties and the presence of a candidate who had the ability to tap that dissatisfaction. If John Anderson had been a successful businessman with a willingness to spend millions of dollars, he too might have made history.

THE CONSEQUENCES OF ROSS PEROT

The importance of Ross Perot, like that of other third party candidates, must be gauged not so much by the number of votes Perot garnered on election day, but by the impact he had on the campaign and on the policies that the major parties felt compelled to adopt in the wake of the election. Although he did not affect the election outcome itself, Perot's entry into the 1992 race helped focus the debate on two issues: the federal budget deficit and political reform. As the major parties had done in the past, Democrats and Republicans alike responded to the third party threat by embracing Perot's positions as their own in an effort to quell Perot and co-opt his supporters.

Just as President Nixon pursued a "Southern strategy" to entice George Wallace's supporters into the Republican fold, so too did President Clinton try to win over those who had voted for Ross Perot. Six weeks after his election, President-elect Clinton staged a two-day economic summit where 300 business, academic, civic, and government leaders offered advice on a broad range of economic issues including deficit reduction, investment for long-term growth, and government reform—a Perotesque electronic town meeting carried live on national television. Weeks into his presidency, Clinton unveiled his first major policy proposal—a program designed to trim the deficit over four years by $500 billion. Like Perot, Clinton called for "shared sacrifice" through tax increases and spending cuts. Clinton even phoned Perot the afternoon he presented his plan before a joint session of Congress to see if Perot would back the proposal.

Clinton also pressed Perot's theme of ethics in government. Within days of the election, the President-elect announced strict ethics guidelines that would prevent transition aides from later representing clients with government ties. Weeks later, Clinton proposed a five-year ban on lobbying by senior political appointees after they left government. In the initial year of his presidency, Clinton introduced proposals to reform campaign finance and eliminate the business tax deduction for lobbyists.

Finally, Clinton aimed his rhetoric at Perot voters. As former Perot pollster Frank Luntz writes: "Proposals to expand government spending and regulation are cloaked in pro-business, pro-entrepreneurship language; tax increases are justified as shared sacrifices for a brighter future; campaign finance reform and cuts in the White House staff are pushed to appeal to the anti-politician mood of the American people. The State of the Union address contained phrases and passages lifted from earlier Perot speeches" (1993, p. 18).

Republicans, too, tried to court Perot and his supporters. Republican National Committee chair Haley Barbour invited United We Stand America organizers to take part in a GOP National Committee meeting. Senate Republican leader Bob Dole met with Perot's regional campaign coordinators. House Republicans invited Perot to speak to them. Prominent congressional Republicans, including Newt Gingrich (who in the aftermath of the 1994 midterm elections became Speaker of the House), sent in membership dues to join United We Stand America (Barnes 1993). Perot themes were among the GOP's top priorities in their "Contract with America": spending cuts to balance the budget; small-business incentives to create new jobs; and congressional reform to streamline the legislative process and make Congress more responsive to the people.

Perot Beyond 1992

Perot's quest, like that of other independent movements in this century, is a story about candidate-centered politics. Unlike third party crusades of the 1800s, Perot did not depend on cadres of grass-roots workers or on vibrant state and local organizations to canvass neighborhoods and mobilize citizens. Instead, Ross Perot relied on the media's coverage of his campaign, on ads, and on infomercials to get his message out to the American people. Perot's campaign was not built from the ground up on the sweat, energy, dedication, or money of ordinary citizens. Instead, Ross Perot bankrolled and controlled the whole operation himself. Unlike the Free Soilers, the Greenbacks, the Populists, and other third party movements of the nineteenth century, United We Stand was organized around and sustained by a single personality.[22]

But unlike Theodore Roosevelt, Robert LaFollette, George Wallace, and John Anderson, who faded from the political scene following their unsuccessful independent presidential bids, Perot endures.

Days after the 1992 election, Perot converted United We Stand into United We Stand America, Inc.—a nonprofit, educational, watchdog group dedicated to promoting Perot's agenda. Perot kicked off the membership drive with an hour-long news conference and a round of television interviews to spotlight the effort. Over the first four months, Perot visited thirty-seven cities in fourteen states to promote the organization. Perot bankrolled the organizational costs, the salaries of the fifty state directors, and the cost of television ads run to lure new members. Perot exercises the same strict central control over this organization that he did over its campaign predecessor (Engelberg and Ayres 1993; Balz 1994).[23]

[22] These fundamental changes in the nature of political campaigns have occurred within the major parties as well. See, for example, Polsby and Wildavsky (1991); Blumenthal (1980); Rosenstone and Hansen (1993).

[23] Perot refuses to release information on UWSA's membership. One estimate, calculated from the National Election Study fielded in the fall of 1993, suggests that about 2.4 percent of the electorate claims that they have joined Perot's organization.

UWSA did not appear as a third party in the 1994 midterm elections. Instead, it acted much like any other interest group—offering its support to whichever major party best met its needs. No United We Stand America candidates ran for governor. None ran for the U.S. Senate. None ran for the U.S. House of Representatives. Even former United We Stand executive director Orson Swindle ran for the House as a Republican, capturing only 43 percent of the vote. Perot urged supporters to elect a Republican Congress. Sixty-three percent of Perot's supporters who voted in 1994 cast a Republican ballot.

It is anyone's guess whether Perot will hear another "call to service" in 1996. To date, he has done nothing to discourage speculation about another run for the White House. He certainly has the resources to bankroll another (and another) presidential bid should he be of mind to do so. He is maintaining an organizational presence in all fifty states to facilitate his candidacy should he decide to revive it.

Perot continues to hug the political limelight. He joined Pat Buchanan and Jerry Brown in a failed effort in 1993 to defeat the North American Free Trade Agreement. Perot promoted his position in a 1993 paperback, *Not for Sale at Any Price*, and faced off against Vice President Al Gore to argue his side in a nationally televised debate. Between October 1994 and June 1995 Perot hosted a radio talk/call-in program, "Listening to America," carried on 153 stations around the country.

In August 1995 Perot hosted a three-day national issues conference—"Preparing Our Country for the 21st Century"— that three thousand of his followers attended. More than three dozen congressional leaders from both parties, representatives from the White House, and all the Republican candidates for President also felt compelled to troop down to Dallas to try to win over Perot's support. In the words of one observer, it was "an extraordinary panderthon." One by one, each speaker paid homage to Perot and his issues: the deficit, political corruption, and untamed foreign influence. And through it all, Perot set the scene for another "call to service" in 1996 by laying out a set of reforms that Congress needed to pass, including a balanced budget amendment, congressional term limits, and campaign finance and election law reform. "I will go away," Perot pledged, if the major parties "pass all the laws and the constitutional amendments."

Perot didn't wait very long to see if Congress would act. Five weeks later, on September 25, 1995, he appeared on *Larry King Live* to announce that he was forming a new "Independence Party." The party would work to get on the ballot in all fifty states and the District of Columbia, would stage a national primary to select a presidential candidate, but would not run any candidates for the House or the Senate. His initial efforts were partially successful, winning ballot access in California as the "Reform Party," but failing in Ohio and Maine.

But to think that Perot's performance in 1992 and his perseverance signal that third parties or independent candidates can now succeed where in the past they have failed is to misread grossly the election results. To be sure, there remains a vast and ideologically diverse pool of citizens with weak allegiance to the major parties, disaffection for the Democratic and Republican nominees, and distrust of politicians in Washington. Third party candidates may well continue to tap into this wellspring of discontent.

The lesson of 1992, however, is not that the pool of potential third party supporters has expanded. The lesson of 1992 is that *Ross Perot had the resources to tap into that pool*. Perot's support stemmed not so much from rising disaffection as much as from his ability to break through the constraints that third party and independent candidates before him faced. Perot's success in 1992 does not so much signal a further eroding of the two-party system or a greater willingness of Americans to support third party candidates as it does an even more familiar theme in American politics: money buys votes.

In 1995 it looked for a while like Perot's "success" in 1992 would inspire political movements from all points on the political spectrum to mount independent electoral campaigns of their own.[24] Former Chairman of the Joint Chiefs of Staff

[24] See, for example, Berke (1995); Cook (1995).

Colin Powell, retiring democratic Senator Bill Bradley of New Jersey, and former Connecticut independent Governor Lowell Weicker spoke openly about running independent campaigns for president. Weicker and Bradley and six other moderately prominent figures (including John Anderson) held discussions about creating a new party. But what was ultimately most telling was not that these leaders flirted with third-party candidacies, but that they all concluded that their efforts would be futile. They confronted the barriers to third parties and found the obstacles too great to overcome.

In all likelihood, they recognized that if they were able to muster the $83 million needed in 1996 to match Perot's 1992 effort, if they managed to capture the media attention that Perot garnered in 1992, and if they were granted a ticket to the presidential debates, they might have stood a chance to match or exceed Perot's vote total. But they would still have finished in third place. Furthermore, they all recognized they were not likely to raise Perot's millions or capture the media's attention, and that they stood a much greater chance of finishing more like John Anderson than Ross Perot.

Again, the key is money. Remember that under the Federal Elections Campaign Act, the Democratic and Republican nominees will each receive about $75 million to mount their 1996 campaigns. An independent candidate who receives at least 5 percent of the vote and appears on the ballot in at least ten states will also receive funding, but not until *after* the election. As one political observer put it, money that arrives in December doesn't buy much television time in October. And although the FECA rules permit candidates to spend as much as their own money as they want, FECA limits to $1,000 the amount that any individual can contribute to an independent's presidential bid. Simply put, any independent candidate (other than a millionaire) will have a hard time keeping pace with Democratic and Republican campaign spending in 1996.

Even if an independent candidate does manage to garner a formidable war chest, the constitutional and legal provisions that govern the conduct of elections in the United States remain inhospitable to third parties. As we argued at the outset of the book, the single-member-district, plurality elections that govern nearly every electoral contest in America favor the two parties. This system prevents third parties from reaping electoral rewards even when they attract 30 percent of the vote; it creates incentives for the major parties to co-opt third party supporters; it makes potential third party supporters feel they are wasting their votes. The Electoral College does the same—discriminating against third parties that do not have regionally concentrated support. Keep in mind that although Perot won nearly one in five votes cast in 1992, he failed to win a single electoral vote. Ballot access laws are still formidable hurdles for third party candidates to jump, and they show no sign of getting more lenient (Winger 1995). These fundamental rules of the political game still limit the potential electoral clout of third parties in America—even those with seemingly unlimited resources.

MINOR PARTY PRESIDENTIAL CANDIDATES,ᵃ 1840-1992

Year	Candidate	Party	Percentage of Presidential Popular Vote
1840	James G. Birney	Liberty	.28
1844	James G. Birney	Liberty	2.30
1848	Martin Van Buren	Free Soil	10.12
1852	John P. Hale	Free Soil	4.91
	Jacob Broom	Native American	.08
1856	Millard Fillmore	Whig-American	21.53
1860	John C. Breckinridge	Southern Democrat	18.09
	John Bell	Constitutional Union	12.61
1864	—	—	—
1868	—	—	—
1872	Charles O'Conor	Straight-out Democrat	.29
	James Black	Prohibition	.05
1876	Peter Cooper	Greenback	.90
	Green Clay Smith	Prohibition	.08
	James B. Walker	American	.01
1880	James B. Weaver	Greenback	3.32
	Neal Dow	Prohibition	.11
	John W. Phelps	American	.01
1884	Benjamin F. Butler	Greenback	1.74
	John P. St. John	Prohibition	1.47
1888	Clinton B. Fisk	Prohibition	2.19
	Alston J. Streeter	Union Labor	1.29
	Robert H. Cowdrey	United Labor	.01
	James Langdon Curtis	American	.01
1892	James B. Weaver	Populist	8.50
	John Bidwell	Prohibition	2.25
	Simon Wing	Socialist Labor	.18
1896	John M. Palmer	National Democrat	.96
	Joshua Levering	Prohibition	.90

Year	Candidate	Party	Percentage of Presidential Popular Vote
	Charles H. Matchett	Socialist Labor	.26
	Charles E. Bentley	National Prohibition	.14
1900	John G. Woolley	Prohibition	1.50
	Eugene V. Debs	Socialist	.62
	Wharton Barker	Populist	.36
	Joseph F. Malloney	Socialist Labor	.29
	Seth H. Ellis	Union Reform	.04
	Jonah F. R. Leonard	United Christian	b
1904	Eugene V. Debs	Socialist	2.98
	Sillas C. Swallow	Prohibition	1.91
	Thomas E. Watson	Populist	.84
	Charles H. Corregan	Socialist Labor	.25
1908	Eugene V. Debs	Socialist	2.82
	Eugene F. Chafin	Prohibition	1.70
	Thomas L. Hisgen	Independence	.55
	Thomas E. Watson	Populist	.19
	August Gillhaus	Socialist Labor	.09
	Daniel B. Turney	United Christian	b
1912	Theodore Roosevelt	Progressive	27.39
	Eugene V. Debs	Socialist	5.99
	Eugene W. Chafin	Prohibition	1.38
	Arthur E. Reimer	Socialist Labor	.20
1916	Allan L. Benson	Socialist	3.18
	James Franklin Hanly	Prohibition	1.19
	c	Progressive	.19
	Arthur E. Reimer	Socialist Labor	.08
1920	Eugene V. Debs	Socialist	3.42
	Parley P. Christensen	Farmer Labor	.99
	Aaron S. Watkins	Prohibition	.70
	William W. Cox	Socialist Labor	.11
	Robert C. Macauly	Single Tax	.02
1924	Robert M. LaFollette	Progressive	16.56
	Herman P. Faris	Prohibition	.19
	Frank T. Johns	Socialist Labor	.10
	William Z. Foster	Communist	.13
	Gilbert O. Nations	American	.08
	William J. Wallace	Commonwealth Land	.01
1928	Norman M. Thomas	Socialist	.72
	William Z. Foster	Communist	.13
	William F. Varney	Prohibition	.09

Year	Candidate	Party	Percentage of Presidential Popular Vote
	Verne L. Reynolds	Socialist Labor	.06
	Frank E. Webb	Farmer Labor	.02
1932	Norman M. Thomas	Socialist	2.22
	William Z. Foster	Communist	.26
	William D. Upshaw	Prohibition	.21
	William H. Harvey	Liberty	.13
	Verne L. Reynolds	Socialist Labor	.09
	Jacob S. Coxey	Farmer Labor	.02
	James R. Cox	Jobless	b
1936	William Lemke	Union	1.96
	Norman M. Thomas	Socialist	.41
	Earl R. Browder	Communist	.17
	David L. Colvin	Prohibition	.08
	John W. Aiken	Socialist Labor	.03
1940	Norman M. Thomas	Socialist	.23
	Roger W. Babson	Prohibition	.12
	Earl R. Browder	Communist	.10
	John W. Aiken	Socialist Labor	.03
1944	Norman M. Thomas	Socialist	.16
	Claude W. Watson	Prohibition	.16
	Edward A. Teichert	Socialist Labor	.09
	Gerald L. K. Smith	America First	b
1948	J. Strom Thurmond	States' Rights Democrat	2.40
	Henry A. Wallace	Progressive	2.38
	Norman M. Thomas	Socialist	.29
	Claude A. Watson	Prohibition	.21
	Edward A. Teichert	Socialist Labor	.06
	Farrell Dobbs	Socialist Workers	.03
1952	Vincent Hallinan	Progressive	.23
	Stuart Hamblen	Prohibition	.12
	Eric Hass	Socialist Labor	.05
	Darlington Hoopes	Socialist	.03
	Farrell Dobbs	Socialist Workers	.02
1956	T. Coleman Andrews	Constitution	.17
	Eric Hass	Socialist Labor	.07
	Enoch A. Haltwick	Prohibition	.07
	Farrell Dobbs	Socialist Workers	.01
	Darlington Hoopes	Socialist	b
1960	Eric Hass	Socialist Labor	.07
	Rutherford L. Decker	Prohibition	.06

Year	Candidate	Party	Percentage of Presidential Popular Vote
	Farrell Dobbs	Socialist Workers	.06
1964	Eric Hass	Socialist Labor	.06
	Clifton Deberry	Socialist Workers	.05
	E. Harold Munn	Prohibition	.03
	John Kasper	National States' Rights	.01
1968	George C. Wallace	American Independent	13.53
	Henning A. Blomen	Socialist Labor	.07
	Fred Halsted	Socialist Workers	.06
	Dick Gregory	Peace and Freedom	.06
	c	Peace and Freedom	.04
	E. Harold Munn	Prohibition	.02
	Eldridge Cleaver	Peace and Freedom	.01
	Charlene Mitchell	Communist	b
1972	John G. Schmitz	American	1.40
	Benjamin Spock	People's	.10
	Louis Fisher	Socialist Labor	.07
	Linda Jenness	Socialist Workers	.05
	Gus Hall	Communist	.03
	Evelyn Reed	Socialist Workers	.02
	E. Harold Munn	Prohibition	.02
	John Hospers	Libertarian	b
	Gabriel Green	Universal	b
1976	Eugene J. McCarthy	Independent	.93
	Roger MacBride	Libertarian	.21
	Lester Maddox	American Independent	.21
	Thomas J. Anderson	American	.20
	Peter Comejo	Socialist Workers	.11
	Gus Hall	Communist	.07
	Margaret Wright	People's Party	.06
	Lyndon H. LaRouche	U.S. Labor	.05
	Benjamin C. Bubar	Prohibition	.02
	Jules Levin	Socialist Labor	.01
	Frank P. Zeidler	Socialist	.01
1980	John B. Anderson	Independent	6.61
	Ed Clark	Libertarian	1.06
	Barry Commoner	Citizens	.27
	Gus Hall	Communist	.05
	John R. Rarick	American Independent	.05
	Ellen McCormick	Right to Life	.04
	Deirdre Griswold	Workers' World	.02

Year	Candidate	Party	Percentage of Presidential Popular Vote
	Percy L. Greaves, Jr.	American	.01
	Benjamin C. Bubar	Statesman	.01
	David McReynolds	Socialist	.01
	Andrew Pulley	Socialist Workers	.01
1984	Sonia Johnson	Citizens	.08
	Bob Richards	Populist	.07
	Dennis L. Serrette	Independent Alliance	.05
	Gus Hall	Communist	.04
	Mel Mason	Socialist Workers	.03
	Larry Homes	Workers' World	.02
	Delmar Dennis	American	.01
	Ed Winn	Workers' League	.01
	Earl F. Dodge	Prohibition	b
	Gavrielle Homes	Workers' World	b
	John B. Anderson	National Unity Party of Kentucky	b
	Arthur J. Lowery	United Sovereign Citizens	b
1988	David E. Duke	Populist	.05
	Eugene J. McCarthy	Consumer	.03
	Lyndon H. LaRouche, Jr.	National Economic Recovery	.03
	William A. Marra	Right to Life	.02
	Ed Winn	Workers' League	.02
	James Warren	Socialist Workers	.02
	Herbert Lewin	Peace and Freedom	.01
	Earl F. Dodge	Prohibition	b
	Larry Homes	Workers' World	b
	Willa Kenoyer	Socialist	b
	Delmar Dennis	American	b
1992	H. Ross Perot	Independent	18.86
	James "Bo" Gritz	Populist	.10
	Lenora B. Fulani	New Alliance	.07
	Howard Philips	U.S. Taxpayers	.04
	John Hagelin	Natural Law	.04
	Ron Daniels	Peace and Freedom	.03
	Lyndon H. LaRouche, Jr.	Economic Recovery	.03
	James Warren	Socialist Workers	.02
	Jack E. Herer	Grassroots	b
	J. Quinn Brisben	Socialist	b

Year	Candidate	Party	Percentage of Presidential Popular Vote
	Helen Halyard	Workers' League	b
	John Yiamouyiannas	Take Back America	b
	Earl F. Dodge	Prohibition	b
	Isabell Masters	Looking Back	b

SOURCE: Congressional Quarterly, *Guide to U.S. Elections* (Washington, D.C.: Congressional Quarterly, Inc., 1975); *Guide to 1976 Elections* (Washington, D.C.: Congressional Quarterly, Inc., 1977); *Guide to U.S. Elections* (Washington, D.C.: Congressional Quarterly, Inc., 1994); Clerk of the House of Representatives, *Statistics of the Presidential and Congressional Election of November 4, 1980* (Washington, D.C.: U.S. Government Printing Office, 1981). *Congressional Quarterly Weekly Report*, January 17, 1981, p. 138.

[a] Only candidates and parties that received popular votes in more than one state are listed in the appendix. People who received votes, but declined the nomination of a party (for example, Orval Faubus in 1960) are also excluded.

[b] Less than .01 percent of the vote.

[c] No candidate recorded.

DESCRIPTION AND CODING
OF VARIABLES

AGGREGATE DATA

Third Party Presidential Vote: proportion of the popular vote cast for non-major party presidential candidates. Source: Congressional Quarterly, *Guide to U.S. Elections*, Washington, D.C.: Congressional Quarterly, Inc., 1975; Congressional Quarterly, *Guide to 1976 Elections*, Washington, D.C.: Congressional Quarterly, Inc., 1977; *Congressional Quarterly Weekly Report*, January 17, 1981, p. 138.

Nationally Prestigious Third Party Candidate Running: years when a third party candidate is both (1) a former president, vice-president, governor, senator, or congressman and (2) has previously run for president or vice-president within a major party or on its ticket = 1; otherwise = 0. Source: Congressional Quarterly, *Guide to U.S. Elections*, Washington, D.C.: Congressional Quarterly, Inc., 1975; Congressional Quarterly, *Guide to 1976 Elections*, Washington, D.C.: Congressional Quarterly, Inc., 1977; *Congressional Quarterly Weekly Report*, October 18, 1980, p. 3144.

Prestigious Third Party Candidate Running: years when a third party candidate is a current or former governor, senator, or congressman, but has not previously run for president or vice-president on a major party ticket = 1; otherwise = 0. Source: see nationally prestigious third party candidate.

Proportion of Voters with a Nationally Prestigious Third Party Candidate on Their Ballot: (number of voters who live in states with a nationally prestigious third party candidate on the ballot) / (the total votes cast for president). In states without an Australian ballot voters are counted as having the candidate on the ballot. Source: Arthur C. Ludington, *American Ballot Access Laws: 1888-1910*, Albany: New York State Library, 1911; Walter Dean Burnham, personal communication; *New York Times*, October 31, 1948, p. 50; Congressional Quarterly, *Guide to U.S. Elections*, Washington, D.C.: Congressional Quarterly, Inc., 1975;

Congressional Quarterly, *Guide to 1976 Elections*, Washington, D.C.: Congressional Quarterly, Inc., 1977; *Congressional Quarterly Weekly Report*, October 18, 1980, p. 3146.

Proportion of Voters with a Prestigious Third Party Candidate on Their Ballot: (number of voters who live in states with a prestigious third party candidate on ballot) / (the number of voters in the electorate). Voters who live in states without an Australian ballot are counted as having the candidate on the ballot. Voters who live in states with two prestigious candidates on the ballot are counted twice. Source: Arthur C. Ludington, *American Ballot Access Laws: 1888-1910*, Albany: New York State Library, 1911; Congressional Quarterly, *Guide to U.S. Elections*, Washington, D.C.: Congressional Quarterly, Inc. 1975; D. Leigh Colvin, *Prohibition in the United States*, New York: George H. Doran Co., 1926; David H. Bennett, *Demagogues in the Depression*, New Brunswick, N.J.: Rutgers University Press, 1969, pp. 267-68; *New York Times*, October 31, 1948, p. 50; *Congressional Quarterly Weekly Report*, October 28, 1972, p. 2794; Congressional Quarterly, *Guide to 1976 Elections*, Washington, D.C.: Congressional Quarterly, Inc., 1977; *Congressional Quarterly Weekly Report*, October 18, 1980, p. 3146.

Third Party Presidential Vote$_{t-4}$ for Non-Prestigious Candidates: (popular third party presidential vote$_{t-4}$) − (vote for prestigious and nationally prestigious third party candidates$_{t-4}$) / (total presidential popular vote$_{t-4}$). Source: see third party presidential vote.

Closeness of Previous Presidential Election: (proportion of popular vote cast for the winning major party candidate$_{t-4}$) − (proportion of popular vote cast for the losing major party candidate$_{t-4}$). Source: see third party presidential vote.

Proportion of the Electorate Eligible to Vote for the First Time: (number of first-time eligible voters$_t$) / (voting age population$_t$); where the number of first-time eligible voters$_t$ = (voting age population$_t$ − voting age population$_{t-4}$ + number of deaths in voting age population between election$_{t-4}$ and election$_t$). Source, voting age population: *Historical Statistics of the United States, Colonial Times to 1970; Statistical Abstract of the United States, 1969; Current Population Reports*, Series P-25, March 1980; *Congressional Quarterly Weekly Report*, January 17, 1981, p. 138. Source, number of deaths: compiled from *Historical Statistics of the United States*,

Colonial Times to 1970 and individual volumes of *Statistical Abstract of the United States*, 1971-1980.

Proportion of the Electorate Eligible to Vote for the First Time Who Immigrated from Countries with Viable Socialist Parties: (number of immigrants from countries with a viable socialist party who arrived 5, 6, 7, or 8 years prior to the election) / (voting age population,). Corrections were made for immigrants who lived in states that permitted aliens to vote. Source, immigrants: *Historical Statistics of the United States, Colonial Times to 1970*; individual volumes of *Statistical Abstract of the United States,*1971-1980; *Economic Report of the President*, 1981. Source, voting age population: see preceding entry.

Age of the Party System: the first year in each system—1828, 1860, 1896, 1932—is counted as the last year of the previous system. The subsequent years—1832, 1864, 1900, 1936—are coded as "2"; 1836, 1868, 1904, 1940 as "3"; and so on.

Major Party Factionalism (National Level): the average, across the two major parties, of the proportion of convention delegates who supported the first runner-up on the last ballot before switches. Source: Richard Bain and Judith H. Parris, *Convention Decisions and Voting Records*, Washington, D.C.: Brookings, 1973; Congressional Quarterly, *Guide to 1976 Elections*, Washington, D.C.: Congressional Quarterly, Inc., 1977; *Congressional Quarterly Weekly Reports*, July 19, 1980, p. 2067, and August 16, 1980, p. 2437.

Major Party Factionalism (Regional Level): the proportion of the convention delegates from the geographic region that most heavily supported the first runner-up on the last ballot before switches who cast nominating ballots for that candidate. Regions: East—Maine, New Hampshire, Vermont, New York, Massachusetts, Rhode Island, Connecticut, New Jersey, Pennsylvania, Delaware, Maryland, District of Columbia; South—West Virginia, Virginia, Kentucky, Tennessee, North Carolina, South Carolina, Georgia, Alabama, Mississippi, Arkansas, Louisiana, Florida, Texas, Oklahoma; Midwest—Ohio, Indiana, Illinois, Michigan, Wisconsin, Minnesota, Iowa, Missouri, Kansas, Nebraska, South Dakota, North Dakota; West—Washington, Oregon, California, Nevada, Arizona, Utah, Idaho, Montana, Wyoming, Colorado, New Mexico, Alaska, Hawaii. Source: see major party factionalism (national level).

Long-Term Change in Agricultural Prices: $((FPI_t-FPI_{t-16}) / (FPI_{t-16}))$ x (proportion of workforce in agriculture$_t$); where FPI = wholesale price index for farm goods. Source, price index: *Historical Statistics of the United States, Colonial Times to 1970*, pp. 199-201; *Statistical Abstract of the United States, 1979*, p. 477; *Statistical Abstract of the United States, 1980*, p. 479; *Economic Report of the President, 1981*, p. 298. Source, percent of workforce in agriculture: 1840-1868—compiled from *U.S. Census*, 1840, 1850, 1860, 1870; 1869-1970—*Historical Statistics of the United States, Colonial Times to 1970*, p. 240; *Survey of Current Business*, Bureau of Economic Analysis, 1972-1980; *Survey of Current Business*, January 1981.

Change in Incumbent Party's Congressional Vote: (proportion of the vote for the U.S. House of Representatives cast for the incumbent president's party$_{t-2}$) − (the proportion of the vote for the U.S. House of Representatives cast for the incumbent president's party$_{t-4}$). Source: "State-Level Congressional, Gubernatorial, and Senatorial Election Data for the United States, 1824-1972," data collected by Walter Dean Burnham and made available through *ICPSR*; *Historical Statistics of the United States, Colonial Times to 1970*; individual volumes of *Statistical Abstract of the United States*.

President Denied His Party's Renomination: if an incumbent or former president sought, but was denied, his party's nomination in year$_t$ or year$_{t-4}$ = 1; otherwise = 0. If the incumbent who was bumped by his party ran as a third party candidate in the year he was denied renomination, the variable is coded 0 in the subsequent year.

Incumbent President Running: when an incumbent president is a major party presidential nominee = 1; otherwise = 0.

Presidential Popularity: proportion of the electorate who approve of the president's performance in office. Source: *Public Opinion Index*, October-November 1980.

Change in Real Disposable Income per Capita: ((real disposal income third quarter, year$_t$)—(real disposable income first quarter, year$_t$)) / (real disposable income first quarter, year$_t$). Source: *Economic Report of the President*, 1953, 1957, 1961, 1965, 1969, 1973, 1977, 1981.

Change in Unemployment: ((average unemployment for the three months of third quarter, year$_t$)—(average unemployment for the three months of first quarter, year$_t$)) / (average unemployment for the three months of first quarter, year$_t$). Source: *Economic Report of the President*, 1953, 1957, 1961, 1965, 1969, 1973, 1977, 1981.

Inflation: ((GNP personal consumption price deflator third quarter, year$_t$)—(GNP personal consumption price deflator first quarter, year$_t$)) / (GNP personal consumption price deflator first quarter, year$_t$). Source: *Economic Report of the President*, 1953, 1957, 1961, 1965, 1969, 1973, 1977, 1981.

INDIVIDUAL-LEVEL DATA

All individual-level data are from the Center for Political Studies 1952-1980 National Election Studies.

Voted for Minor Party Candidate = 1; Voted for Major Party Candidate = 0.

Evaluation of the Major Party Candidates: respondents were asked what they liked and disliked about the major party candidates. The respondent's value on this variable is equal to the number of positive comments minus the number of negative comments for the candidate he feels most positive about. This score was recoded to the 0-1 interval (0 = most negative evaluation; 1 = most positive evaluation).

Evaluation of the Major Parties: respondents were asked what they liked and disliked about the two major parties. The respondent's value on this variable is equal to the number of positive comments about the major parties minus the number of negative comments. This score was recoded to the 0-1 interval (0 = most negative evaluation; 1 = most positive evaluation).

Concern with Issues: proportion of all comments made about the major parties and their nominees that cite issues.

Distance from the Major Party Candidates on Urban Unrest Issue in 1968: coded in 1968 as the distance between the respondent's position and the nearest major party candidate's position. The original urban unrest scale ranged from 1 (solve problems of poverty and unemployment) to 7 (use all available force). Nixon is coded 5, Humphrey 2. The absolute value of the arithmetic distance between the respondent's and the closest major party candidate's position was set to the 0-1 interval (0 = the respondent's position is equivalent to a major party candidate's position; 1 = the respondent's position is very far away from a major party candidate's position). Years other than 1968 = 0.

Distance from the Major Party Candidates on Racial Issues in 1968: constructed in the same manner as the urban unrest variable except that the distance on two issues was averaged. The two items used were: (1) the federal government's role in ensuring job equality ("see to it that Negroes get fair treatment in jobs" = 1; "leave these matters to the states and local communities" = 5; Nixon is coded 2, Humphrey 1); and (2) the federal government's role in ensuring school integration ("see to it that white and Negro children go to the same schools" = 1; "stay out of this area as it is none of its business" = 5; Nixon is coded 3.5, Humphrey 1). The average absolute value of the arithmetic distance between the respondent's and the closest major party candidate's position was set to the 0-1 interval (0 = the respondent's position is equivalent to a major party candidate's position; 1 = the respondent's position is very far away from a major party candidate's position). Years other than 1968 = 0.

Political Disaffection: a scale that ranges between 0 (least disaffected) and 1 (most disaffected). The scale is constructed from responses to four questions: "Would you say that the government is pretty much run by a few big interests looking out for themselves or that it is run for the benefit of all the people?" "Do you think that people in the government waste a lot of the money we pay in taxes, waste some of it, or don't waste very much of it?" "Do you think that quite a few of the people running the govenment are a little crooked, not very many are, or do you think hardly any of them are at all?" "How much of the time do you think you can trust the government in Washington to do what is right—just about always, most of the time, only some of the time?" Responses to each item were factor analyzed; the factor scores were used to weight the items in constructing the scale.

National Economic Conditions: national economic conditions are worse now than they were a year ago = 0; about the same = .5; economic conditions are better now than they were a year ago = 1.

Personal Financial Well Being: personally worse off financially than a year ago = 0; about the same = .5; personally better off financially than a year ago = 1.

Nationally Prestigious Third Party Candidate on Ballot = 1; not on the Ballot = 0.

Prestigious Third Party Candidate on Ballot = 1; not on the Ballot = 0.

New Deal Cohort: respondent came of voting age in 1932 or 1936 = 1; otherwise = 0.

New Deal Children Cohort: respondent came of voting age between 1937 and 1956 = 1; came of voting age before 1937 or after 1956 = 0.

Post–New Deal Cohort: respondent came of voting age in or after 1960 = 1; came of voting age before 1960 = 0.

Age (logged): $\log_e$ of age of respondent (in years).

Southern White (1968 only): Southern white in 1968 = 1; otherwise = 0.

Student = 1; non-student = 0.

Black = 1; white or other race = 0.

Male = 1; female = 0.

First-Time Voter: respondent is eligible to vote for the first time = 1; otherwise = 0.

Education: 0-8 years of education = 1; some high school = 2; high school diploma = 3; trade or technical school = 4; some college = 5; college degree = 6.

Unemployed = 1; not unemployed = 0.

Professional or Manager: head of household is a professional or manager = 1; otherwise = 0.

Unskilled Worker: head of household is an unskilled worker = 1; otherwise = 0.

Service Worker: head of household is a service worker = 1; otherwise = 0.

Union Family: the respondent or a member of his family belongs to a labor union = 1; otherwise = 0.

Upper-Income Bracket: respondent's family income is in the top third of the nation = 1; otherwise = 0.

Lower-Income Bracket: respondent's family income is in the bottom third of the nation = 1; otherwise = 0.

Catholic = 1; otherwise = 0.

Jew = 1; otherwise = 0.

Democrat: respondent identifies with the Democratic Party or is an independent who "leans" to the Democratic Party = 1; otherwise = 0.

Party Identification Relative to Party of Incumbent President: respondent's party identification is the same as the president's =

1; respondent's party identification is the opposite of the president's $= -1$; otherwise $= 0$.

Lives in an Eastern State: respondent lives in Maine, New Hampshire, Vermont, Massachusetts, Rhode Island, Connecticut, New York, New Jersey, Pennsylvania, Delaware, or the District of Columbia $= 1$; otherwise $= 0$.

Lives in a Border State: respondent lives in West Virginia, Oklahoma, Missouri, Kentucky, or Maryland $= 1$; otherwise $= 0$.

Lives in a Southern State: respondent lives in Virginia, North Carolina, South Carolina, Georgia, Florida, Tennessee, Alabama, Mississippi, Arkansas, Louisiana, or Texas $= 1$; otherwise $= 0$.

Lives in a Rocky Mountain State: respondent lives in Montana, Arizona, Colorado, Idaho, Wyoming, Utah, Nevada, New Mexico $= 1$; otherwise $= 0$.

Lives in a Western State: respondent lives in California, Oregon, Washington, Hawaii, or Alaska $= 1$; otherwise $= 0$.

Not Interested in the Campaign $= 1$; "very much interested in the campaign" or "somewhat interested in the campaign" $= 0$.

Very Much Interested in the Campaign $= 1$; "not interested in the campaign" or "somewhat interested in the campaign" $= 0$.

Contacted by a Major Party: respondent was personally contacted by a major party campaign $= 1$; not contacted $= 0$.

Post-1964 Elections: 1968 $= 1$; 1972 $= 2$; 1976 $= 3$; 1980 $= 4$; 1952-1964 $= 0$.

REFERENCES

Abramson, Paul R., John H. Aldrich, Phil Paolino, and David W. Rohde. 1994. "The Problem of Third-Party and Independent Candidates in the American Political System: Wallace, Anderson, and Perot in Comparative Perspective." Paper read at the 1994 annual meeting of the American Political Science Association, New York, September 1-4, 1994.

Achen, Christopher, H. 1983. *Statistical Analysis of Quasi-Experiments.* Berkeley: University of California Press.

Alexander, Herbert E. 1976. *Financing the 1972 Election.* Lexington, Mass.: Lexington Books.

———. 1979. *Financing the 1976 Election.* Washington, D.C.: Congressional Quarterly, Inc.

———. 1983. *Financing the 1980 Election.* Lexington, Mass.: Lexington Books.

Alvarez, R. Michael, and Jonathan Nagler. 1994. "Change or Continuity in Presidential Politics: A Multinomial Probit Model of Candidate Choice in the 1992 Election." Unpublished manuscript. California Institute of Technology.

American Civil Liberties Union. 1943. "Minority Parties on the Ballot." Unpublished manuscript. New York: American Civil Liberties Union.

American Political Network, Inc. 1992. "Those Crazy Talking Heads and Their Nutty Crystal Balls." *Hotline*, November 2, 1992.

Anderson v. Babb (E.D. N.C. August 21, 1980).

Anderson v. Celebrezze (S.D. Ohio July 18, 1980).

Anderson v. Hooper (D. N.M. July 8, 1980).

Anderson v. Mills (E.D. Ky. August 14, 1980).

Anderson v. Morris (D. Md. August 6, 1980).

Anderson v. Quinn (D. Maine August 11, 1980).

Arnett, Alex M. 1922. *The Populist Movement in Georgia.* New York: Columbia University Press.

Asher, Herbert. 1980. *Presidential Elections and American Politics.* Homewood, Ill.: Dorsey.

Associated Press. 1980. "Democrats Ready to Fight to Keep Anderson off Ballot." *New York Times,* June 6, 1980, p. 30.

Balz, Dan. 1993. "A Year Later, Perot's Purpose Is Still Unclear." *Washington Post,* June 22, 1993, pp. A1, A8.

———. 1994. "Internal Battles Shake Foundation of Perot's Political Structure." *Washington Post,* April 24, 1994, p. A20.

Barnard, William D. 1974. *Dixiecrats and Democrats.* University of Alabama Press.

Barnes, Fred, 1993. "Loving too much." *The New Republic,* August 9, 1993, pp. 10-11.

Barrett, Laurence I. 1992. "Perot Takes a Walk." *Time,* July 27, 1992, pp. 32-33.

Bass, Paul S. 1982. "No Alternatives: Third Parties and the Fourth Estate." Unpublished manuscript. Yale University.

Beck, Paul Allen. 1974. "A Socialization Theory of Partisan Realignment." In Richard G. Niemi and Associates (eds.), pp. 199-219. *The Politics of Future Citizens.* San Francisco: Josey-Bass.

Bennett, David H. (1969. *Demagogues in the Depression.* New Brunswick, N.J.: Rutgers University Press.

Berke, Richard L. 1995. "The Specter of Perot Haunts Major Parties." *New York Times,* June 6, 1995, p. A20.

Berman, William C. 1970. *The Politics of Civil Rights in the Truman Administration.* Columbia: Ohio State University Press.

Billington, Ray Allen. 1933. *The Protestant Crusade, 1800-1960.* New York: Macmillan.

Binkley, Wilfred Ellsworth. 1961. *American Political Parties, Their Natural History,* 3rd edn. New York: Knopf.

Bishop, Joseph Bucklin. 1920. *Theodore Roosevelt and His Time.* Vol. II. New York: Charles Scribner's Sons.

Black, Gordon. 1972. "A Theory of Political Ambition: Career Choices and the Role of Structural Incentives." *American Political Science Review* 66: 144-59.

Black, Gordon S., and Benjamin D. Black. 1992. "Americans Want and Need a New Party." *The Public Perspective,* November/December 1992, pp. 3-6.

———. 1994. *The Politics of American Discontent; How a New Party Can Make Democracy Work Again.* New York: Wiley.

Blackorby, Edward C. 1963. *Prairie Rebel: The Public Life of William Lemke.* Lincoln: University of Nebraska Press.

Blue, Frederick J. 1973. *The Free Soilers.* Urbana: University of Illinois Press.

Blum, John Morton. 1973. *The Price of Vision: The Diary of Henry A. Wallace.* Boston: Houghton Mifflin.

Blumenthal, Sidney. 1980. *The Permanent Campaign: Inside the World of Elite Political Consultants.* New York: Basic Books.

Bone, Hugh A. 1943. "Small Political Parties—Casualties of War?" *National Municipal Review* 32: 524-26.

Boulding, Kenneth E. 1953. *The Organization Revolution.* New York: Harper.

Brams, Steven J. 1978. *The Presidential Election Game.* New Haven: Yale University Press.

Brams, Steven J., and Samuel Merrill III. 1994. "Would Ross Perot Have Won the 1992 Presidential Election under Approval Voting?" *PS* 27 (March 1994): 30-44.

Broder, David S. 1971. "Election of 1968." In Arthur M. Schlesinger and Fred L. Israel (eds.), pp. 3705-52. *History of American Presidential Elections, 1789-1968.* New York: McGraw-Hill.

————. 1980. "Carter, Reagan Camps Focusing on Suburbs in the Swing States." *Washington Post,* September 28, 1980, pp. A1, A4-5.

————, et al. 1980. *Pursuit of the Presidency.* New York: Berkley Books.

Buchanan, Bruce, 1993. "A Tale of Two Campaigns or Why '92's Voters Forced a Presidential Campaign Better than '88's and How It Could Happen Again." Paper read at the 1993 annual meeting of the American Political Science Association, Washington, D.C., September 2-5, 1993.

Burner, David. 1971. "Election of 1924." In Arthur M. Schlesinger and Fred L. Israel (eds.), pp. 2459-90. *History of American Presidential Elections, 1789-1968.* New York: McGraw-Hill.

Burnham, Walter Dean. 1955. *Presidential Ballots 1836-1892.* Baltimore: The Johns Hopkins University Press.

————. 1970. *Critical Elections and the Mainsprings of American Politics.* New York: W. W. Norton.

Cain, Bruce E. 1978. "Strategic Voting in Britain." *American Journal of Political Science* 22: 639-55.

Cameron, David R. 1981. "Presidential Elections and the Mobilization of Nazism: The Growth of a Catch-All Party." Unpublished manuscript. Yale University.

Campbell, Angus, Philip Converse, Warren E. Miller, and Donald Stokes. 1960. *The American Voter.* New York: Wiley.

Carlson, Jody. 1981. *George C. Wallace and the Politics of Powerlessness.* New Brunswick, N.J.: Transaction Books.

Ceaser, James, and Andrew Busch. 1993. *Upside Down and Inside Out; the 1992 Elections and American Politics.* Lanham, Md.: Rowman and Littlefield.

Chambers, William Nisbet. 1967. "Party Development and the American Mainstream." In William Nisbet Chambers and Walter Dean Burnham (eds.), pp. 3-32. *The American Party Systems.* New York: Oxford University Press.

———. 1971. "The Election of 1840." In Arthur M. Schlesinger and Fred L. Israel (eds.), pp. 643-90. *History of American Presidential Elections, 1789-1968.* New York: McGraw-Hill.

Citrin, Jack. 1974. "Comment. The Political Relevance of Trust in Government." *American Political Science Review* 68: 973-88.

Clubb, Jerome M., William H. Flanigan, and Nancy H. Zingale. 1980. *Partisan Realignment.* Beverly Hills, Calif.: Sage.

Columbia Law Review. 1937. "Limitations on Access to the General Election Ballot." 37: 86-101.

Colvin, D. Leigh. 1926. *Prohibition In the United States.* New York: George H. Doran Co.

Congressional Quarterly Weekly Report. 1968. "The Public Record of George C. Wallace." September 27, 1968, pp. 2553-67.

———. 1975. "The Presidency: Harris, McCarthy Candidacies." January 18, 1975, p. 164.

Converse, Philip E. 1976. *The Dynamics of Party Support.* Beverly Hills, Calif.: Sage.

———, Warren E. Miller, Jerrold C. Rusk, and Arthur C. Wolfe. 1969. "Continuity and Change in American Politics: Parties and Issues in the 1968 Election." *American Political Science Review* 63: 1083-1105.

Cook, Rhodes. 1980a. "High Hurdles for the Anderson Campaign." *Congressional Quarterly Weekly Report,* May 17, 1980, pp. 1315-18.

———. 1980b. "Public Financing Obstacles: Money Woes Limit Anderson, Third Party Presidential Bids." *Congressional Quarterly Weekly Report,* August 16, 1980, pp. 2374-78.

———. 1995. "Assault on Two-Party System May Find Toehold in '96." *Congressional Quarterly Weekly Reports,* September 9, 1995, pp. 2735-41.

Cox, D. R. 1970. *The Analysis of Binary Data.* London: Methuen.

Crespi, Irving. 1971. "Structural Sources of the George Wallace Constituency." *Social Science Quarterly* 52: 115-32.

DeWitt, Benjamin Parke. 1915. *The Progressive Movement.* New York: Macmillan.

Dillon, Merton L. 1974. *The Abolitionists.* New York: W. W. Norton.

Dinnerstein, Leonard. 1971. "Election of 1880." In Arthur M. Schlesinger and Fred L. Israel (eds.), pp. 1491-516. *History of American Presidential Elections, 1789-1968.* New York: McGraw-Hill.

Downing, Kimberly. 1994. "Media Coverage and Interpretation of Campaign Events: Evidence from the 1992 Presidential Debates." Paper presented at the 1994 annual meeting of the American Political Science Association, New York, September 1-4, 1994.

Downs, Anthony. 1957. *An Economic Theory of Democracy.* New York: Harper and Row.

Duverger, Maurice. 1954. *Political Parties.* New York: Wiley.

Engleberg, Stephen, and B. Drummond Ayres Jr. 1993. "Perot's Organization Shows Fissures and Sagging Morale." *New York Times,* June 1, 1993, p. A1.

Evans, Rowland Jr., and Robert D. Novak. 1971. *Nixon in the White House: The Frustration of Power.* New York: Vintage Books.

Fair, Ray C. 1970. "The Estimation of Simultaneous Equation Models with Lagged Endogenous Variables and First Order Serially Correlated Errors." *Econometrica* 38: 507-16.

———. 1978. "The Effect of Economic Events on Votes for President." *Review of Economics and Statistics* 60: 159-73.

Fine, Nathan. 1928. *Labor and Farmer Parties in the United States: 1828-1928.* New York: Rand School of Social Science.

Fiorina, Morris. 1981. *Retrospective Voting in American National Elections.* New Haven: Yale University Press.

Foner, Eric. 1970. *Free Soil, Free Labor, Free Men: The Ideology of the Republican Party Before the Civil War.* New York: Oxford University Press.

Frady, Marshall. 1968. *Wallace.* New York: World Publishing.

Franklin, Ben A. 1973. "$100 for Wallace is Called Illegal." *New York Times,* October 31, 1973, p. 22.

Gaither, Gerald H. 1977. *Blacks and the Populist Revolt.* University: University of Alabama Press.

Germond, Jack, and Jules, Witcover. 1980. "Anderson's Aides Doubt His Viability." *Washington Star,* September 26, 1980, pp. A-1 and A-3.

———. 1993. *Mad as Hell Revolt: At the Ballot Box, 1992.* New York: Warner Books.

Gilbert, Christopher P., Timothy R. Johnson, and David A. Peterson. 1994. "Patterns of Support and Defection for Third Party Presidential Candidates: A Comparison of Anderson, Perot, and Wallace Voters." Paper read at the annual meeting of the Midwest Political Science Association, Chicago, April 14-16, 1994.

Gold, Howard J. 1994. "Third Party Voting in Presidential Elections: A Study of Perot, Anderson, and Wallace." Paper read at the 1994 annual meeting of the American Political Science Association, New York, September 1-4, 1994.

Goldman, Peter. 1980. "John Anderson: The Wild Card." *Newsweek,* June 9, 1980, pp. 28-38.

Goldman, Peter, and Thomas M. DeFrank. 1992. "How He Won." *Newsweek Special Election Issue,* November/December 1992.

Goldman, Peter, Thomas M. DeFrank, Mark Miler, Andrew Murr, and Tom Mathews. 1994. *Quest for the Presidency 1992.* College Station: Texas A & M University Press.

Goodwyn, Lawrence. 1978. *The Populist Movement.* New York: Cambridge University Press.

Greer, Thomas H. 1949. *American Social Reform Movements.* New York: Prentice-Hall.

Gusfield, Joseph R. 1963. *Symbolic Crusade.* Urbana: University of Illinois Press.

Hamilton, Holman. 1971. "Election of 1848." In Arthur M. Schlesinger and Fred L. Israel (eds.), pp. 865-905. *History of American Presidential Elections, 1789-1968.* New York: McGraw-Hill.

Hanushek, Eric A., and John E. Jackson. 1977. *Statistical Methods for Social Scientists.* New York: Academic Press.

Haynes, Fred E. 1916. *Third Party Movements Since the Civil War.* Iowa City, Iowa: The State Historical Society of Iowa.

———. 1919. *James Baird Weaver.* Iowa City, Iowa: The State Historical Society of Iowa.

———. 1924. *Social Politics in the United States.* Boston: Houghton Mifflin.

Heard, Alexander. 1952. *A Two-Party South?* Chapel Hill: University of North Carolina Press.

Heberle, Rudolf. 1970. *From Democracy to Nazism.* New York: Grosset and Dunlap.

Heckman, James. 1976. "The Common Structure of Statistical Models of Truncation, Sample Selection and Limited Dependent Variables and a Simple Estimator for Such Models." *Annals of Economic and Social Measurement* 5: 475-92.

Herring, Pendleton. 1965. *The Politics of Democracy.* New York: W. W. Norton.

Hersh, Seymour. 1973. "Anti-Wallace Aid Laid to Kalmbach." *New York Times,* May 29, 1973, p. 1.

Hesseltine, William B. 1962. *The Rise and Fall of Third Parties.* Princeton: D. Van Nostrand.

Hicks, John D. 1933. "The Third Party Tradition in American Politics." *Mississippi Valley Historical Review* 20: 3-28.

———. 1960. *Republican Ascendancy: 1921-1933.* New York: Harper and Row.

————. 1961. *The Populist Revolt*. Lincoln: University of Nebraska Press.

Hirsch, Mark D. 1971. "The Election of 1884." In Arthur M. Schlesinger and Fred L. Israel (eds.), pp. 1561-81. *History of American Presidential Elections 1789-1968*. New York: McGraw-Hill.

Hirschman, Albert O. 1970. *Exit, Voice, and Loyalty.* Cambridge: Harvard University Press.

Hofstadter, Richard. 1955. *The Age of Reform*. New York: Vintage Books.

Isikoff, Michael, and Lauri Goodstein. 1992. "Perot Spot on NY Ballot Seen Assured." *Washington Post*, August 26, 1992, p. A6.

Jacobson, Gary C. 1978. "Effects of Campaign Spending on Congressional Elections." *American Political Science Review* 72: 469-91.

————. 1980. *Money in Congressional Elections*. New Haven: Yale University Press.

Jacobson, Gary C., and Samuel Kernell. 1981. *Strategy and Choice in Congressional Elections*. New Haven: Yale University Press.

Jones, Rochelle. 1975. "McCarthy: Calling for New Electoral Process." *Congressional Quarterly Weekly Report*, October 25, 1975, pp. 2279-83.

Josephson, Matthew. 1963. *The Politicos: 1856-1896*. New York: Harcourt, Brace and World.

Kelly, Michael. 1992. "Charges Ignite Perot Temper as They Surface." *New York Times*, June 25, p. 1.

Kernell, Samuel. 1977. "Toward Understanding 19th Century Congressional Careers: Ambition, Competition, and Rotation." *American Journal of Political Science* 21: 669-93.

Key, V. O., Jr. 1949. *Southern Politics in State and Nation*. New York: Random House.

————. 1955. "A Theory of Critical Elections." *Journal of Politics* 17: 3-18.

————. 1964. *Politics, Parties and Pressure Groups*, 5th edn. New York: Thomas Y. Crowell.

Kinder, Donald R., and Robert P. Abelson. 1981. "Appraising Presidential Candidates: Personality and Affect in the 1980 Campaign." Paper read at the annual meeting of the American Political Science Association, New York, September 3-6, 1981.

Kirkendall, Richard S. 1971. "Election of 1948." In Arthur M. Schlesinger and Fred L. Israel (eds.), pp. 3099-145. *History of American Presidential Elections, 1789-1968*. New York: McGraw-Hill.

Kramer, Gerald H. 1971. "Short-Term Fluctuations in U.S. Voting Behavior, 1896-1964." *American Political Science Review* 65: 131-43.

Lachicotte, Alberta. 1966. *Rebel Senator: Strom Thurmond of South Carolina*. New York: Devin-Adair Company.

LaFollette, Bella C., and Fola LaFollette. 1953. *Robert M. LaFollette*. New York: Macmillan.

Leiser, Ernest. 1980. As stated on *The MacNeil/Lehrer Report*, September 10, 1980.

Lemieux, Peter. 1977. *The Liberal Party and British Political Change: 1955-74*. Ph.D. dissertation. Massachusetts Institute of Technology.

Leuchtenburg, William E. 1971. "The Election of 1936." In Arthur M. Schlesinger and Fred L. Israel (eds.), pp. 2809-49. *History of American Presidential Elections, 1789-1968*. New York: McGraw-Hill.

Lewis, Anthony. 1980. "The Anderson Factor." *New York Times*, August 25, 1980, p. A23.

Link, Arthur S., and William M. Leary, Jr. 1971. "Election of 1916." In Arthur M. Schlesinger and Fred L. Israel (eds.), pp. 2245-70. *History of American Presidential Elections, 1789-1968*. New York: McGraw-Hill.

Lipset, Seymour Martin. 1963. *Political Man*. New York: Doubleday.
———. 1968. *Agrarian Socialism* (revised and expanded edition). Berkeley: University of California Press.
———, and Earl Raab. 1970. *The Politics of Unreason*. New York: Harper and Row.

Loomis, Charles, and J. Allan Beegle. 1946. "The Spread of Nazism in Rural Areas." *American Sociological Review* 11: 724-34.

Lubell, Samuel. 1965. *The Future of American Politics*. New York: Harper and Row.

Ludington, Arthur C. 1911. *American Ballot Laws: 1888-1910*. Albany: New York State Library.

Luntz, Frank I. 1993. "Perovian Civilization; Who Supported Ross, and Why," *Policy Review* 64: 18-23.

Lynch, Dennis Tilden. 1929. *An Epoch and a Man: Martin Van Buren and His Times*. New York: Horace Liveright.

McCarthy, Eugene J. 1980. *The Ultimate Tyranny*. New York: Harcourt, Brace and Jovanovich.

McCormick, Richard P. 1966. *The Second American Party System*. Chapel Hill: University of North Carolina Press.

McCoy, Donald R. 1958. *Angry Voices: Left-at-Center Politics in the New Deal Era*. Lawrence: University of Kansas Press.

MacKay, Kenneth Campbell. 1947. *The Progressive Movement of 1924*. New York: Columbia University Press.

Maddala, G. S., and Lung-Fei Lee. 1976. "Recursive Models with Qualitative Endogenous Variables." *Annals of Economic and Social Measurement* 5: 525-45.

Magoon, Michael. 1994. "Media Coverage of Third Party Presidential Candidates." Paper read at the annual meeting of the American Political Science Association, New York, September 1-4, 1994.

Mann, Thomas E., and Raymond E. Wolfinger. 1980. "Candidates and Parties in Congressional Elections." *American Political Science Review* 74: 617-32.

Market Strategies Inc., 1994. "National Focus Group Report," April 25-29, 1992. In Peter Goldman, Thomas M. DeFrank, Mark Miler, Andrew Murr, and Tom Mathews, pp. 666-74. *Quest for the Presidency 1992.* College Station: Texas A & M University Press.

Martin, Roscoe C. 1933. *The People's Party in Texas.* Austin: University of Texas Bulletin.

Matalin, Mary, and James Carville. 1994. *All's Fair; Love, War, and Running for President.* New York: Random House.

Mayhew, Anne. 1972. "A Reappraisal of the Causes of Farm Protest in the United States." *Journal of Economic History* 32: 464-75.

Miller, Warren E., and J. Merrill Shanks. 1995. "The American Voter Revisited." Unpublished manuscript. Arizona State University.

Morgan, Wayne H. 1971. "Election of 1892." In Arthur M. Schlesinger and Fred L. Israel (eds.), pp. 1703-32. *History of American Presidential Elections, 1789-1968.* New York: McGraw-Hill.

Morison, Samuel Eliot, and Henry Steele Commager. 1962. *The Growth of the American Republic.* Vol. II. New York: Oxford University Press.

Mowry, George E. 1946. *Theodore Roosevelt and the Progressive Movement.* New York: Hill and Wang.

———. 1971. "Election of 1912." In Arthur M. Schlesinger and Fred L. Israel (eds.), pp. 2135-66. *History of American Presidential Elections, 1789-1968.* New York: McGraw-Hill.

Murray, Robert K. 1955. *Red Scare; A Study in National Hysteria, 1919-1920.* Minneapolis: University of Minnesota Press.

Nash, Howard P., Jr. 1959. *Third Parties in American Politics.* Washington, D.C.: Public Affairs Press.

Neuborne, Burt, and Arthur Eisenberg. 1980. *The Rights of Candidates and Voters.* New York: Avon.

Newport, Frank, and Alec Gallup. 1992. "Half of Swing Voters Say Debates Could Make a Difference." *The Gallup Poll Monthly* (October): 9-24.

Nichols, Roy F., and Philip S. Klein. 1971. "The Election of 1856." In Arthur M. Schlesinger and Fred L. Israel (eds.), pp. 1007-33. *History of American Presidential Elections, 1789-1968*. New York: McGraw-Hill.

Nichols, Stephen M., and Paul Allen Beck. 1995. "Reversing the Decline: Voter Turnout in the 1992 Election." In Herbert F. Weisberg (ed.), pp. 29-71. *Democracy's Feast*. Chatham, N.J.: Chatham House.

Nielsen Media Research. 1993. *Nielsen Tunes in to Politics: Tracking the Presidential Election Years (1960-1992)*. New York: Nielsen Media Research.

Noah, Timothy. 1992. "Perot Waters His Grass Roots Heavily, Paying 'Volunteers' and Orchestrating Poll of Supporters." *The Wall Street Journal*, September 30, 1992, p. A16.

Olson, Mancur. 1965. *The Logic of Collective Action*. Cambridge: Harvard University Press.

Page, Benjamin I. 1978. *Choices and Echoes in Presidential Elections*. Chicago: University of Chicago Press.

———, and Richard Brody. 1972. "Policy Voting and the Electoral Process: The Vietnam War Issue." *American Political Science Review* 66: 979-95.

Pear, Robert. 1992. "The 1992 Elections: Disappointment—The Turnout: 55% Voting Rate Reverses 30-Year Decline." *New York Times*, November 5, 1992, p. B4.

Perot, Ross. 1992. *United We Stand; How We Can Take Back Our Country*. New York: Hyperion.

Peterson, Bill. 1980a. "Campaign Sagging, Cash Short, Anderson Shakes Up His Staff." *Washington Post*, August 29, 1980, pp. A1, A4.

———. 1980b. "Anderson: Hoping Punch Will Connect: Independent Challenger Continues to Bid for Notice by Major Candidates." *Washington Post*, October 13, 1980, p. A2.

Pinchot, Amos R. E. 1958. *History of the Progressive Party, 1912-1916*. New York: New York University Press.

Pindyck, Robert S., and Daniel L. Rubinfeld. 1976. *Economic Models and Economic Forecasts*. New York: McGraw-Hill.

Pollard, Edward A. 1962. "The Road to Disunion." In William B. Hesseltine (ed.), pp. 44-66. *The Tragic Conflict*. New York: George Braziller.

Polsby, Nelson W., and Aaron Wildavsky. 1991. *Presidential Elections: Contemporary Strategies of American Electoral Politics*. 8th ed. New York: Free Press.

Pomper, Gerald M. 1993. *The Election of 1992*. Chatham, N.J.: Chatham House.

Potter, David M. 1976. *The Impending Crisis, 1848-1861*. New York: Harper and Row.

Rae, Douglas W. 1971. *The Political Consequences of Electoral Laws*. New Haven: Yale University Press.

Ranney, Austin, and Willmoore Kendall. 1951. *Democracy and the American Party System*. New York: Harcourt, Brace and Company.

Rayback, Joseph G. 1970. *Free Soil: The Election of 1848*. Lexington: University Press of Kentucky.

Riker, William H. 1982. "The Two-Party System and Duverger's Law: An Essay on the History of Political Science." *American Political Science Review* 76: 753-66.

Roberts, Steven V. 1980. "Fear of Electing Reagan Cutting Anderson Support." *New York Times*, October 7, 1980, p. D22.

Rogin, Michael. 1969. "California Populism and the 'System of 1896'." *Western Political Quarterly* 22: 179-96.

Rosebaum, David E. 1973. "Kalmbach Says Strangers Got $400,000 From Him." *New York Times*, July 18, 1973, p. 1.

Roseboom, Eugene H., and Alfred E. Eckes, Jr. 1979. *A History of Presidential Elections*, 4th edn. New York: Macmillan.

Rosenstone, Steven J. 1983. *Forecasting Presidential Elections*. New Haven: Yale University Press.

———. 1993. "Electoral Myths, Political Realities." *Boston Review* (January/February): 11-13.

Rosenstone, Steven J., and John Mark Hansen. 1993. *Mobilization, Participation, and Democracy in America*. New York: Macmillan.

Rosenstone, Steven J., John Mark Hansen, Paul Freedman, and Marguerite Grabarek. 1993. "Voter Turnout: Myth and Reality in the 1992 Election." Paper read at the 1993 annual meeting of the American Political Science Association, Washington, D.C., September 2-5.

Ross, Irwin. 1968. *The Loneliest Campaign*. New York: Signet Books.

Ross, Michael J., Reeve D. Vanneman, and Thomas F. Pettigrew. 1976. "Patterns of Support for George Wallace: Implications for Racial Change." *Journal of Social Issues* 36: 69-91.

Rusk, Jerrold G. 1968. "The Effect of the Australian Ballot Reform on Split Ticket Voting: 1876-1908." Ph.D. dissertation. University of Michigan.

———. 1970. "The Effect of the Australian Ballot Reform on Split Ticket Voting: 1876-1908." *American Political Science Review* 64: 1220-38.

Sartori, Giovanni. 1976. *Parties and Party Systems*. Cambridge: Cambridge University Press.

Schattschneider, E. E. 1942. *Party Government*. New York: Holt, Rinehart and Winston.

Schlesinger, Arthur M., Jr. 1960. *The Politics of Upheaval*. Boston: Houghton Mifflin.

Schlesinger, Joseph A. 1966. *Ambition and Politics: Political Careers in the United States*. Chicago: Rand McNally.

Schmidt, Karl M. 1960. *Henry A. Wallace: Quixotic Crusade 1948*. Syracuse, N.Y.: Syracuse University Press.

Schram, Martin. 1977. *Running for President 1976*. New York: Stein and Day.

———. 1980. "Florida Democrats Plan Suit to Knock Anderson Off Ballot." *Washington Post*, September 8, 1980, pp. A1, A12.

Sewell, Richard H. 1976. *Ballots for Freedom: Anti-Slavery Politics in the United States 1837-1960*. New York: W. W. Norton.

Shade, William G. 1981. "Political Pluralism and Party Development: The Creation of a Modern Party System, 1815-1852." In Paul Kleppner, Walter Dean Burnham, Ronald P. Formisano, Samuel P. Hays, Richard Jensen, and William G. Shade (eds.), pp. 77-112. *The Evolution of American Electoral Systems*. Westport, Conn.: Greenwood Press.

Shanahan, Eileen. 1974. "Nixon Asked Data on Wallace Tax, Panel Was told." *New York Times*, July 17, 1974, p. 1.

Shanks, J. Merrill, and Bradley Palmquist. 1981. "Intra-Party Candidate Choice in 1980." Paper presented at the 1981 meeting of the Midwest Political Science Association, Cincinnati, Ohio, April 16-17, 1981.

Shannon, David A. 1955. *The Socialist Party in America*. New York: Macmillan.

Shaw, Daron R. 1993. "Electoral Models and Presidential Preference Polls in the 1992 Election." Paper read at the annual meeting of the American Political Science Association, Washington, D.C., September 2-5, 1993.

———. 1994. "The Effect of Campaign Events in the 1992 Presidential Election." Paper read at the 1994 annual meeting of the Western Political Science Association, Albuquerque, N.M., March 10-12, 1994.

Smallwood, Frank. 1983. *The Other Candidates*. Hanover, N.H.: University Press of New England.

Sombart, Werner. 1976. *Why is There no Socialism in the United States?*

Patricia M. Hocking and C. T. Husbands (trans.). London: Macmillan Press.

Sorauf, Frank J. 1992. *Inside Campaign Finance; Myths and Realities*. New Haven: Yale University Press.

Stanwood, Edward. 1898. *A History of the Presidency from 1788 to 1897*. Boston: Houghton Mifflin.

Starks, John F. 1980. "Squeezed Out of the Middle." *Time Magazine*, November 17, 1980, p. 52.

Stedman, Murray S., Jr., and Susan W. Stedman. 1950. *Discontent at the Polls, A Study of Farmer and Labor Parties, 1827-1948*. New York: Columbia University Press.

Storms, Roger C. 1972. *Partisan Prophets*. Denver: National Prohibition Foundation, Inc.

Sundquist, James L. 1973. *Dynamics of the Party System*. Washington, D.C.: The Brookings Institution.

Swanson, Doug J. 1992. "Voters Turn Out in Record Numbers; Economic Worries Loom Large Over U.S." *The Dallas Morning News*, November 4, 1992, p. K1.

Time Magazine. 1948. "Third Parties 'In the Interests of Peace'." May 31, 1948, p. 16.

Tufte, Edward R. 1974. *Data Analysis for Politics and Policy*. Englewood Cliffs, N.J.: Prentice-Hall.

———. 1978. *Political Control of the Economy*. Princeton: Princeton University Press.

Tull, Charles J. 1965. *Father Coughlin and the New Deal*. Syracuse, N.Y.: Syracuse University Press.

Turque, Bill. 1992. "Power Ploy: How Perot Got Back In." *Newsweek*, October 12, 1992, pp. 30-41.

Unger, Irwin. 1964. *The Greenback Era*. Princeton: Princeton University Press.

Vaden, Ted. 1977. "New Congress Faces Familiar Issues." *Congressional Quarterly Weekly Report*, January 1, 1977, pp. 16-18.

Visgaitis, Gary. 1992. "How Viewers View Political Ads." *USA Today*, November 5, 1992, p. 1A.

Warner, Edwin. 1980. "The Long Shot Takes Aim." *Time Magazine*, June 30, 1980, pp. 21-22.

Weaver, Warren Jr. 1980a. "Election Commission Staff Backs Subsidy of Anderson." *New York Times*, September 3, 1980, p. B12.

———. 1980b. "Anderson Campaign Is Running Short Of Both Time and Financial Resources." *New York Times*, October 7, 1980, p. D22.

Weinstein, James. 1967. *The Decline of Socialism in America, 1912-1925.* New York: Monthly Review Press.

———. 1968. *The Corporate Ideal in the Liberal State 1900-1918.* Boston: Beacon Press.

Whittle, Richard. 1980. "John Anderson Still Trying to Dump His 'Spoiler' Image." *Congressional Quarterly Weekly Report,* September 27, 1980, pp. 2833-38.

Wilentz, Sean. 1993. "Ross Perot and the Corruption of Populism." *The New Republic,* August 9, 1993, pp. 29-35.

Williams v. *Rhodes* (393 U.S. 23 [1968]).

Wilson, James Q. 1973. *Political Organizations.* New York: Basic Books.

Winger, Richard. 1992. *Ballot Access News.* Quoted in "Perot: 50-State Roundup of Independent Ballot Access Laws." American Political Network, *The Hotline,* April 8, 1992.

———. 1995. "1996 Petitioning for President." *Ballot Access News,* August 24, 1995, p. 4.

Wiseheart, Malcolm B. Jr. 1969. "Constitutional Law: Third Political Parties as Second-Class Citizens." *University of Florida Law Review* 21: 701-68.

Woodward, C. Vann. 1951. *Origins of the New South.* Baton Rouge: Louisiana State University Press.

Yale Law Journal. 1948. "Legal Obstacles to Minority Party Success." 57: 1276-97.

Yarnell, Allen. 1974. *Democrats and Progressives.* Berkeley: University of California Press.

Zaller, John. 1995. "Rules of Press Coverage in Presidential Elections, 1948-1992." Paper read at the 1995 annual meeting of the American Political Science Association, Chicago, September 4, 1995.

Zaller, John, and Mark Hunt. 1996. *Politics as Usual; Ross Perot and the Popularization of Politics.* Chicago: University of Chicago Press.

INDEX

Abelson, Robert P., 138
abolitionists, 27, 33n, 49–50, 75, 133. *See also* Free Soil Party; Liberty Party
Abramson, Paul R., 244n, 250n, 254
Achen, Christopher H., 151n, 157n
age cohort, 113, 116, 119, 145, 176–78, 182, 183, 225, 226, 244–45
age of party system, 144, 201–203. *See also* realignment
Agnew, Spiro T., 112
agricultural adversity, 134–38, 165–67, 207–209. *See also* farmers
agricultural prices, 69, 93–94, 134–35, 137, 165–67, 207–209
Alexander, Herbert E., 35n, 45, 261
allegiance to the major parties, *see* major parties
allegiance to the political system, 147–48, 179–81, 233–34, 248, 249–51
Alvarez, R. Michael, 244n, 250n, 251n, 254
American Anti-Slavery Society, 49. *See also* Liberty Party
American Federation of Labor, 96, 101
American Independent Party, 5, 45, 111, 115, 142, 188–89. *See also* Wallace, George C.
American Labor Party, 105
American Party, 115. *See also* Fillmore, Millard; Know-Nothing Party
Americans for Democratic Action (ADA), 104
Anderson, John, 6, 7, 10n, 17, 21, 30, 116–19, 120, 121, 139, 141, 145, 174, 175n, 182, 183, 189, 197, 198, 213n, 217, 255, 260; attacked by major parties, 45; ballot access fight, 23, 24; campaign expenditures, 27, 29; compared to H. Ross Perot, 244–67; electorate's perception of, 38, 39, 39n-40n; elite backing of, 33; FEC ruling,

26; media coverage of, 33–35; motivation for running, 190; positions, 117–18; support for, 41, 119, 182, 183
Anderson v. Babb, 23n
Anderson v. Celebrezze, 23n
Anderson v. Hooper, 23n
Anderson v. Mills, 23n
Anderson v. Morris, 23n
Anderson v. Quinn, 23n
Anderson, Thomas, 115
Anthony, Susan B., 75
anti-monopoly movement, 63, 67
Anti-Monopoly Party, 64, 66
Anti-Saloon League, 75, 77, 78
Arnett, Alex M., 148
Arthur, Chester, 199
Asher, Herbert, 132
Australian ballot, 20, 21, 25, 149
Ayres, B. Drummond, Jr., 269

ballot access laws, 19–25, 96, 115, 149, 171 74, 213, 260, 273
balloting, in the nineteenth century, 19–20
Balz, Dan, 242, 269
Barnard, William D., 108, 109
Barnburners, 52, 53
Barnes, Fred, 268
Barrett, Laurence I., 240
barriers against third parties, 16–27, 191, 213, 224, 232, 260, 272–73. *See also* constraints on third parties; major parties, strategies against third parties
Bass, Paul S., 35, 36n
Beck, Paul Allen, 144, 254n
Beegle, J. Allan, 138n
Bell, John, 59, 62. *See also* Constitutional Union Party
Bennett, David H., 24, 30, 32, 36, 101
Berke, Richard L., 271n
Berman, William C., 101, 105
Bidwell, John, 77
Billington, Ray Allen, 56, 57, 58